Amazon Connect: Up and Running

Improve your customer experience by building logical and cost-effective solutions for critical call center systems

Jeff Armstrong

BIRMINGHAM—MUMBAI

Amazon Connect: Up and Running

Group Product Manager: Wilson D'souza

Publishing Product Manager: Vijin Boricha

Senior Editor: Rahul Dsouza

Content Development Editor: Nihar Kapadia

Technical Editor: Sarvesh Jaywant

Copy Editor: Safis Editing

Project Coordinator: Neil D'mello

Proofreader: Safis Editing

Indexer: Pratik Shirodkar

Production Designer: Joshua Misquitta

First published: April 2021
Production reference: 1240321

Published by Packt Publishing Ltd.
Livery Place
35 Livery Street
Birmingham
B3 2PB, UK.

ISBN 978-1-80056-383-4

www.packt.com

Contributors

About the author

Jeff Armstrong has 25 years of information technology experience, working in several industry verticals for start-ups and Fortune 100 companies alike.

For the past six years, he has been working as an architect in the application modernization space. Jeff is also an avid programmer, having worked in nine different languages throughout his career. He has obtained nine AWS certifications and is also CISSP certified.

Jeff believes in self-innovation and continued education. He holds a bachelor's degree in business administration and a master's degree in information technology and assurance. He also holds a certificate in strategy and innovation from MIT Sloan and a certificate in executive leadership from Cornell.

About the reviewer

Venkata Maniteja Alapati is a proven product manager with extensive experience in contact center technologies, digital experience, AI, UX, and SaaS technologies. His expertise spans multiple contact center technologies, such as Genesys, Avaya, Cisco, and Amazon Connect. He has been working on Amazon Connect since its release and has delivered projects with it in cloud contact centers. He holds a double bachelor's degree in electronics and computer science engineering and has certifications in multiple contact center products. He believes self-motivation and self-learning are key aspects for success.

I would like to thank my parents, wife, and daughter for supporting me throughout the review process.

Table of Contents

Preface

Section 1: Planning

1

Benefits of Amazon Connect

Exploring the benefits of Connect	4	Reducing hard costs	10
Customer experience	4	No circuit costs	10
Improved interaction	5	No long-term contracts	11
Interfacing with enterprise applications	6	No long delays for implementation and upgrades	12
Self-service	7	No demarcation extension costs	12
AI services	7	Extra equipment	13
Multi-channel experiences	8	Reducing soft costs	13
Surveys	9	Summary	15
Sentiment analysis	9		

2

Reviewing Stakeholder Objectives

Extracting critical information	18	Deployment influencers	24
Contact flow influencers	19	Management	24
Business hours	19	Reframing the conversation	30
Queues	20	Summary	32
Transfers	21		
Callbacks	22		
Voicemail	23		
Integrations	24		

3

Sketching Your Contact Flows

Types of flows	**34**	**Flow components**	**37**
Inbound contact flow	34	Interactions	38
Customer queue flow	35	Settings	42
Customer hold flow	35	Branch	48
Customer whisper flow	35	Integrate	51
Outbound whisper flow	36	Terminate/transfer	52
Agent hold flow	36	Putting the pieces together	54
Agent whisper flow	36	**Summary**	**55**
Transfer to agent flow	37		
Transfer to queue flow	37		

4

Connect Costing

Base Connect charges	**58**	**Analytics costing**	**65**
Communications costs	**60**	Kinesis Firehose	66
Lambda costing	**62**	Glue	66
Invocations	63	Athena	67
RAM and duration	63	QuickSight	67
Lex bot costing	**64**	**Summary**	**68**
Contact Lens costing	**65**		

Section 2: Implementation

5

Base Connect Implementation

AWS account prerequisites	**72**	Logging in to your instance	78
VPC	72	**Picking or transferring your phone number**	**80**
Federation	73		
Management roles	73	Setting your hours of operation	84
Deploying Connect	**74**	**Creating your call queues**	**87**

Creating security profiles   90   Summary   100
Adding users   97

6
Contact Flow Creation

Creating a contact flow   102   Exporting and importing
     Editing an existing flow   103   contact flows   130
     Creating a contact flow from scratch   111   Putting it all together   136
Copying contact flows   121   Summary   138

7
Creating AI Bots

Amazon Lex capabilities crash   Modifying the bridging contact
course   140   flow   157
Creating your first bot   140   Summary   162
Connecting to Amazon Connect   154

8
Interfacing Enterprise Applications

Learning about your API   Deploying the solution via
capabilities   164   CloudFormation   169
Understanding Lambda's   Connecting Lambda to Connect   173
capabilities   165   Creating the contact flow   175
Solution overview   167   Testing the solution   187
Retrieving required information   168   Summary   191

9
Implementing Callbacks

Solution overview   194   Implementing the callback
Capturing the caller's number   195   contact flow   200
Number validation   200   Summary   202

10
Implementing Voicemail

Voicemail solution overview   204
Launching the solution   207
Configuring your instance   215
Using the management portal   220
Importing voicemail contact
flows   225

Completing the settings   232
Testing the solution   233
Other ways to integrate into
contact flows   234
    Removing the extension prompt   234
Summary   239

11
Implementing Call Analytics

Understanding the data flow   242
Configuring the
CloudFormation Template   243
Capturing the ARN from a
voicemail   248
Deploying the CloudFormation

template   250
Setting up S3 access   254
Establishing analysis   259
Dashboarding with QuickSight   263
Summary   267

12
Implementing Contact Lens

Enabling Contact Lens   270
Assigning user permissions   275
Understanding Contact Lens'

capabilities   277
Creating Contact Lens rules   282
Summary   289

13
Implementing Chat

Chat requirements   292
    Application requirements   292
Connect instance requirements   293
Deploying contact flows   294

Gathering required information 301
Deploying the solution   303
Testing your chat experience   306
Summary   310

Why subscribe?   311

Other Books You May Enjoy

Index

Preface

Amazon Connect is by far one of the most powerful customer engagement services offered by AWS. Today, SMS and email are purely table stakes capabilities. If you want to up your customer service game, you need to address the elephant in the room: your outdated call center.

It doesn't matter what type of company you work for; you will most likely need a call center to handle customer calls. Those calls might be in the form of customer orders, customer issues, or maybe for facilitating scheduling. No matter what form your calls take, if you want to stand out from your competition, you need to provide customer value during those calls.

You might be wondering what customer value looks like in a call center. After all, aren't we just answering a phone? Absolutely not. You are providing your customer with an experience that will leave an impression just as much as your showroom, advertising, or website. It might even leave more of an impression. Many call centers are built to address customer problems. It doesn't matter what the problem was. If they have a terrible experience, they are going to let everyone know.

This book provides the critical information you need to make your call center the showcase of your customer's next-generation experience. It will walk you through all the latest technologies and show you first their benefits to your organization and then how to implement the various technologies. You want your new call center to leave your customers happy, and this book will help you do just that.

Who this book is for

This book is for a range of staff at a company. It is laid out in two separate parts. Part one lays out the benefits, costings, and how to work with stakeholders for requirements gathering.

The second part of the book covers the technical implementation of Amazon Connect. It provides a detailed step-by-step implementation guide along with caveats, best practices, and personal anecdotes from my experience of working with the platform.

If you are technical and working on the implementation side of your call center, the entire book will be important material to cover. You will get a sound base and understanding of the capabilities and how to implement them.

If you're a project manager, manager, or C-suite executive, part one will be vitally important for you to review. It will allow you to make sound business decisions and ensure you understand all the capabilities.

What this book covers

Chapter 1, Benefits of Amazon Connect, teaches you about the benefits of Connect so you have a strong foundational understanding of what kinds of capabilities your company can implement.

Chapter 2, Reviewing Stakeholder Objectives, covers how understanding your stakeholders' objectives is critical to ensure your implementation's success. This chapter will cover the kinds of questions to ask your stakeholders to extract the correct information.

Chapter 3, Sketching Your Contact Flows, details how, after you understand your stakeholders' needs, it's best to create contact flow strawmen to create something tangible to be used later in the process. This chapter will cover the types of contact flows and contact flow components, and how to put them together to meet your stakeholders' objectives.

Chapter 4, Connect Costing, outlines how, since a proper Amazon Connect deployment includes many AWS services, costing can be complicated. In this chapter, we review all the services used in the book and how to estimate costs for your operations.

Chapter 5, Basic Connect Implementation, details the deployment of a basic Amazon Connect implementation. It will form the base to which we will add the rest of the functionality in the remainder of the book.

Chapter 6, Contact Flow Creation, outlines the creation and modification of contact flows as the most common administration function performed in Connect. This chapter will cover common ways to create, copy, and import/export contact flows.

Chapter 7, Creating AI Bots, shows how using Lex to provide advanced AI bot capabilities is one of the easiest ways to improve your customer's experience. In this chapter, we will demonstrate how to change an **Interactive Voice Response** (**IVR**) into an intelligent AI branching system.

Chapter 8, Interfacing Enterprise Applications, demonstrates that using advanced enterprise application interfaces is the best way to reduce your call center costs. Interfaces allow Connect to perform advanced operations and self-service without the need for expensive agents. In this chapter, we cover how one of these interfaces might work using a mock interface.

Chapter 9, Implementing Callbacks, teaches you how to implement callbacks. Callbacks increase customer satisfaction by allowing them to go about their business without having to wait on the phone for an agent. We will focus not only on the technical implementation, but also on some customer issues that should be addressed to reduce concerns about line position.

Chapter 10, Implementing Voicemail, covers how, although it's true that callbacks are superior for clients over voicemail, there may be situations where voicemail is still a necessary option. We will cover what these options might look like in this chapter, as well as how to implement a solution.

Chapter 11, Implementing Call Analytics, outlines the built-in analytics that come with Connect, but shows that they aren't highly customizable. We will cover how to implement more advanced analytics capabilities using additional AWS services.

Chapter 12, Implementing Contact Lens, discusses the ability to know how your customers feel as a vital aspect in improving overall customer satisfaction. In this chapter, we will cover how to implement Contact Lens to gather customer sentiments.

Chapter 13, Implementing Chat, shows how Connect allows you to use the same staff and contact center to address both typical voice communication and chat. Chat offers another channel that allows your customers to communicate directly from your website or mobile application. We will cover how to implement and configure chat in your Connect instance in this chapter.

To get the most out of this book

To make the best use of the content in this book, a remedial understanding of AWS services and the AWS console is required. It is recommended that if you are working with production workloads, critical client data, or internet-facing capabilities, you should have a thorough understanding of AWS security as security concepts outside of Connect permissions themselves are not covered in this book.

Some CloudFormation experience is required. Although the CloudFormation work can be performed with any text editor, an IDE that supports CloudFormation syntax would be helpful.

If you are using the digital version of this book, we advise you to type the code yourself or access the code via the GitHub repository (link available in the next section). Doing so will help you avoid any potential errors related to the copying and pasting of code.

Download the example code files

You can download the example code files for this book from your account at www. packt.com. If you purchased this book elsewhere, you can visit www.packtpub.com/support and register to have the files e-mailed directly to you.

You can download the code files by following these steps:

1. Log in or register at www.packt.com.
2. Select the **Support** tab.
3. Click on **Code Downloads**.
4. Enter the name of the book in the **Search** box and follow the onscreen instructions.

Once the file is downloaded, please make sure that you unzip or extract the folder using the latest version of:

*   WinRAR/7-Zip for Windows
*   Zipeg/iZip/UnRarX for Mac
*   7-Zip/PeaZip for Linux

The code bundle for the book is also hosted on GitHub at https://github.com/PacktPublishing/Amazon-Connect-Up-and-Running. In case there's an update to the code, it will be updated on the existing GitHub repository.

We also have other code bundles from our rich catalog of books and videos available at https://github.com/PacktPublishing/. Check them out!

Download the color images

We also provide a PDF file that has color images of the screenshots/diagrams used in this book. You can download it here: http://www.packtpub.com/sites/default/files/downloads/9781800563834_ColorImages.pdf.

Conventions used

There are a number of text conventions used throughout this book.

`Code in text`: Indicates code words in text, database table names, folder names, filenames, file extensions, pathnames, dummy URLs, user input, and Twitter handles. Here is an example: "In my experience, there is a message that says something like, `something went wrong, goodbye`."

A block of code is set as follows:

```
<code>,
{
    "Name": "ContactFlowEvent",
    "Details": {
      "ContactData": {
        "Attributes": {},
        "Channel": "VOICE",
```

Bold: Indicates a new term, an important word, or words that you see onscreen. For example, words in menus or dialog boxes appear in the text like this. Here is an example: "Once you click on **Amazon Connect**, you will be greeted with the Connect service."

> **Tips or important notes**
> Appear like this.

Get in touch

Feedback from our readers is always welcome.

General feedback: If you have questions about any aspect of this book, mention the book title in the subject of your message and e-mail us at `customercare@packtpub.com`.

Errata: Although we have taken every care to ensure the accuracy of our content, mistakes do happen. If you have found a mistake in this book, we would be grateful if you would report this to us. Please visit www.packtpub.com/support/errata, selecting your book, clicking on the Errata Submission Form link, and entering the details.

Piracy: If you come across any illegal copies of our works in any form on the Internet, we would be grateful if you would provide us with the location address or website name. Please contact us at `copyright@packt.com` with a link to the material.

If you are interested in becoming an author: If there is a topic that you have expertise in and you are interested in either writing or contributing to a book, please visit `authors.packtpub.com`.

Reviews

Please leave a review. Once you have read and used this book, why not leave a review on the site that you purchased it from? Potential readers can then see and use your unbiased opinion to make purchase decisions, we at Packt can understand what you think about our products, and our authors can see your feedback on their book. Thank you!

For more information about Packt, please visit `packt.com`.

Disclaimer

The information within this book is intended to be used only in an ethical manner. Do not use any information from the book if you do not have written permission from the owner of the equipment. If you perform illegal actions, you are likely to be arrested and prosecuted to the full extent of the law. Packt Publishing does not take any responsibility if you misuse any of the information contained within the book. The information provided in this book is only for demonstration and will need to be adjusted based on their specific use case. The information herein must only be used while testing environments with proper written authorization from the appropriate persons responsible.

Section 1: Planning

Welcome to Amazon Connect: Up and Running. I designed this book to take you from idea inception to the implementation of your Amazon Connect deployment. To help you better absorb the information, the book has been split into two parts. The first part, comprising the first four chapters, focuses on some of Connect's planning items. The second part consists of the implementation.

I have seen many IT projects fail over my career. Most often, this is due to a lack of planning at the beginning of the project. I don't want to tell you cliches, such as if you fail to plan, you plan to fail. But then again, I guess I just did. We also won't go in-depth about how to plan and manage a project. We will cover in part 1 the planning aspects that are unique and directly related to Connect.

One of the most important things to understand when you're kicking off a new project is why you're doing it. Figuring out what and how is the easy part. Where it gets more complicated is communicating the why. Business units outside of IT often view projects as frivolous and unnecessary, making it harder to get buy-in and cooperation. If you can figure out the why and adequately communicate it, it will make your job significantly easier. Chapter 1, Benefits of Amazon Connect, details the benefits of Amazon Connect and how it will help your company improve operationally and boost your customer experience. These benefits will help you realize your individual why and help you communicate that to the constituents of your company for increased buy-in.

Once we understand all the benefits of Connect and how it relates specifically to your business, we will move on to calculating costs in Chapter 2, Reviewing Stakeholder Objectives. The reduction of costs may not be the primary motivator for the implementation of Connect in your company. However, you need to calculate costs to get approval for your project. Now that we have discussed how the book is laid out, let's move on to Chapter 1, Benefits of Amazon Connect, and discuss Connect's benefits.

This part of the book comprises the following chapters:

- *Chapter 1, Benefits of Amazon Connect*
- *Chapter 2, Reviewing Stakeholder Objectives*
- *Chapter 3, Sketching Your Contact Flows*
- *Chapter 4, Connect Costing*

1
Benefits of Amazon Connect

Now that you are getting started on your Amazon Connect journey, let's start by discussing its benefits. Remember, we don't want the rest of the company's stakeholders thinking that this project is the next shiny penny for IT. For that to happen, we need to discuss the benefits and how they might potentially impact your company.

To do that, we will cover the benefits, and then I will go through a couple of scenarios on how those benefits have played out for other companies. These scenarios will help you see the similarities and enable you to draw conclusions that apply to your own company. Once you have drawn your conclusions on how Connect will benefit your company, you will have the necessary information to establish your *why*. The *why* will be your critical business drivers that can be communicated to other corporate stakeholders.

In this chapter, we'll work through the following topics:

- Customer experience
- Reducing hard costs
- Reducing soft costs

Exploring the benefits of Connect

You will notice, in the introduction, that I used the term *business drivers* and not *technology drivers*. This nomenclature is an important distinction. Individuals outside of technology don't care all that much about how things work. They don't care that new technology is driven by serverless technology or uses object storage. Those items might be great from a technology perspective, but it isn't going to light a fire under someone like cutting call duration by a minute per call would. Those minutes of employee time add up quickly and end up being significant savings.

Think for a minute about a situation where you could save a minute per call that ended up reducing just one employee on the call center staff. That would mean that there is one less of the following to worry about:

- A salary
- A set of benefits
- A desk that needs to be occupied
- A person to train and onboard
- An annual review that needs to be completed
- A computer, phone, and headset

The list doesn't stop there; I'm sure that I forgot some essential expenses. You should be able to see that there is a significant impact possible with Connect, even with something as seemingly insignificant as a minute of call savings. Now that we have covered why the *why* is such an essential part of your project plan, let's discuss the benefits of Amazon Connect.

Customer experience

I believe that one of the most significant benefits of using **Connect** is to improve your user experience. Let's face it, who likes calling into a call center? If you have arrived at the point of calling into a company, you have already exhausted everything you can do on your end to resolve your issue. You have already tried to place an order online, return a product, or fix your problem, but nothing has worked. Now you have to call in to talk to a person to get the assistance that you need. Needing to talk to someone isn't the issue. The issue is the endless question-and-answer loops, the poor menu choices, and the failed call transfers. If you are like me, you might be wondering if they are just trying to get rid of you as a customer sometimes.

You don't want to run your call center like this. You want to provide an excellent experience where your customers on the other end of the line are wowed. Today there are a million companies that do a horrible job with customer experience. It wouldn't take much to wow a customer and ensure they become a repeat customer. Here is an excellent example.

My wife and I shop mostly on Amazon. Sometimes issues arise with what we purchase, and we must send it back. Amazon has built its entire business on being customer-centric. When we need to return something, it takes a few clicks and dropping the item off at the UPS store down the street. We couldn't ask for a better process. However, my wife and kids buy things online from clothing retailers. Many of these companies have horrible return procedures that require you to call in and plead to send back something that didn't fit. With some of these companies, especially during COVID-19, the customer service was so bad that they refused to shop there again. Does it cost Amazon more with their process? Maybe, maybe not. What I can tell you is that it cost the other companies a small fortune in lost sales from my wife and kids.

Connect makes it easy for your company to provide the kinds of experiences that make your customers happy. We will cover improved interaction, self-service, AI services, single-channel experiences, surveys, and sentiment analysis in the following sections to demonstrate these benefits.

Improved interaction

Practically everyone has been on a phone call where you have a horrible interaction experience with the call center's contact flow. A **contact flow** is a path that is programmed into the system to lead callers down an intended path. The problem with conventional systems is that they are hard to program, and the engineers that run them would rather be performing more interesting work. This situation is where you, as the caller, get frustrated because the menu has twenty-seven options that you have to listen through. Another common problem is when there isn't an option that fits your needs, and there is no way to get to a person to explain it to. Ultimately, you end up choosing any of the options and hoping that the person that answers your call can transfer you to the right individual.

The beautiful thing about Connect is that it's easy to set up your contact flows using a graphical interface. Everything is done via point-and-click and drag-and-drop motions. This is not to say that everything is rosy. You can get yourself into trouble if you don't know how to set up contact flows properly and allow them to get too large and unruly. We will cover this later in *Part Two* of the book to save you from that frustration. However, as the implementation engineer, the system allows you a more accessible and efficient way to configure and make changes to the system. Instead of a static system that gets changed rarely, you can change and adapt to the changing market and customer needs efficiently. Customers' needs change, and your interactions need to change as well.

Interfacing with enterprise applications

As we have covered before, Amazon Connect allows interfacing with other AWS services to expand its capabilities. One of the capabilities that you can add is interfacing with external enterprise applications. By itself, Connect is like any other telecom system. It doesn't contain any information about your customers, products, or operations. To provide capabilities such as AI bots, you need to interface with the systems and databases that contain all of this information. This interface is much more difficult in a conventional system and wouldn't have as rich a feature set as AWS.

I guess that you would say that interfacing with AWS services is the biggest background benefit to your company. However, these AWS services by themselves aren't very useful. They are the building blocks for you to construct your individualized services. The second biggest benefit of Amazon Connect is being able to use these services to create interfaces to your applications and databases. These application interfaces are what will make your AI bots, surveys, and sentiment analysis more impactful for your business.

The most effective way to interface between Connect and your applications is via an API. APIs allow you to query information for clients as well as update information easily using standard web calls. Most modern applications have some form of API interface for integrations. If your application does not have an API, all is not lost. Some instances of applications that might not have an API are older applications or potentially internally developed applications. You can still create interfaces for these applications, but you will have to have access to read the database directly. This method is a bit more complicated. You will need to know the data layout to query the data properly. Also, this method would best be left to read-only operations. Writing and mirroring the operations of the application can be quite complicated. You could corrupt data accidentally if there isn't a strong understanding of the application's operations.

Self-service

I'm willing to bet that you have run into a situation where you were stuck on a call waiting for someone to answer a straightforward question. Wouldn't it be better if you could get that information for that simple question yourself? The fact of the matter is that most call centers don't have self-service capabilities. Sure, the big banks do. They let you get your account balance and make transfers and such. But many companies do not have this capability. This inconvenience exists primarily because the big banks and retailers are the only ones that could afford to have this kind of interfacing set up for them. An advanced self-service functionality was outside the reach of the everyday company before Amazon Connect.

Since Connect allows you to utilize AWS services as part of the call center operations, you have at your disposal all the pieces required to provide self-service capabilities. To provide self-service, you need to tie your call center to your enterprise applications that hold vital data, such as your **Enterprise Resource Planning (ERP)** and **Customer Relationship Management (CRM)** systems. The interfaces for conventional on-premises call centers are very costly. The problem is further exacerbated by the lack of availability of these interfaces for your application. With the plethora of applications available on the market, the probability of an interface for yours declines. With Connect, as long as you have a way to communicate with your application via an API, you will be able to interface the two systems together. This ability to connect to an API gives you nearly unlimited capabilities to create a self-service experience for your customers.

AI services

Just like the self-service capabilities we just discussed, Connect also allows you to incorporate AI services. AWS has several off-the-shelf AI services that don't require any machine learning capabilities or massive training data. They are ready to use with a simple configuration and can then be interfaced with Connect. Typically, on-premises AI capabilities are out of reach for most companies. Even large corporations such as banks and large-scale retailers don't have elaborate AI capabilities. You might recall a situation where you called into one of these large organizations. You were prompted with a question where you could say *"yes"* or *"no"* to the prompt. The natural language processing power of these systems is relatively limited to understanding only a small response set.

There are several AI services that Connect can interface with that fit very well. The two major ones that most call centers will use would be Amazon Polly and Amazon Lex. **Polly** is a text-to-speech service that allows your call center to communicate with your customers verbally. **Lex** is a chatbot that uses natural language understanding and automatic speech recognition to provide a lifelike communication experience with your clients. These services work to reduce the burden on your call center staff by removing mundane workloads such as identity verification from them. Also, these AI services serve as the foundation of your self-service capabilities that improve customer satisfaction. We will cover the implementation of Polly and Lex later in *Part Two* of this book.

Multi-channel experiences

The internet and mobile applications have changed the way that we as consumers communicate with companies. Back in the olden days, when I was young, and rocks were soft, we only had three ways to communicate with a company. I could go to their place of business and speak in person, I could call them on the phone, or write them a letter. Later, you could send a fax, but it would be some time before people had fax machines in their homes. Today, we have dozens of pathways. You can still call them on the phone, but you can also use mobile applications and websites. When utilizing these different paths, you want to accomplish two things. The first is that you want your customers to have a unified experience no matter what method they use. Secondly, you want to minimize your staff requirements and utilize the staff you have to the fullest effect.

Before late 2019, if you had chat functionality in your application or website, it would have to be serviced independently from your call center staff. At least, it should have been. If you were utilizing your team, they would be operating in two different systems and would have to move in or out of the call center system while servicing individuals in the chat system. This set-up is suboptimal as it distorts your reporting and analytics, as it becomes hard to determine how efficiently your staff is operating. Seeing this deficiency, Amazon created a chat integration in Connect and released it in late 2019. Having chat integrated into your call center solves a lot of problems for your company. Issues such as the productivity issue discussed earlier, staff reduction, and providing customers a consistent experience become moot.

Surveys

One of the best ways to get feedback from your clients is to perform a survey about their experience. Using conventional on-premises systems conducting a survey wasn't the easiest to accomplish. You obviously wouldn't want to have the operator taking the call also perform a survey at the end. This conflict would mean that you would have to transfer the call to another operator to do a survey. This method is costly and uses staff for a function that might not utilize their expertise. After all, you hired them to take orders or answer support questions, not to take surveys. Often, these surveys would be handled by an outside firm. This mode saves your employees time but at a considerable operating expense to the company.

Since Connect allows the utilization of AWS services, you can create an entirely automated survey interface, utilizing the AI capabilities of Polly and Lex. This method will allow you to gather your customers' insights without impacting your staff or bottom line. Best of all, you can utilize this feedback to improve your overall customer experience. You can modify your contact flows to achieve a better experience and get nearly immediate feedback through the survey mechanism. You are essentially creating a continuous feedback loop on how your call center is operating.

Sentiment analysis

The last benefit of Connect that I wanted to cover is the ability to do sentiment analysis. **Sentiment analysis** is when you take a look at the conversations happening in your call center and determine the sentiment of the client's interaction by the words they use – to put it bluntly, to see if they are happy or not. Utilizing this information, you can tell if they are unhappy with a particular product or feature, if the call center agent needs more training, and when they like their experience. Before Connect, the implementation of this capability would have been too costly. You would have needed specialized processing power to handle this type of AI computation.

AWS makes sentiment analysis possible through the implementation of Contact Lens. **Contact Lens** uses several underlying AWS AI services to construct the sentiment analysis. You might be thinking it is complicated to set up the ability to recognize the speech in a phone call and then analyze it for sentiment. However, it is relatively straightforward, and although not easy, it's not complicated. Similar to surveys, you can use sentiment analysis to create feedback loops that continually improve your products and your customer experience. We will cover how to implement sentiment analysis using Contact Lens in *Part Two* of this book.

Now that we have covered the customer experience benefits, you will hopefully see that Connect can provide a far superior experience; that is, if you implement the correct technologies and set up the proper processes and feedback loops to improve continually. Using Connect, you should think of your call center as a living, evolving organism. You will need to break free of the contemporary patterns of *set it and forget it* used with conventional systems. You should find at least one, if not more, compelling *why* business stories for Connect's implementation within these benefits. We can now move on to the reduction of hard costs, which will help make a compelling financial story.

Reducing hard costs

I've been in IT for over 25 years, and it seems that no matter how hard I try to drive projects with business value, it always comes back to costs. It probably originates from the fact that at most companies, IT is a cost center and doesn't drive any revenue directly. That is, unless you are a **Software-as-a-Service (SaaS)** company. As you are reading this, you might be thinking the same thing: *I'm going to have to show how this implementation project will save us some money, or at least not cost us any more than we are paying today.*

I'm reasonably confident that Connect will save you money over operating on-premises with a conventional system. However, there are two types of costs associated with a call center. They are the soft costs and hard costs. The soft costs are things like time savings, and hard costs are the real dollars you pay for equipment and services. Hard costs are easier to substantiate, and typically where I focus the majority of my efforts, so we will cover those first. Although they are genuine, soft costs are often qualitative versus quantitative and don't sway people into decisions easily. We will cover soft costs in the next section.

No circuit costs

One of the more apparent savings with Connect is that you no longer have to pay for any circuits for telecommunications for your call center. These would typically be in the form of **T1** or **T3** circuits that come into your building from the telephone company. Conventional phone carriers charge you for both the circuit and the phone calls going out over that circuit. Since Connect is an over-the-internet product, you won't need these phone circuits. AWS will handle all of your circuit needs for you. Like the phone company, AWS will charge you for the minutes you use only.

The Connect model is attractive to businesses because there are no sunk monthly costs with the pay-as-you-go model. For instance, let's say that your company sells Christmas ornaments, and your busy sales season is from June to November. However, in December, since all the store displays are already set up, and everyone has their inventory, your call volume drops to near zero. On premises with a conventional system, you would still have to pay for those circuits even though they aren't being used. If using Connect, your costs would drop to near zero along with your call volume.

It should be reasonably easy for you to identify the costs for your circuits that you currently use. If you are setting up a new call center, it might make sense to call a phone company and find out how much a circuit would cost, so that you can include an on-premises comparison. This comparison will help paint a picture as to how Connect is more cost-effective than other solutions.

No long-term contracts

If you have ever worked with a phone company with any circuit larger than a standard phone line, you will know how they lock you into a long-term contract. Typically, a T1 circuit could have a contract as long as three years. While this might not sound like an expense above and beyond the circuit costs we just talked about, it can be. The contracts that you enter with a phone company lock you into a specific usage pattern at a particular location. If any of those two things change, you might be on the hook for expenses to terminate the contract early. If you were to move to a different state where the provider didn't have a presence in order to move your circuit, you would probably owe them termination fees. These fees immediately recoup the cost of the installation from you.

Phone companies lock you into a contract because it costs them money to bring the circuits to your building. They spread this cost out over time to recoup them. It's similar to how you used to get a cell phone for nearly nothing but had to sign up for a two-year contract with the cell carrier. The cell carrier was just recouping the cost of the phone from you over a longer period.

Since Amazon Connect uses a pay-as-you-go model, these costs will never exist in the first place. You can create and remove phone numbers, call flows, or even whole Connect instances with no penalty. Although you might not be in a situation where this kind of hard cost would affect you, it does make a compelling argument against a conventional system.

No long delays for implementation and upgrades

With conventional telephone circuits, there is a lengthy delay with the installation. At best, you can get a circuit installed within 30 days. However, it wouldn't be uncommon to see an install timeline in the 90-day range. Unfortunately, there isn't much that can be done to accelerate the phone companies and get the line installed faster. While you're waiting for the circuits to be installed, your business isn't stopping. This delay is where the costs come in. You can't expand to meet increasing customer demand or launch that new product. While at a standstill, your company is burning real dollars in lost revenue and decreasing your customers' satisfaction.

Again, since Connect is a pay-as-you-go internet-based product, you don't have to wait for anything to be installed. You get to start using it the second that you want to. This lack of delay means that you can immediately address increased customer demand or launch that new product line. This agility and speed mean that your company can start to reap the benefits as quickly as you implement your Connect instance. Once Connect is up and online, it will scale to meet your needs, big or small. I might sound like a broken record right now because I keep stating all of the pay-as-you-go benefits, but they are numerous and essential.

No demarcation extension costs

Unless you are fortunate in terms of the layout of your building and where the phone companies' circuits come in, you will probably run into some costs associated with extending the circuit to your suite or telecom room. The phone company will only bring your circuits into the building. They aren't responsible for the rest of the way. The responsibility to extend that circuit is up to you. Typically, these costs are not astronomical, maybe a couple of thousand dollars. However, it is an inconvenience as another piece in an already complex puzzle.

Since we already discussed that with Connect, you wouldn't have any circuits in the first place, you wouldn't then need to extend the circuit. However, this is another instance where it's an important cost to incorporate when making a financial comparison against an existing or potential on-premises deployment. Many of these small costs get lost when performing an analysis since they don't occur often. Employee churn is very common in IT, and it wouldn't be unheard of for someone who installed a circuit to leave before the next one is provisioned. When the employee left, they took the tribal knowledge required for the circuit extension. These types of oversights lead to cost overruns or incomplete comparisons.

Extra equipment

I have saved the best hard cost for last: extra equipment. Since Connect is based on a software platform, there isn't any need to buy phones, cards for a telephone system, or special power over Ethernet switches. Suppose you take a second to think about all of the world's phones out there, sitting on desks unused. I'm sure the costs of those phones are in the hundreds of millions. The COVID-19 pandemic made this problem even worse. Phones are a depreciating asset that you don't have to purchase when using Amazon Connect.

With Connect, your users will use the computers and headsets that they already have. You won't need to purchase any extra equipment that depreciates or sits unused. Determining how much phones would cost is an important variable when comparing Connect to typical call center systems. The cost of phones alone adds up to be a significant expense. To make matters worse, the phones themselves depreciate very quickly. At one company I worked for, we purchased our phones second-hand and saved significantly. Others' misfortunes were our gain.

We have now covered the hard cost savings that can be attributed to utilizing Connect. If you can allocate costs appropriately for an existing system, you should be able to compare to your current system and show how migrating to Connect will save you a small fortune. Likewise, suppose you are going to be creating a new call center. In that case, you can properly compare and contrast costs and demonstrate how a software- and internet-based solution is far superior to on-premises systems.

Reducing soft costs

The interfacing of other AWS services gives Connect the ability to reduce soft costs in your organization. In the *User experience* section, we touched on several capabilities that also decrease your soft costs. Before we start reviewing these savings opportunities, let's review a comment made earlier that soft costs are more qualitative and harder to use for financial decisions. Since soft costs are items such as reducing employee efforts and reducing staff, they become harder to quantify. Employees are different. They work at different speeds, have different career objectives, different skill sets, and so on. Therefore, whenever you estimate these soft costs, there is always some amount of doubt. This doubt is what makes crafting a financial decision based on them much more difficult.

To demonstrate this, let's take a look at this scenario. You have designed your Connect implementation and have created an AI bot that allows your customers to use self-service. Your customers can now call in and check their last order's status without speaking to an agent. You have chosen this self-service option because you spoke to the call center staff and asked them the most frequent question. You then asked the staff how long they would spend on the phone with a client looking up their order and letting them know the status. After you gathered all of the information, you took the average hourly cost of a call center agent and calculated the savings based on the estimated number of calls. In total, you have figured that the new self-service AI bot will save the company $124,546 in employee time.

Based on this scenario, you should be able to see how Connect can save you a significant amount of money. Unfortunately, soft cost savings are more of a bonus when seeking financial and project approval. If you were to base the entire project on the merits of the $124,546 alone, you would run into a lot of questions, such as the following:

- Do you have exact numbers on how many times this question was asked of staff?
- Are the time savings are based on an average of employees, efficient employees, or poor performers?
- Does the volume of this question ebb and flow based on the time of year?

There's almost an infinite number of permutations of the questions you will be asked. You won't have answers for all of them. That is why I suggest building your solid foundation for approval on hard costs first, and make the soft cost savings the icing on the cake.

We have already covered how an AI bot may potentially save you money by reducing staff commitments. This reduction is probably one of the biggest contributors to saving you cash with Connect. The possibilities for self-service using bots are nearly endless. Some possible options to think about are as follows:

- Order status
- Shipping status
- Last paycheck deposit amount
- Current vacation balance
- Repeating a customer's last order
- Pausing a standing order
- Canceling an order
- Getting test results

These are some examples of what can be automated with self-service. Of course, this is highly dependent on the industry that you are engaged in. The only way that you will be able to extract what these automations might look like would be to communicate with the call center team. They will be able to provide the required insight as to what would be most effective to implement. If you are implementing a new call center, you might extract information from the business unit requesting the call center. However, I would suggest a follow-up post-implementation after a few months to revisit and see what improvements can be made. All of these self-service automations are reliant on a very important concept. This concept is the interfacing of Connect with enterprise applications. We will cover these interfaces in depth in the next chapter.

Summary

Now that we have covered the benefits of Connect, you have hopefully created some strong stories as to how your company can use these benefits to its advantage. The customer experience benefits should give you some great "why" stories to communicate with other business units. The hard and soft cost savings will give you a great financial story to show. Finally, all of these things are possible by utilizing AWS services to create application interfaces. You may have some additional effort to complete the costing analysis and estimates. However, you should be well on your way to crafting the initial parts of your implementation plan.

The next part of the planning process involves gathering the business requirements from your stakeholders. You will not be able to judge the project scope, or how much the finished implementation will cost, unless you know what the business is trying to achieve. In the next chapter, we are going to cover how to extract this information, and how views will need to change to adapt to Connect's capabilities.

2
Reviewing Stakeholder Objectives

Before you can start deploying your call center or even move on to the planning process costs phase, you will have to gather your stakeholders' objectives. Establishing what your call center contact flows will look like is an essential step in the planning process. By establishing a rough draft of what the overall call structure will look like, you will have a better idea of what additional AWS services you will use and where. This would be impossible without meeting with your stakeholders and learning about their needs. It's essential to establish this upfront as it helps you determine the costs of operating your call center. We will cover costs in depth in *Chapter 4, Connect Costing*. This chapter will focus on the conversations that need to be had with stakeholders and how to convert their objectives into contact flows.

We aren't going to stop there either. We are going to have to break some proverbial eggs to make our new call center omelet. When you first sit down and talk through the contact flows with the stakeholders, you and they will have a propensity to stick to conventional methods. What I mean by conventional methods is what you are used to experiencing when you call a call center. We will push you further to make you start thinking outside of the box to provide better service, reduce costs, and break the existing mental barriers.

In this chapter, you will learn about the following:

- What probing questions should you ask
- Contact flow influencers
- Deployment influencers
- Reframing the conversation

Extracting critical information

Many of the contact flows within Connect are necessary for operations and don't need a lot of customization. These are items such as callback, customer hold, and agent hold. There may be some minor tweaks to the messaging, but for the most part, these flows remain mostly unchanged. The brunt of your work in designing call flows will occur in the specialized call flows designed for your particular use case. It is from these contact flows that you will need to extract the experience from the stakeholder. By experience, I mean how the stakeholder expects the customer to progress through the system and end up where they need to be.

Since we are talking to the stakeholders, we will also want to cover some additional items that aren't directly related to the contact flows. I'm a firm believer in having fewer meetings rather than more. These days, I know it feels like I'm a dying breed, but I'm keeping up the good fight. While you have the stakeholder's attention, you can cover things such as where the call center will be located and save you and them time. The things that we need to cover are as follows:

- Region
- Agent location
- Identity management
- Business hours
- Queues
- Callbacks

- Voicemail
- Outbound calling
- Management
- Integrations

You will need this information at some point, so it's best to get it out of the way now. Just make sure to document it in a way that you can reference it later. I myself have captured information such as this and then was unable to find it later. It's not a good look to re-ask questions, so don't follow in my footsteps there.

Contact flow influencers

We need to extract two different kinds of information from the stakeholders. The first kind of information that we are going to cover is the contact flow influencers. These are items that directly influence the way that the contact flows are created. They are tightly coupled with the customers' experience. In this section, we will cover the following:

- Business hours
- Queues
- Transfers
- Callbacks
- Voicemail
- Integrations

Let's dive deep into each of these categories.

Business hours

The first and probably most important item to cover is business hours. **Business hours** are necessary because they can dictate how queues will operate when the center is or is not staffed. It's obvious that we will cover how the stakeholder wants calls to be answered during business hours. However, there are several ways you might want to handle calls outside of regular business hours. The stakeholder might want to have the system ask for a callback number for a caller to be called by the first available agent the next business day. Another option might be to record a voicemail that someone will check later. There also might be a need to accept information and page someone in the event of an emergency.

Having this information will help you determine what kind of branching will need to occur after hours. There might be some **Interactive Voice Response (IVR)** capabilities required to gather client information as well. Having this information will also help you identify some potential additions to the queue configuration, which we will cover in the next section.

Queues

Queues are one of the basic components of a Connect instance. Essentially, a queue is a line that customers will be put into when they proverbially walk in to your call center. When a caller first enters your system, they will be presented with a greeting and your first set of options. These options determine what queue they should be placed in for service. For instance, let's say that we have called in to a support center for some software we just purchased.

Along with that software, we also bought a premium support plan. This plan allows us priority access to support. When we call in, we will be prompted for our support contract number. Once the Connect instance knows what support options we have, it can route our call to the right queue. In this case, we are calling about a widget mobile app, and so we are placed in the widget premium support queue.

You are probably wondering why it's essential to ask your stakeholders about what kind of queues they want. The way the queues get laid out will significantly impact how your contact flows are created. The number of queues is going to directly affect your costs both from an operational and implementation standpoint.

Types and quantity of queues

There are technically two types of queues in Connect: **standard** and **agent**. But that isn't what I mean by types here. You will need to determine the kinds of queues required from a business perspective. Some questions you might want to ask are as follows:

- Do you require calls to be answered according to different priorities?

- Do you need to have calls answered by agents with special knowledge?

- Do agents need the ability to transfer from one queue to another?

To demonstrate what a queue structure looks like, let's look at a hospital's hypothetical setup. If you were setting up a call center for a hospital, there would be several queues required. Think about all the departments that may be available on a call menu when customers first call. There would be appointments, billing, accounts payable, radiology, oncology, pediatrics, geriatrics, ICU, NICU, and emergency, just to name a few. Then within some of these queues, there might be a need for sub-queues.

> **Important note**
> There is no such thing as a sub-queue. I'm just using this terminology to help you visualize. For instance, say someone lands in the billing queue and their call is answered, but they end up having a dispute about their bill. From there, the agent might route them into another queue for billing disputes. This queue would have a subset of agents in it with specialized training to handle these particular calls.

It's important to note that Connect has a soft limit of 50 queues per instance. "Soft" means that you can enter a support ticket to have that number increased. If you are going to get close to that number, you will probably want to open that support ticket as soon as you create your Connect instance so that it's resolved before your deployment.

Once you have a layout of the queues and sub-queues, you can picture the glue required between them. This glue might consist of IVR, Lex Bots, or manual agent transfers.

Transfers

After you have the details about the queue, you are going to have to inquire about **transfers**. Nearly every call center is going to need to transfer users at some point. I don't think that I have run into a single instance where this wasn't necessary. It's important to understand the types and how your stakeholders might use them. There are three ways to do transfers in Connect:

- Transfer to queue
- Transfer to agent
- Transfer to an external number

Transfer to queue

The **transfer to queue** capability will be your go-to function for transferring customers to get specialized answers. The capability is as it sounds: an agent can transfer a caller into another queue directly without sending them through some sort of IVR or another system. For instance, say that you called to make a change to your hotel reservation, and you ended up pressing one for reservations. Unfortunately, you didn't listen to the rest of the message, and option two was to make changes to an existing reservation. When you were connected to the agent and asked to make a change, they could not do that in the system. The agent then transfers you to another queue, option two, for you. When speaking with your stakeholder, it will be important to draw out what kinds of transfers they want and which should be unavailable.

Transfer to agent

The ability to **transfer to an agent** is self-explanatory. A client calls in, has a special need, and is transferred to the agent to help them. However, I will advise against asking your stakeholder if they want the ability to transfer calls to an agent. If you think about it for a second, you can probably see how that agent might be on vacation, lunch, or be otherwise unavailable. Then what would you do? I would reserve the transfer to agent capability for transferring calls to managers to resolve issues and recommend using transfer to queue for special skills requests. You then resolve the issue of agent availability. Even if there is only one agent in the queue, you would be able to offer a callback to the customer using this method.

Transfer to an external number

The last form of transfer that you will need to ask your stakeholder about is the ability to **transfer to an external number**. This type of transfer typically shows up in two situations:

- The first is where you transfer as part of the contact flow itself, such as to a support number that goes to a cell phone after hours.
- The second type is when you are transferring from the agent to an external number.

Transferring to an external number is expected when you need to transfer a call to another Connect instance. One thing to keep in mind is that when you transfer from one Connect instance to another, the call is still based on the first instance and is essentially relayed to the second. This hopping might cause additional latency delays.

Callbacks

Now that you have discussed transfers with your stakeholder, we need to move on and discuss callbacks. **Callbacks** are a newer development in call centers. A callback is when a client calls in to a center, the hold times are long, and the system offers them the option to receive a callback. They then enter their number or confirm their caller ID number, and the system will call them back. This feature is a massive improvement to customer satisfaction. How many times have you had to wait on the phone for potentially over an hour? How much happier would you have been if you could be doing what you needed to get done and could just pick up your phone when it rang? Unless you love the horrible hold music, I doubt you will say you prefer the old method.

Callbacks are also a very useful alternative to using voicemail for after-hours calls. With voicemail, someone has to check it, take notes, and then call someone back. Some things happen in this process that don't provide excellent customer service. Is the voicemail going to be checked first thing in the morning? Are calls going to be returned in order? Will a customer call position be preserved before new calls come in? Will all calls be returned and not lost? The answer to all these questions is a big maybe, with a heavy weighting toward no.

With callbacks, these problems go away. The Connect instance will manage all queue callbacks and remove human error and delays from the equation. You should recommend callbacks over voicemail when anyone asks for it. They are most likely looking for the ability to get back to clients after hours and are unaware of how callbacks can improve the overall experience. By highlighting voicemail's previously mentioned pitfalls, you will probably persuade them to ditch the older voicemail model.

Voicemail

You might be wondering why I'm mentioning voicemail after I just slammed it and said it was inferior to callbacks. Well, **voicemail** can be used in a different way, not only for clients calling after hours. I run a non-profit and use Connect as my phone system. It's not the intended use for Connect, but guess what: Connect is so flexible that you can use it for a phone system anyway. How cool is that? In the phone system model, voicemail makes perfect sense. If I'm not available or just don't want to receive any calls, I can have them sent to voicemail instead. In this situation, it's not a random call that wants to talk to an agent, nor is there any concern about when and in what order the call will be returned. The caller is looking to speak to another employee or me directly.

You might not require this in your call center, but it's important to discuss it with the stakeholder. There might be a situation where an agent has such specialized knowledge that having voicemail set up for their overflow calls makes sense. You will want to leave all the options on the table. Now that we have covered the Connect features to deal with overflow and after-hours calls with voicemail and callbacks, we need to cover outbound calling.

Integrations

The last component that we need to talk about that affects contact flows is **integrations** into third-party systems. You will want to find out from your stakeholder what kinds of systems they have that might be possible integration points. These systems might be **Customer Relationship Management (CRMs)**, **Enterprise Resource Planning (ERPs)**, **Software as a Service (SaaS)** solutions, or potentially internally built applications. You might need to interface directly with a database to extract information as well. It's highly probable that your stakeholder hasn't even thought of what these interfaces might look like. The capabilities of Connect and the ancillary AWS services are uncharted waters for many people and companies.

You just want to extract what applications might be possible interfaces and not get into the nitty-gritty of what they might look like at this phase of your review. You are just looking for a rough idea of how many connections might need to be made and how that will affect your contact flows at a high level. Later, in the section about reframing the conversation, we will discuss how to draw out what these interactions will look like at a detailed level. You will want to review the information you have been collecting up to this point. You don't want to move forward immediately with reframing. Think about the current requirements for some time. You will want to let your mind wander and think about the what-if situations. But more on that in the later section.

Deployment influencers

Integrations were the last of the contact flow influencers that we are going to discuss. Now we are going to move on to deployment influencers. These items influence the deployment in a more general and overarching way. They do not have any direct effect on the customer's experience but rather the experience and capabilities of agents and managers.

Management

We have just finished covering all the items that directly affect the contact flows and how they are laid out. Now you will need to consider a few more items that are relevant to your deployment but around administration. Amazon Connect comes with four default security profiles to attach users to. These profiles are as follows:

- **Admin**: Grants full admin rights
- **Agent**: Grants access to the **Contact Control Panel (CCP)**
- **Call Center Manager**: Grants permissions for user management, routing, and more
- **Quality Analyst**: Grants access to metrics

In my experience, these permissions are not quite granular enough, and more security profiles will need to be created to fine-tune the access permissions. For instance, one of my frustrations is that the call center manager profile doesn't give access to the CCP to accept calls. Nearly every manager I've talked to has wanted to accept calls and help in times of high volume. Another common issue is that the call center manager profile can change routing. For a large organization that uses Connect for multiple call centers, these rights should be limited to IT staff.

When you discuss permissions with your stakeholder, you will want to review the six major access permissions categories that create a security profile. These categories and their permissions are as follows:

Category	Sub Items
Routing	Routing profiles Quick connects Hours of operation Queues
Numbers and flows	Prompts Contact flows Phone numbers Chat test mode
Users and permissions	Users Agent hierarchy Security profiles Agent status
Contact Control Panel	Access Contact Control Panel Make outbound calls

Category	Sub Items
Metrics and Quality	Access metrics
	Contact search
	Search contacts by conversation characteristics
	Search contacts by keywords
	Restrict contact access
	Contact attributes
	Contact Lens – speech analytics
	Rules
	Recorded conversations (redacted)
	Login/logout report
	Manager monitor
	Recorded conversations (unredacted)
	Saved reports
Historical changes	View historical changes

We won't dive into each of the permissions at this time. The message that I want to convey is that you should review the groups of users and what each group should do. You won't want to talk in strictly technical terms, such as does a user need to *publish contact flow?* Instead, ask: should the manager group be able to change a contact flow? Your stakeholder might not understand the tenchnical terms. You can use the information conveyed from your stakeholder to align with existing security profiles and identify additional ones that need to be created. There is no fee for creating security profiles, so there should be no reason to try and artificially constrain yourself to what is already available. Bend Connect to fit your needs as much as necessary. It allows the use of up to 100 security profiles. With our review of user permissions done, it's time to move on to monitoring.

Monitoring and recording

Most call centers you will contact today have some form of monitoring for quality, training, or security purposes. Connect also allows you to perform monitoring and call recording. You would want to ask your stakeholder if they want to record and monitor calls. The activation of monitoring and recording does have a small impact on how you design your contact flows. One important thing to note is that you cannot do call monitoring without activating call recording; it's a packaged deal. After you ask about monitoring and recording, you should follow that up by asking about what kind of messaging should be attached to meet privacy regulations. This message is pretty standard most of the time, but it's best to cover your bases.

Another thing you will probably want to discuss is whether they're going to record outbound calls. The recording of outbound calls would require a change to the outbound whisper to enable call recording and provide a message to the callee that their call was being monitored and recorded. Another option would be to have the agent notify them verbally once the call was connected. However, this message could be forgotten and could potentially open you up to liability and fines. Connect offers the whisper contact flow option, and I would stick with that.

Outbound calling

Your stakeholder might need for individuals to be able to call out of the call center. In this instance, we are not talking about the ability to perform a callback. Outbound calls, in this sense, are when the agent dials the phone like a house or cell phone. There might be several use cases for this type of call initiation, but it's essential to understand the difference. Inbound and outbound calls are metered at different rates with Amazon Connect. We will cover these costs later in *Chapter 3, Sketching Your Contact Flows*. For now, you need to discuss this option with the stakeholder so you can get an idea as to the ratio of inbound and outbound calls to assess costs correctly.

To help the stakeholder understand the use case, let's look at this scenario. You just launch a new start-up during the COVID-19 pandemic to do COVID testing. You set up a call center to field the calls for customers to get their results. A significant component of your strategy is to have a nurse call out for any positive test results. You don't want your customers to have to call in and potentially wait longer for those results. You're estimating that 25% of cases will be positive.

In this scenario, you now have a use case for outbound calls and the percentage of calls in this category. The one caveat you should address is that some users may call in to get the results before the nurse has time to call them back. You will still want to account for the 25%, but you will want to add 5% for the incoming calls to account for overlap. You might be asking about callbacks – are they not outbound calls too? You would be correct, but we will address callbacks as outbound calls and costs in *Chapter 3, Sketching Your Contact Flows*.

Region

Like with the rest of the AWS services, you will have to deploy Connect into a specific region. The region location should be located as close as possible to the bulk of the agents. Having the agents close to the Connect instance provides the best experience in terms of latency. You don't want to have your customers calling in to your brand new call center and getting choppy and hard-to-hear audio out of your agents. Amazon Connect isn't available in every region; as of the publishing of this book, these are the available regions:

- US East
- US West
- Asia Pacific (Sydney)
- Asia Pacific (Singapore)
- Asia Pacific (Tokyo)
- EU (Frankfurt)
- EU (London)

AWS is always changing its offerings, and it's best to check to see whether a new region is supported when you deploy Connect.

When clients call in to your Connect instance, they are traversing the telecom networks using standard phone communications. They won't be using the internet to connect like your agents. Agents use **Voice over IP** (**VoIP**) technology to connect via a web interface. Although the distance between the caller and your Connect instance can create a latency issue, I haven't experienced any noticeable delays within the continental US. If your callers are making international connections or your clients are in more underdeveloped regions, you might want to balance the distance between your agents and customers when selecting an AWS region.

Agent location

Once you have identified which region you want to use, the next question that needs to be asked of your stakeholder is where the agents will be located. In this case, we are not looking for a region as before but rather for where they will perform their work. Will the agents be working from home? Will they be in an office? This question needs to be asked to determine whether there is enough bandwidth available to handle all communications. Again, you don't want your clients to have a poor experience with jittery and unintelligible chatter.

If your agents are going to be working from home, you will have a bandwidth advantage. Each agent will have an internet connection and will probably have adequate bandwidth. Connect requires 100 Kbps of bandwidth for each agent connection. Unless your agents are in a pandemic and have kids doing distance learning on Zoom, they should be just fine.

You might need to break out your calculator when your call center has many agents in a single location. If you were to have about 200 agents in a single site, you would need 20 Mbps of bandwidth. This amount might not seem like a large number, but some internet connections can be asynchronous, meaning the upload bandwidth does not match the download bandwidth. Asynchronous communications are pervasive in cable-based broadband internet. Your connection might have 300 Mpbs for download, but the upload might be maxed out at 20 Mpbs. Now that you know how much bandwidth the call center might need, it's time to determine where the users will be sourced.

Identity management

You are going to need to find out how users will authenticate to your new Connect instance. Connect offers three ways to authenticate users, but in my opinion, there are only two options. The three options are as follows:

- Store users with Amazon Connect
- Link to an existing directory
- **Security Assertion Markup Language (SAML)** 2.0-based authentication

The two options that I recommend are to store the users within Connect and SAML. I only recommend keeping users within Connect for minimal deployments of just a few agents where you don't have an existing SAML provider. However, if possible, I highly suggest that you build out a SAML provider anyway. It doesn't make sense for your users to have yet another password to track, lose, or have poor password hygiene with. With SAML, your users will use your existing directories such as Microsoft Active Directory, Azure Active Directory, or Google GSuite. Single sign-on is preferred by users and security teams alike. Plus, by using SAML, you can implement **Multi-Factor Authentication (MFA)** as well.

I don't recommend linking Connect to an existing directory because you have to use the AWS directory services. You will need to use either the full or Simple Microsoft directory service, or the Active Directory Connector offered by AWS. Most often, these are just additional costs for inferior products to the SAML authentication. Odds are, with all the SaaS applications in use today, you probably have a SAML implementation already anyway.

Your business stakeholder might not be able to answer this question for you. You might need to talk to someone in the IT department to discuss the options. One question that would make sense to ask the stakeholder is whether they would find it acceptable to use separate user accounts for a small deployment. They might not find it to be a significant inconvenience. Also, getting SAML configured through IT might take more time and delay a small group project.

Reframing the conversation

Congratulations on making it this far in the process. You've collected all the necessary information from the stakeholders, and you have a good mental picture of what it would take to implement their needs in Amazon Connect. This is where we need to spice things up a bit. I'd venture to guess that you have received conventional answers for everything you have asked your stakeholders. They probably didn't throw any ideas your way that would leverage any of the more advanced capabilities of Amazon Connect. To reframe the conversation, you will have to have a new conversation and introduce some new possibilities.

I suggest that you let the information you have gathered sit and stew in your mind for a couple of days. This time gives you the ability to think about more *what if* scenarios. The next time you talk to the stakeholder, you want to bring the *art of the possible* to the table. Some of your ideas might not be achievable, but it will get them thinking in the right way. With all Connect's capabilities, you don't want just to set up a standard boring call center, do you?

As we discussed in *Chapter 1, Benefits of Amazon Connect*, most of the benefits of Connect enable improved user experience. Up till now, most of the conversations have probably been around standard IVR capabilities. Think back to our hospital example: if you want the billing department, press one; for radiology, press two. You won't exactly be getting any usability awards for that kind of customer interaction. The two new capabilities that Connect offers that we will use to reframe are Amazon Lex and Interfaces.

Lex offers you an AI chatbot to receive customer information. This augmentation can make the contact flows feel more natural and quicker for customers. For instance, our hospital example had many potential departments that a caller might want to reach. This menu creates a very long session for your user before they even have the potential to speak to someone. Another good example of this is calling a large-box home improvement retailer. I've had to sit on the phone and hit 22 before being able to speak to the department I was looking for. No one wants to sit there and listen to all the options.

With Lex, you can build a bot that asks what department you would like to speak to. The bot then waits for the user to reply with whom they wish to speak. The customer reply is then processed via natural language processing to identify what the user wants. Lex calls these intents. We won't get any deeper into how Lex works. We will cover that in a later chapter with its technical implementation. Using Lex for customer input rather than IVR is just one way that you can improve your experience.

Another way in which Lex can improve your call center is when it's coupled with an interface to create self-service. Using Lex in this way, you not only increase customer satisfaction but also drive down costs. Your agents may potentially not need to answer that customer's call. Let's go back to our hospital example. You have to call in and find out the amount of your last bill because your kids decided to use it to make papier-mâché. Without Lex, you would have to go through an IVR system to speak to billing and then talk to an agent to determine your last bill.

Utilizing Lex, you will still call in to the system but then tell Lex that you wanted to speak to billing. At this point, you would be transferred to the billing contact flow. This contact flow would prompt you with a new Lex bot that would inquire as to what kind of help you needed, such as paying a bill or getting your last balance. You would then ask for your last balance, and Lex would then reply to get additional information such as your social security number and zip code to validate your identity. When Lex identifies your identity and intent, this information gets passed to Lambda, the heart of your integration. Lambda reaches out to the hospital system that holds this billing information and looks up your last statement's balance. Lambda then passes this information back to Connect, which tells you what your balance was.

As you can hopefully see, not only did you get the information you needed quickly, but you also didn't have to speak to an agent. The agent was free to continue taking calls that couldn't be answered by the Lex bot. These are the types of conversations you will want to think about, given the information you have gathered and how the overall flow might be improved. You can then craft stories such as the example shared to demonstrate your stakeholder's new capabilities. In turn, they should give you a host of new ideas and functions that they would like to be built in to the system.

Summary

We covered a lot of material in this chapter. But it's important to drive home how to gather the system's needs early in the planning process. It makes the whole endeavor significantly easier in the long run. There is nothing worse than having to come back later and re-work significant parts. The probing questions you have learned, and how they affect the contact flows and the deployments, will help you take a shortcut to a more refined system at launch. Finally, our discussion about reframing the conversation assisted you in taking the capabilities of your call center to the next level.

Now that we have a firm understanding of what the contact flows should contain, it's time to move on to sketching out your contact flows in *Chapter 3, Sketching Your Contact Flows*.

3
Sketching Your Contact Flows

Since you have discovered all your call center's objectives from the business stakeholder, it's now time to sketch out your contact flows. The reason that I recommend defining them now is that it will help you with estimating costs. With a conventional call center, all your costs will be related to minutes on the phone. However, with Connect, there are many more services at your disposal. The costs for these additional services should be included in your financial analysis for the overall project. In addition to helping you with cost estimation, sketching out your contact flows now helps you to demonstrate the actions callers will take visually. This picture will help people within your company understand the project better as a whole.

Before we can cover how to sketch out the contact flows, we must cover some basics about contact flows themselves. There are several types of contact flows and several components that create the flows. Once we learn about these concepts, we can cover what rules need to be followed and finally put our thoughts on paper or the screen.

In this chapter, we will work through the following topics:

- Types of contact flows
- Contact flow components
- Putting all the pieces together

Types of flows

Connect has nine different types of contact flows. They each serve a specific purpose, and we will cover those in depth in the next few sections.

The nine contact flow types are as follows:

- Inbound contact flow
- Customer queue flow
- Customer hold flow
- Customer whisper flow
- Outbound whisper flow
- Agent hold flow
- Agent whisper flow
- Transfer to agent flow
- Transfer to queue flow

The important thing to remember is that of these nine different types, most of your work will be performed using the inbound contact flow. The others will be used in your call center, but you won't have to do as much work with them as you will with the inbound contact flow type.

Inbound contact flow

This is the default kind of flow in Connect when you click the button to create a contact flow. Inside of the inbound flow, you will put your AI bots, **Interactive Voice Response** (**IVR**), interfaces, and other advanced features such as callbacks. Inbound contact flows work with both voice and chat functions. The best practice is to have more than one inbound flow. If you try and do everything in one flow, it will quickly become unruly and hard to manage. I liken the way that I design contact flows to microservices. You want to segment the workloads, in the case of Connect themes, so that you can make things more manageable and distribute your risk.

For instance, I would create an inbound flow to accept the call and then set various settings. Rather than continue with playing messages and moving the flow forward, I transfer to a second flow. Within this second inbound flow, I play a message and continue with the flow of the call. By creating segmentation, you make your contact flows easier to manage and reduce risk by minimizing your blast radius.

Customer queue flow

The customer queue flow is used when a customer is put into a queue. Typically, this flow is used to set things such as hold music or messages apologizing for delays or how many people are in the queue ahead of them. In this type of flow, you might also want to offer the option to have the customer select a callback, so they don't have to wait on the phone any longer. You will want to have a customer queue flow, but you probably won't have to edit it often.

I have found that once these flows are set up, they are fairly static. There are, of course, some minor changes to messaging. You might want to change messages for the holidays or highlight currently running sales. You may want to have more than one customer queue flow depending on how many queues you have and the business's objectives.

Customer hold flow

The customer hold flow is used when the customer is put on hold by an agent. It isn't used when the customer is sitting in the queue waiting for an agent to answer. In that instance, you would use the customer queue flow that we just discussed. Again, this type of flow is usually set up and doesn't see a lot of changes. Typically, I have seen these flows changed for holidays, where the music is changed. Otherwise, they are rather static.

I would recommend that you have some sort of background sound, either music or messaging, while on hold so that your customer knows that they were not hung up on. Nothing is more awkward to someone than sitting on the phone listening to dead air. This type of flow only works with voice, as there isn't any hold for chat messages.

Customer whisper flow

A whisper flow controls what happens as someone is connected to an agent or called during an outbound call. In the case of a customer whisper flow, it controls the messaging a customer receives just before an agent answers. The customer whisper flow works for both chat and voice calls.

You might not have a customer whisper flow, but typically they contain a message that the call may be monitored or recorded. You could put this message in an inbound flow or a queue flow. However, by using the customer whisper flow, you ensure that this message is played and not missed. You wouldn't want to get yourself into any legal trouble by not playing this message. This flow will be static and will probably not change.

Outbound whisper flow

When an agent or callback outbound call is made, the outbound whisper flow is used. This flow is important, and it is used to enable call recording for outbound calls and plays disclaimer messages. Technically, you don't need to have anything in your outbound whisper flow. You might just choose not to record outbound calls, and then you won't have to play a disclaimer. I would suggest that there is some form of messaging that is played so that your customer knows what is going on.

For callbacks, I typically recommend a message noting that they are receiving a callback. This way, your customer knows that it's the call they were expecting. Then, notify them that the call can be reordered and follow up with a message about being connected to an agent. I recommend this approach so that the client does not have any dead air on the phone. You won't want them to think that they are receiving a spam call from a robot-dialer.

Agent hold flow

The agent hold flow is probably the simplest of all the contact flows. When an agent puts a customer on hold, this is the flow that is used. Typically, there is some form of message informing the agent that the customer is on hold on a loop. Although simple, it serves a very important purpose of reminding the agent that they have a customer on hold. It would be very rare to change this flow once it is created.

Agent whisper flow

With all Connect's added benefits, the agent whisper flow becomes an important part of your call center design. The agent whisper flow is played to the agent before a customer is connected. It can be a powerful tool when combined with application interfaces. For instance, it can look up the customer's name and notify the agent.

You can use it for more impactful things as well. Let's say that you run a non-profit, and you want to make your donors feel more appreciated. You could create an interface that uses the caller ID number to look up the caller's last donation. You could set up an agent whisper to play this information to the agent connected to the caller. With this information, your agent could thank them for their donation, with the exact amount they gave. Imagine how this would make your donor feel.

Keep how you can use agent whisper flows to improve your customers' experience in the back of your head. You may need to put some precursor work into your inbound contact flow first to pass the required information on to the agent whisper.

Transfer to agent flow

Sometimes an agent needs to transfer to another agent. This transfer typically needs to occur because the agent in question has some specific knowledge or capability required by the caller. The transfer to agent flow is used when this form of transfer occurs.

The transfer to agent flow can be useful in relaying information about the customer to the next agent. This interaction ensures a smooth transition between agents and a great user experience. Nothing is worse when you get transferred to a call center and must answer many questions over again just to pick up the conversation. Once the transfer to agent flow is set up, there probably won't be many changes made long term.

Transfer to queue flow

Finally, we arrive at the transfer to queue flow. This flow controls what an agent hears or reads when they transfer to another queue. This flow mainly has controls to ensure that the queue isn't full and that there are agents staffed. You wouldn't want to transfer a customer call into a queue that wasn't manned or was already full from a customer experience perspective. If there are no agents staffed, the customer might get sent directly to voicemail or a callback. That wouldn't be an exceptionally good experience. It would be equally bad to transfer into a queue that was already full as well. In that case, they would receive a fast busy signal and get disconnected. This is also very undesirable from a customer experience perspective.

This type of contact flow works with both chat and voice and is yet another flow that isn't modified all that often. Now that we have covered all the flows, we can move on to the flow components. The flow components are the individual pieces that create the actual contact flow look and feel.

Flow components

The flows in Connect are created by stringing together several flow components to create your call center feel. AWS has broken these flow components down into five categories. We will cover each of these categories as well as all the components in each. Where applicable, I will include some examples of where and when you might use a particular component. The five categories that we are going to cover are as follows:

- Interactions
- Settings

- Branch
- Integrate
- Terminate/transfer

For each of the components, we will cover what the component does and what its output paths are. The output paths are what you will use to connect your components to create a flow. Moving from one component to the next one changes based on the outputs and inputs of each.

Interactions

The interactions grouping is used to interface with the customer on the phone or chat window. It is used to either deliver or extract information from the customer. You will use these components many times over in your call center. They may be the most used of all. The interactions components are as follows:

- Play prompt
- Get customer input
- Store customer input
- Hold customer or agent
- Start media streaming
- Stop media streaming

Let's review how you can use these components to provide a positive user experience.

Play prompt

The play prompt component plays a prompt to your customer, and there are three ways you can communicate. You can play a prompt from your audio library. For instance, if you paid for Samuel L. Jackson to record your hello greeting for your call center, that audio file would be selected and played via this component. Another way would be to use text-to-speech, in which Amazon will use AI to produce a lifelike-sounding voice using the text you entered, such as Amazon Alexa. Finally, the last option is to use text-to-speech for chat. You wouldn't use voice in a chat session, but you would choose for text-to-voice. It's the same selection. The actual field in the configuration is **Text-to-speech or chat text** but I have found that people find this confusing and don't understand.

The play prompt component also can dynamically play a prompt under the text-to-speech option. This option is very useful when creating contact flows that engage with the customer. You could use this for something as simple as letting them know how many people are in the queue ahead of them or as complex as retrieving information from a **Customer Relationship Management (CRM)** or sales system.

The other uses for play prompt abound. It will probably be your number-one-used component in all your contact flows. Obvious uses are your greeting, asking survey questions, or asking for a callback number to be entered. The play prompt component also prefaces more advanced capabilities, such as AI bots. Play prompt also plays a vital role when an error occurs in your contact flow, and you need to notify the customer that something went wrong. You wouldn't want to just hang up on them.

The play prompt component only has one output path. The path available for this component is okay and denotes that the prompt was played. You will use this output to connect to the next input in your contact flow.

Get customer input

When you need to receive data back from your customer, you will use the customer input component. This component is the play prompt component and the ability to capture input combined. From a prompt perspective, it does everything that the play prompt component does, so you won't have to preface the get customer input component with a play prompt component in many cases. The get customer input prompt allows you to receive information from the customer via **Dual Tone Multi-Frequency (DTMF)**, that is, a button press, or an Amazon Lex bot.

With the get customer input component, you can build meaningful contact flows to deliver a self-service experience. A classic example of using the get customer input component would be to ask which department the caller wishes to speak to and receive a DTMF response. It is an effective way to move clients through your call flow without assistance from an agent or receptionist. You can also use this component to ask what department the caller would like to speak to, but rather than DTMF, use a Lex bot to receive back a department name. This method saves your customer from wading through a list of options and provides a better experience.

This component has three default outputs and a dynamic number of configurable outputs. Since you are receiving customer input, you can add new outputs based on that input. In the case of DTMF, you will add button presses, 1, 2, 3, and 4. These button presses will show up as new inputs. Similarly, if you use Lex, you will see intents as outputs, such as plumbing, electrical, paint, and flooring. For these dynamic outputs, you will connect them to the next component in your contact flow. For instance, if someone selected plumbing, that output might go to a transfer component that sends it to another plumbing department flow.

The three default outputs of this component are timeout, default, and error. The timeout output is used when the component doesn't receive back information from the customer. Typically, you will want to loop the timeout back to the same get customer input component so that you can re-prompt for an answer. Sometimes, users enter something that wasn't an option, such as 7 when the highest option was 4. In this case, the default output would be enabled. You may want to send the default to a play prompt component to let them know they entered a bad option and then loop back to the input component to try again.

Finally, there is the error block. The error block is when something goes wrong and it needs to be handled. You might have run into this before when you have called a call center. In my experience, there is a message that says something like, Something went wrong, goodbye. Not helpful for you as a customer or for the company. Errors do happen. Instead of the example message just mentioned, I recommend saying that something went wrong, identifying an error code, apologizing for the inconvenience of needing to call back, and asking them to relay the error code back to an agent when they speak to someone.

Handling errors in this way does several things. It provides your customer with a sense that something will get taken care of by giving the error code. When they give it to an agent, you will be able to trace down where the error occurred in your contact flow and what might have gone wrong. It also gives the message that you are sorry; I know it seems simple, but there is nothing worse than being told that someone screwed up some programming and then being hung up on. Many of the contact flow components will have error handling. Instead of repeating the information just covered; I will just let you know when a block has an error output or not. How you handle errors should be universal.

Store customer input

The store customer input is very similar to getting customer input. The big difference is that you're asking for some form of information rather than a selection. The store customer input component doesn't have dynamic outputs; instead, it stores data for use later in the contact flow. Like get customer input, the store customer input component also plays a message, so you don't need to preface this component with a message component.

You use the store customer input block for capturing things such as phone numbers for callbacks, social security numbers to access account details, ZIP codes, and more. You will probably have a couple of store customer input instances in your call center, especially if you are moving toward self-service capabilities. You can store two different kinds of values, either a custom value or a phone number. If you select a phone number, there are several options and error checks available.

The store customer input has three outputs: success, error, and if you select that you are storing phone numbers, the invalid number output is available. Errors should be handled with your standard error-handling routine. Success is used to move the contact flow forward to the next component. If you selected a phone number type, the invalid phone number output will allow you to handle that error specifically and allow another attempt by looping back to the store customer input again.

Hold customer or agent

Hold customer or agent is a very interesting and useful component. At first glance, you might be asking yourself why putting an agent on hold would be so special. What makes this component awesome is that you can interrupt a call, place an agent on hold, receive some form of secure information using the store customer input component, and then rejoin the agent again. By following this pattern, you ensure that secure information, such as credit card numbers or social security numbers, is never disclosed to agents. You can also encrypt the data for even more protection (the details on how to accomplish this are outside of this book's scope). You might not need this kind of functionality in your call center, but it's important to know that it's available if the need arises.

The hold customer or agent component has only two outputs: success and error. Errors should be handled in the standard way, and the success output connects to the next component in the contact flow.

Start media streaming

Sometimes you might want to take audio from a customer call and route it so that it can be analyzed, processed, or used for training. To accomplish this with Connect, you can use the start media streaming component. This component sends the audio from the call to Kinesis for further processing. There are two configuration options available with this component. You can opt to start streaming the audio from the customer, to the customer, or both at the same time.

Kinesis streaming is a very advanced capability that requires a significant amount of knowledge around programming and other AWS services to properly utilize its outputs. An interesting use case is streaming audio to a third-party application used to detect fraud, specifically, the kind of fraud that happens when people try to call cell phone providers and act like you so that they can get free iPhones sent to them to sell on the black market.

At this point in the development stage, you might not have enough information to formulate whether this type of integration is necessary or what it might look like. Advanced capabilities that would require this kind of integration might be better suited for the second phase of implementation. A complex integration might slow down the initial implementation and increase the risk.

Since start media streaming is a simple component, it only has success or error output. These outputs should be connected like any other component that we have already discussed.

Stop media streaming

After you start media, you need a way to stop it, and that's what this component does. There isn't much to discuss as it has no options to configure. The stop media streaming component has two outputs, the standard success and error, and should be connected in the standard fashion.

The stop media streaming component is the last in the interactions class. Now that we have covered all the ways you can interact with a client in your call center, we can move on to how you can set configuration options within your contact flow.

Settings

While working in Connect, there are several settings that you will need to configure to customize Connect and your customers' experience to your specific business requirements. For instance, one setting configures the voice that is used for prompts, and there are several options. Another configures if calls are logged or not.

Although Connect offers defaults for many of these components, such as using the Johanna voice option in the United States, they might not fit your business requirements. Based on your individual requirements, you may have to include many of the settings components to achieve your desired effect. On the contrary, maybe the defaults meet your needs.

Either way, as a best practice, I recommend including the settings components even if you are using the defaults. This is because it's easier and less error prone to change a setting in an existing component than it is to recraft a flow to include a new component.

> **Important note**
> Although the default flows that Amazon Connect comes with will do the job, they aren't robust and just offer the minimum required settings. For instance, error handling on many of the flows just says goodbye and hangs up on the customer.

Typically, I create a contact flow just for configuring all the necessary settings for the call center. Most of the time, you will only set this one time. I guess if you wanted to continually change the voice used everywhere in your call center, you could, but I'm not sure what the value would be in that. The setting components we are going to cover are as follows:

- Set working queue
- Set contact attributes
- Change routing priority/age
- Set logging behavior
- Set recording and analytic behavior
- Set hold flow
- Set customer queue flow
- Set whisper flow
- Set disconnect flow
- Set callback number
- Set voice
- Get queue metrics

We will now review the capabilities of these components and discuss some of their use cases.

Set working queue

For Connect to be able to handle calls, you need to set a working queue. This setting tells Connect what agents are going to handle the calls. If you are running a small contact center, you will probably set the working queue early in a contact flow setting. However, if you have a large call center with many departments or groups that will be answering calls, then you will probably hold off on setting this until you have more information about the caller's intentions. Once you have those intentions, you need to set the queue before transferring the call to the queue. Set working queue has two outputs, success and error, and they should be handled in the standard fashion.

Set contact attributes

When you start working with Connect's more advanced integration features, you will probably run into a situation where you need to store some information about the caller for later processing. Set contact attributes allows you to store additional information about the client. For instance, you might look to use the caller ID phone number to look up the caller's name in your CRM system. After your Lambda function runs and pulls the customer name, you can store it using the set contact attributes component.

You can also use the set contact attributes block to identify whether compliance messages have been played. For instance, you can play a message about call recording and immediately set a contact attribute that can be used later to ensure that the customer heard the message. If not, the agent can notify them when they are connected to the call. The outputs for this component are the standard success and error outputs.

Change routing priority/age

In the last chapter, we discussed how you might have a paid subscription in which some customers might have a higher level of priority support. There are two ways in which you can implement priority in Amazon Connect. The first one is to set up a separate queue where a special team of agents answers those calls. Sometimes this isn't practical or cost-effective, and another solution is needed. In this case, you can use the change routing priority component.

Here is an example of how you would use this component. You have a premium support line that allows for shorter hold times for priority customers. However, you can't afford a complete team dedicated to these customers. Instead, you opt to set up a separate phone number for priority customers. When a customer calls into this number, the contact flow uses the change routing priority component to set the priority to one for all calls coming into that number (the highest priority). The clients are then placed into a queue. For normal customers, there is a separate number that they call. When they call into the standard support number, the contact flow sets the priority of those calls to 5, the lowest priority.

Using this method allows you to keep the same call queue and the same agents yet have higher priority calls answered first. You can also use this component to manually set the age of the caller. However, I don't see this technique used often. This component only has the success output and should be connected using standard methods.

Set logging behavior

Logging is a vital function in pretty much any IT service or software. Without logging, it becomes very difficult to trace any errors and figure out how to repair them. The same holds with Amazon Connect. The volumes of calls and the sheer number of possible pathways in a large call center would make it nearly impossible to trace errors. Thankfully, Connect offers the ability to send all the contact flow data to CloudWatch Logs for investigation. To enable this capability, you need to use the set logging behavior component. This component has two values, enable and disable, and I typically recommend setting it early in the contact flow to capture as much data as possible. We will discuss this in more detail in *Chapter 5, Base Connect Implementation*. The set logging behavior component has only one output for success.

Set recording and analytic behavior

At this point, call recording is a de facto standard for call center quality control and corporate risk mitigation. As we discussed previously in *Chapter 2, Reviewing Stakeholder Objectives*, Amazon Connect also offers the ability to record call center calls. This feature needs to be enabled in your contact flow. There is no overarching control to enable it for everything, which is probably a good thing. There may be situations where you don't want to record. For instance, we talked before about putting the agent on hold to capture sensitive data. During this part of a call, you probably wouldn't want the call to be recorded at all.

You can use the set recording component to enable and disable call recording at will. This component gives you some flexibility when it comes to security and cost savings. There may be parts of a call that you don't want to be recorded for cost-savings measures, or for security. The recording settings offer the option to turn a recording on or off.

Also, this component allows you to turn the Contact Lens analytics capability on. Contact Lens offers the ability to redact sensitive information for several languages. Because of this, you won't need to turn Contact Lens on and off for certain areas of your contact flow for security reasons. The only output for this component is success and should move your flow to the next component.

Set hold flow

The agent hold flow component allows you to set the hold flow for both the agent and the customer. If you recall, the agent and customer hold flows are what play when either is put on hold and is a vital component of your call center to ensure that no one thinks they were hung up on. The set hold flow component has the standard success and error outputs for connecting to your contact flow components.

Set customer queue flow

The customer queue flow is the prompts, music, and potential callback options offered to customers as they sit in your queue waiting to be connected to an agent. The set customer queue flow component lets you set this setting. It has the standard success and error outputs for connecting to the rest of your contact flow.

You may have different messages that you want to play based on the target queue for the call. For instance, you might want to tell someone waiting in the plumbing queue that sump pumps are on sale this week. In contrast, someone calling electrical would hear that ceiling fans are on sale. Since this setting can be queue-specific, it would be best to set it before a caller is put into a queue.

Set whisper flow

Whisper flows are messages that are played to only one party when a call is connected. You may use set whisper flow to set both the agent and customer whispers. Whispers can be used for things such as notifying the agent of the caller's name or potentially a special status such as a premium member. Another use case would be to notify the agent about how long the caller has been waiting in the queue to apologize if the wait was long and start the conversation on a better footing.

Whisper flows for clients can be used for messages such as telling the customer that the call will be recorded or that they are being connected to an agent. The whisper flow can also perform other functions such as what to do after an agent disconnects from a call, such as to perform a satisfaction survey. The set whisper flow component uses the standard success and error outputs to connect to other flow components.

Set disconnect flow

As we just discussed, one of the options in a whisper flow is to set a disconnect flow where the caller would receive a survey to complete on their call or product satisfaction. You configure the disconnect flow using the set disconnect flow component. The set disconnect flow component is very simple to configure, as it only has one option to set. This component has the standard success and failure outputs.

Set callback number

In *Chapter 1*, *Benefits of Amazon Connect*, we covered how giving callers the ability to receive a callback versus sitting on hold for extended periods is a great benefit with Connect. To make this work in your contact flow, you need to set a callback number before sending it to a callback queue. The set callback number component configures this setting. You set the callback number using an Amazon Connect attribute that was captured using the get input component.

I have found that the default examples for customer callbacks with Connect ask the user to input a phone number to call back on. I prefer using the system attribute for the customer's number as the primary source instead. Then, instead of asking the caller to enter a number, you can play a prompt asking whether they wish to receive a callback on the number they are calling from. I follow this up with a Lex bot that can capture their intent, and if they wish to supply another number, I then prompt. If they are OK with using the number they called from, I move the contact flow forward and set the callback number to a variable of the system category and customer number.

Set callback number has three outputs. It has the default success output for when the callback number is set properly. Also, it has two more outputs if something went wrong. They are not dialable and invalid number to address phone number issues. Typically, I loop both of these outputs back to capture the customer's input again to re-enter the phone number.

Set voice

The set voice component is straightforward. This component allows you to change the voice that is used to play prompts. Most of the time, I don't see this changed from the default of Joanna with the new neural speaking style. If you don't have a problem with this voice, you don't even need to use the set voice component. If you live in another country where English isn't the primary language, you might want to investigate the voices and pick one that sounds best to you. Set voice only has the standard success output.

Get queue metrics

Sometimes you may want to make routing decisions based on the metrics of a queue. For example, you might want to see the oldest call in the queue and then forward the call to another queue with a shorter time to balance customer hold times. The get queue metrics component allows you to filter based on channel (chat and voice) and by queue or agent. Get queue metrics offer the standard success and error outputs.

We finally made it through all the set components. There were quite a few. Thankfully, there are fewer branch components for Connect flows. We will cover branching components next.

Branch

The branching components allow you to take deeper control of how the contact flow operates and aren't related to the caller's experience. The way I typically explain the branch controls is that they control the logistics of your call center. The branch components we are going to cover are as follows:

- Check queue status
- Check staffing
- Check hours of operation
- Check contact attributes
- Distribute by percentage
- Loop
- Wait

Let's look at how we can use these components in Connect flows.

Check queue status

Within your contact flow, you might want to have the ability to check on the status of your queue so that you can make branch decisions. The check queue status component does exactly this. You can check the status of your queue with conditions such as greater than or less than. These conditions then create a new dynamic output in which you can route the call to different contact flow components. For instance, you might want to check the queue time to see how long the oldest call has been in the queue and automatically shift newer calls directly to a callback contact flow, so they are not waiting on hold. If your conduction doesn't match, then those calls are routed to the no-match output for a different action. In the case just discussed, the call would move forward to be put in the agent's queue. If something goes wrong, the call is routed to the error output for error processing.

Check staffing

When working with your contact flows, an important step in the flow is to check for available staff before putting someone in the queue. If you don't, you have the potential for a customer to be listening to your hold music for quite some time until an agent logs in. I see this component as more of a fail-safe check. Let's say that you messed up your hours of operation for the call center and left Saturday as an available day, even though the call center isn't staffed. A customer calls in, and you're not checking that your queue is staffed. The client gets put into the queue and just sits there forever until they get tired of waiting on hold for an agent. This experience isn't the best and leaves them irritated.

In this same scenario, by using the check staffing component, you can detect that no one is available for the queue and route any calls directly to a callback queue. This pattern would save your customers some frustration. This example isn't the only use case for this component, but it demonstrates its capabilities.

There are three available items that check staffing can look for: available, staffed, and online. Available will return true if there are agents that are in the available status, that is, they can immediately answer the call. Staffed will return true if agents are on a call, available, or performing post-call work. Typically, I use staffed as the indicator in my contact flows. The final condition is online, which checks whether agents are in the previous two states or offline. If the condition doesn't match, the call is routed to the false output. If something goes wrong, the component offers the standard error output.

Check hours of operation

The check hours of operation component is straightforward. If the call is made within the hours of operation, it will be sent to the in hours of operation output. On the flip side, calls made outside of hours are routed to the out of hours output. Like most other components, errors are routed to the error output for processing.

Check contact attributes

One of the more interesting branching components is check contact attributes. You can do some pretty cool things with this component. My favorite example follows. Say your company has a few A-list clients. One of these clients is Denzel Washington. You want to make sure that Mr. Washington always gets white-glove service from your best agents. To accomplish this, you can use check contact attributes and branch when this component detects that the customer that is calling has a phone number that matches Mr. Washington's.

In this use case, a dynamic output of = his number would appear in the component, where you could route the call down the white-glove path. If the number doesn't match, the call would be routed out the no match output.

Distribute by percentage

The cloud is all about being agile and adapting to changes in your business and the market quickly. There are many capabilities developed in DevOps to help companies quickly deploy updates to applications and capabilities. Many times, new software will be deployed using techniques such as canary and blue/green deployments. Connect also offers your company a way to test new contact flows using a canary method. You can accomplish canary testing using the distribute by percentage component. Canary testing is when you release a change to only a subset of users to fully test and vet the changes before releasing it at scale. IT prevents you from impacting your whole userbase at the same time, lessening customer dissatisfaction if something goes wrong.

The distribute by percentage component creates dynamic outputs based on the conditions you create in it. For canary testing, you might want to create a condition where you send 10% of your calls to a canary test flow, and the default will be 90% leftover. The distribute by percentage component will then have two outputs that you direct to two separate contact flows. The 10% output would direct to the new contact flow, so only a small subset of your customers would be affected. The default output of 90% would be directed to the existing contact flow, where no changes were made.

Loop

The loop component allows you to loop your contact flow several times and can be configured up to 100 times. This component has two outputs: looping, in which you can direct back to a starting point to start the loop over, and complete. The complete output is used to move your contact flow forward after the loop completes.

You can use the loop component for a use case where you might want to progress messages. During the first three loops, you play one message, and then the loop progress. The next loop then plays another message three times before progressing. Finally, you reach the end of your flow, where you play yet another message. Typically, I haven't seen loops used very often. Most people favor looped prompts, but there are still a few use cases, and it's good to keep a loop in the bottom of your toolbox for those special occasions.

Wait

The wait component does exactly what it sounds like. You can configure it to wait a certain amount of time before it progresses. It has two outputs: when the time is expired and a second in case of an error. Wait only works for chat, not for voice.

Integrate

The integrate class of components only has one component, but it's an important and powerful one if you want to interface into your enterprise applications to create automations and self-service capabilities. If you aren't going to have any application interfaces or have no need to store and retrieve data, this section won't be relevant to your contact flows.

Invoke Lambda

The invoke Lambda component allows you to call a Lambda function and return a set of values that can be used later in the contact flow. Lambda integration is one of the two major components for creating self-service. Lambda allows you to access the APIs and databases of your applications to retrieve and update information for your clients. This information can be coupled with Lex bots to create the rest of your customers' self-service experience.

An example of how you can use a Lambda integration is to look up a customer's name. Let's build on my example with Denzel. You have your system check the phone number and then send it to your white-glove service. But you want to make sure that Mr. Washington gets greeted the way he should, by name. You pass his phone number that you already have to the invoke Lambda component. The Lambda executes, connects to your CRM, and pulls his name. The Lambda output is consumed and passed to the agent whisper flow, notifying the agent of the name.

This example is just one of many showing how Lambda can be implemented in your contact flow. If you are integrating with an enterprise application, you will potentially have dozens of Lambdas throughout your contact flows, depending on your self-service components' complexity. The invoke Lambda component offers standard success and error outputs.

Terminate/transfer

We have finally arrived at the last group of contact flow components: the terminate and transfer group. You have probably already deduced what this group is used for, so I won't get into the details right now. I will tell you that you will use this several times in your call center contact flows. You will probably use one of these in every contact flow. The terminate group has these items:

- Disconnect/hang up
- Transfer to queue
- Transfer to phone number
- Transfer to flow
- End flow/resume

Let's dive into these last components we need to cover and discover their uses.

Disconnect/hang up

It probably goes without saying, but this component hangs up and has no outputs.

Transfer to queue

You will use transfer to queue at least once in your contact flows. It wouldn't be much of a call center if there wasn't at least one queue where people were sent. This component is also used to send people to a callback queue as well. So, most likely, you will have at least two of these components in your contact center. The only time you wouldn't use a transfer queue is when you are using Connect as a phone system rather than a call center. In that case, you would use transfer to phone number. However, using Connect as a phone system replacement is outside the scope of this book.

When you use the transfer to queue component, there are two outputs: at capacity and error. If everything works as expected, callers are placed in the queue. If the queue is full, as it can't take any more callers, then the call will be output at capacity. At capacity allows you to handle the situation better, such as offering a callback. Finally, if something goes wrong, the call is sent to the error output.

Transfer to phone number

Sometimes in your call center, you want to forward to an external number. This number might route to a cell phone that's used for after-hours support. Another use case might be where you forward from one Connect instance to another by dialing the next Connect instance's phone number.

There are two options for the transfer to phone number component, both relating to how it operates. The first option transfers the call to a phone number. When you select this option, you only get the error output from the component. The second option continues the contact flow after the transfer and disconnect. In this second case, three other outputs can be used to control what happens after the call. The three additional outputs are success, call failed, and timeout. These additional outputs allow you to add additional features, such as a survey after an after-hours support call.

Transfer to flow

If you recall, I stated earlier that you should split up your contact flows to minimize your blast radius when you make changes to your environment. To accomplish this, you use the transfer to flow component. This component takes the name of a contact flow as the setting. It then transfers the call to this next flow when the component is reached. You will use this component in every contact flow where you want to continue to another flow. This component only has the error output.

End flow/resume

The end flow/resume component is another self-explanatory component. You use this component in a limited number of places, mainly at the end of whisper flows.

Putting the pieces together

Now that you have covered all the components that go into a contact flow, we need to discuss how you will put all these pieces together. At this point in the process, we don't want to get into the nitty-gritty. You don't need to be concerned about error handling, or sometimes even timeouts and other secondary outputs. Right now, you just want to focus on the main outputs and sketch out how the general feel of the contact flow will look.

You also don't need to worry about whisper flows at this point in the process, either. Those can be put together later because they don't have any complex items that will drive up costs or project complexity. For now, you are just concerned with the general flow and where integrations will happen.

There is also a reason as to why I used the word *sketch* and not *paint a masterpiece*. We aren't going for perfection here. That can be achieved later when we are building the contact flows in Connect. I can tell you that if you aim for perfection at this point, you won't achieve it. There will always be some gotcha that you will run into when you start testing that you didn't account for. So, don't go overboard on trying to be precise. You can see what a Connect contact flow looks like in *Figure 3.1*. You can use this as a blueprint for how your sketches should look:

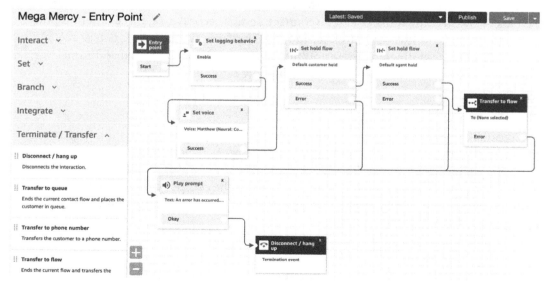

Figure 3.1 – What a contact flow looks like

I also don't mean to sketch. Well, I guess you can if that's your method. But any method will do. You can use a drawing program, or you can sketch it out on paper; I've even used sticky notes on a whiteboard with connections drawn in with dry-erase markers. Although low-tech, the last method is my favorite. It allows everyone in the room to participate, even the stakeholders, and it's fast. Not everyone knows how to use Visio, but everyone knows how to use a marker and a sticky note. This anecdote also brings up a good point. I said *stakeholders*, and yes, it's good to have them involved in the process, so they understand what the flows will ultimately resemble once the call center is complete. Additionally, it helps you to weed out unforeseen issues before you have put any work into the project.

Summary

In this chapter, we covered all the types of flows and all the components that go inside of those flows. Altogether, you just learned about 38 new pieces, way to go! Finally, we wrapped up how you can put the pieces together to build out your contact flows. The final step was a very important one. In the next chapter, we will cover costing your Connect instance. The information you created as part of this process will help you build your cost estimates.

4
Connect Costing

Whenever you migrate or deploy something to the cloud, one of the most significant changes in mindset is to do with costing. No company is going to move forward with a project without knowing the costs. With typical on-premises deployments, this is usually a large capital expenditure with ongoing maintenance expenses. When you migrate to a cloud-based solution, you won't have those capital expenditures. Instead, the cloud is a pay-as-you-go model where you pay for what you use. Some of these costs are straightforward. For instance, Amazon QuickSight has a per-user consumption model. This model is relatively straightforward to forecast. However, when you start looking at services such as Lambda, things can get a bit more complicated. Lambda has three consumption models, making it much more complicated to estimate costs.

The good news is that when we are talking about these services concerning Amazon Connect, things get a bit easier for you. The primary reason for this is the reduction of volume. Let's take another look at Lambda. If you were to run a serverless website with Lambda, there would be potentially millions of users making millions of different requests. All these requests add up to huge numbers. However, with Connect, the number of potential visitors, that is, phone calls, is much lower. The total number of Lambda executions is lower, but the number of possible Lambda functions is lower. A website may have hundreds of individual Lambda functions whereas a Connect implementation might have a couple of dozen on the high end. In this chapter, we will review how you properly cost Connect and its ancillary AWS services.

In this chapter, we'll work through the following topics:

- Base Connect charges
- Communications costs
- Lambda costing
- Lex bot costing
- Contact Lens costing
- Analytics costing

Base Connect charges

You might think that Connect is just like an on-premises phone system, and there is a barrier-to-entry cost. But you would be wrong. This is one of those times where it feels good to be incorrect, right? One of the most significant cost savings with Connect is that you don't have that huge upfront expenditure as you do with other systems. The software, since there isn't any hardware, is free. This fact will put your project at least tens of thousands or even hundreds of thousands in capital ahead of any conventional system.

> **Tip**
> A word of caution: prepare to explain this discrepancy to management if you are replacing an existing system. This explanation will become even more critical if you aren't running other cloud workloads and management isn't used to the costing models. You won't want them to think that you are somehow misrepresenting the costs for a favorable outcome. The discussion shouldn't be that difficult, but it might make sense to have a copy of the AWS Connect pricing page (`https://aws.amazon.com/connect/pricing/`) just in case.

Since Connect is a pay-as-you-go service, we do have some costs that we need to account for when it comes to the base costs of Connect. There are two primary price structures for Connect. You pay for allocating phone numbers and for voice and chat minutes. For voice and chat, the costs are straightforward. They are $0.018 for voice and $0.004 per message for chat. We will cover this in more detail in a minute. These costs are universal for Connect across all regions. Phone numbers are a bit more complicated. There are two classes of numbers: **Direct Inward Dial** (**DID**) (standard phone numbers) and toll-free numbers (where callers don't pay). Also, the costs are different based on the country where the number was sourced. We will come back to numbers. For now, let's get back to the voice and message costs.

If you migrate from a conventional system, you will have a good idea of how many minutes you will use based on your previous phone bills. I recommend adding up the minutes used from the last 12 months and obtaining an average. You can utilize this number to estimate your monthly voice charges for Connect. For instance, if you used 250,000 minutes over the year, you would end up with 20,833 per month. The ultimate cost for Connect voice capability would be $375 per month based on your historical usage. There are some organizations that may want to look for usage spikes and compensate for months with higher usage. Companies that might experience huge surges in usage would be retail around the holiday season or tax preparers near the tax deadline.

On the other hand, if you create a new call center, you will have to estimate the call volume since you don't have any other metric to use. I typically use a figure of 5 minutes per call and then estimate how many calls would come in to the center. It's not an exact science, but you will have to put a stake in the ground and say this is where you are starting. This number will be your foundation, and you may have to adjust it once you are up and running. For instance, if you estimate that you will have 1,000 calls a month, your cost will be $90 (1,000 X 0.018 X 5). If you run a helpdesk or vacation planning call center, your call times will generally be much longer. You will need to consider the purpose of your call center and adjust the average minutes accordingly.

One often-overlooked aspect of call time is the time that customers are on-hold for. Your average call time might 5 minutes, but the average hold time before callers get to speak to an agent may be 10 minutes. In this case, your actual call time would be 15 minutes, not 5, and your costs will reflect that. If you migrate, you don't have to worry about adjusting for hold time since your phone bill minutes already reflect it. But if you are building a new center, you will need to account for how busy the agents will be. It can be a challenge, and you will probably need some insight from the stakeholders to determine the expected wait time. Once you have that number, you can adjust your calculation as necessary to arrive at your new base cost.

For most companies, the ability to use chat with your call center from your website will be a new capability. Like starting a call center from scratch, you will have to estimate how many chats you will have to develop some baseline. When I'm estimating, I begin with 15 chat messages per session. You will have to produce an estimate of how many users will opt to use your chat on your website rather than calling your call center. Once you have arrived at that number, you can calculate your baseline for chat costs. For instance, if you estimate that 323 people will use your chat service, then your cost would be $19.38 per month (323 X 0.004 X 15).

Now that we have the cost of voice and messages out of the way, we can finally return to the phone numbers' cost. You will have to reference the cost of the numbers directly from the AWS Connect pricing page (https://aws.amazon.com/connect/pricing/) as there are too many options to list here. For the costing example here, we will say that the Connect instance will be deployed into the US East region, and we want to use a US toll-free number. The price for a toll-free US number is $0.06 per day. To get the monthly fee, you multiply by 30.42 (the average number of days in a month) to get a cost of $1.8252 per month. This cost is per number, so if you have a couple of numbers, you will have to combine these costs.

Now that we have covered the base costs for Connect, you should have the foundation for building your cost model. Next, we will cover how to account for communications costs, equivalent to your telephone bill in a conventional deployment.

Communications costs

AWS charges per minute for telecommunications in addition to the per-minute voice charges that we just discussed. The way that Amazon charges for line usage is broken into three separate categories:

- Regions where Connect is deployed

- Whether an inbound call is toll-free or DID

- Outbound calls

The primary selector for fees is the region to which the Connect instance is deployed. You are going to have to select this first. The primary location should be close to your base of operations. You wouldn't want to run Connect outside of the country where your agents are located if it can be avoided. Once you have selected the region, we can start diving into the inbound and outbound costs. For all the cost explanations in this book, we will always use the us-east-1 region.

The first part of the telecommunications estimate has already been completed by the previous section's exercises on base costs. The number or estimate you produced for the voice costs will be the starting point for communications. One of the features that Connect offers that is valuable for customer service is callbacks. Callbacks allow a client to leave their number and Connect will call them back when the next agent is available. This process saves your customer valuable time that would otherwise be wasted on hold. Of course, call back also changes traffic flow from an inbound call to an outbound call. It wouldn't make sense to account for 100% of your inbound volume and then allocate more for an outbound callback. We will need to make some assumptions as to how many calls will be converted to callbacks.

To assess the callback quantity, you need to make some assumptions about how loaded your call queue will be. What I mean by that is how often your call queue and hold time will get large enough that people will opt for a callback. If you are migrating from a conventional system, you should have some metrics that you can use to arrive at this percentage. For those of you who are building a new system, you will need to bust out a calculator. To figure out how many people could be sitting on hold, you will need to use the following equation:

(estimated number of calls per day/open hours X average call time)/(number of agents X 60)

This equation will provide you with the call load and the available work minutes of your staff. The result will show you how many more minutes are or are not committed to your call center staff. Let's look at the next two scenarios to demonstrate this.

No hold time:

$$\frac{\left(\frac{800}{8\cdot5}\right)}{(10 \cdot 60)} = .833$$

Hold time:

$$\frac{\left(\frac{1200}{8\cdot5}\right)}{(4 \cdot 60)} = 3.125$$

The second equation shows that the call center has three times more work than can be completed. This equation is an extreme example, and you would have some upset customers and employees. However, a ratio of 1:1 would mean that 10% of your calls will be on hold and need a callback. If you had 800 minutes of calls per day, then 80 of those minutes would be callbacks. This number isn't exactly correct. After all, customers call in and then ask for a callback. But it's a good enough estimation. Once you have the number of minutes that will be outbound calls, you can calculate your total telecommunications cost.

> **Important note**
> Unfortunately, calculating the cost is a little more complicated than calculating the inbound and outbound minutes if you have international calls. If you are going to have global communications, you will have to estimate how many minutes by country. The costs per country are located on the Amazon Connect pricing page (https://aws.amazon.com/connect/pricing/).

For our examples, we are going to assume that all calls are to and from the US. Calls from a US caller to the us-east-1 Connect instance will run you $0.0022 for DID, $0.0120 for toll-free calls, and $0.0048 for outbound calls per minute. Using our earlier numbers, the inbound calls for our toll-free 720 minutes will be $8.64 per day. The 80 minutes of outbound calls will cost a total of $0.384. The total communication costs for this scenario are $180.48 per month based on 20 workdays.

Now that we have the base Connect costs and the telecommunication costs, we can move on to the more advanced costing items. These items are the ones that create sophisticated user interactions for your call center, such as Lambda and Lex.

Lambda costing

Remember that we stated that one of the most significant benefits of Amazon Connect is the ability to interface with third-party applications in *Chapter 1, Benefits of Amazon Connect*. It is these interfaces that create a rich user experience. How you make these interfaces is through a service from Amazon called Lambda. Lambda allows the execution of snippets of code without the use of a server. This lack of dedicated compute power will enable you to reduce your ongoing operations costs significantly. An issue arises when you want to estimate how much Lambda is going to cost you. With a confidential application, you can estimate how many CPUs you need and how much RAM and then pick an AWS instance accordingly. This sizing, in turn, will allow you to look up the pricing for that instance, and you can easily calculate the monthly expenditure.

When it comes to costing Lambda, three different consumption models need to be calculated:

- The number of invocations, that is, the number of times the code is run
- The amount of RAM required to run the code
- The duration of code execution

At first glance, it might not seem that difficult to calculate. However, let's take a closer look at these three items.

Invocations

Determining how many invocations you have is the easiest to do when it comes to Connect. When working with a serverless application or website, the usage patterns are random and based on users' whims. With Connect, the usage patterns of your contact flows are very well defined. This standardization of pattern allows you to identify the number of invocations more easily. We discussed contact flows in detail in *Chapter 3, Sketching Your Contact Flows*. For demonstration purposes, we will say that our contact flow has 18 Lambda invocations in total. Of these 18 Lambda invocations, a caller will only execute six in any given call. You might wonder why there are only six. It's because a contact flow is based on a decision tree and options. A single user will only select one option at a time, moving through the path. Some users might make a mistake and go back and do it again, but we'll get back to this later. Now that we know how many Lambda invocations a caller will execute, we will multiply the six Lambda invocations by the number of callers we have in a day and then multiply that by the number of workdays in a month.

Invocations * Callers per day * Workdays = Total monthly Lambda invocations

6 * 423 * 20 = 50,760

In our example, we will have around 51,000 invocations of Lambda per month. In this instance, our Lambda will be free. Amazon allows one million Lambda invocations per month in the free tier. Based on our number, we won't even come close to that. However, let's say that we have a web application that uses Lambda, so we are going well over the free tier. As of the time of writing, Lambda in us-east-1 costs $0.20 per million requests. As you can probably see, Lambda isn't going to cost us a lot for this scenario.

RAM and duration

The second and third aspects of Lambda pricing go hand in hand. The duration cost is based on how much RAM is allocated to a Lambda function. All the examples that will appear later in this book are written in Python and use 128 MB of RAM each. We will use that configuration for our example here as well. We will say that each of our 18 Lambda invocations will use one second at 128 MB. The current pricing for 128 MB in us-east-1 is $0.0000002083 per 100 milliseconds, which means that our cost per invocation is $0.000002083. To get our total cost for duration and RAM, we need to multiply the duration cost by our 76,140 invocations. We arrive at a total cost of $0.15859962 for duration and RAM.

Altogether, Lambda will cost a total of around $0.35 per month for our hypothetical call center executions. That works out to 20 cents for the invocations and 15 cents for the duration and RAM allocation.

Lex bot costing

Just like the other services that we talked about here, Amazon Lex is also a pay-as-you-go service. With Connect, Lex provides the bot interfaces and **Natural Language Processing (NLP)** required for your contact flow to offer the user experience enhancements that we talked about in *Chapter 1, Benefits of Amazon Connect*. How AWS charges for Lex is by voice and text request. Amazon charges $0.004 per voice request and $0.00075 per text request. As with Lambda, the costs for Lex are meager. Like Lambda, the nature of call centers and the amount of service use will also keep your costs low.

Lex is another service where you can't estimate costs until you sketch out some ideas about how your contact flows will operate. You will need to estimate the number of locations at which you will be using Lex. I want to be clear on the types of interactions that Lex works with. Lex is not used in a situation where you would have a prompt saying, "*press one to check order status*." That functionality is covered with native Connect capabilities. Lex is used for the type of interaction when you would have a prompt such as, "*what do you need help with today*?" This prompt is open-ended and can receive several responses: "*check the status of my order*." Lex's power is that it doesn't restrict your customers to a few options. It allows you to provide a much more dynamic user experience.

If you have an existing system that you are replacing with Connect, it should be easy for you to identify where you could put Lex in your contact flow. It will also be easy to draw on your existing experience to identify the options to be programmed into Lex based on your previous experience. If you are setting up a new system, this task might be a bit more complicated as you won't have prior experience to draw on. For new deployments, I recommend starting with a small number of Lex bots so that you can gather the necessary information to craft a great user experience.

Once you have the number (at least an estimate) of Lex bots, you will use it in your contact flow. You can estimate the costs. For this example, we will use 3,500 callers per day to demonstrate the costs more effectively. In this example, we have six different Lex bots that prompt users and send them to different support queues based on products and required support types. We need to take the total bots (six) and the total number of callers, 3,500, and multiply them together. This calculation gives us 21,000 total interactions with Lex. Once we know the total number of interactions, we can multiply that by the cost of Lex at $0.004. When we calculate that, we end up with $84, or $1,680 for an entire month, which might look like a significant number, but remember that we had 3,500 callers a day, six Lex bots, and we didn't need to run the servers and GPUs required to do NLP. Overall, Lex is a pretty good deal.

Contact Lens costing

Contact Lens is an Amazon service that performs sentiment analysis on your phone calls and determines whether people are happy or upset with your product or service. Although Contact Lens is a powerful and complex system behind the scenes, the cost estimation is straightforward. Contact lens costs $0.015 per minute for the first 5 million minutes and then $0.0125 for everything over 5 million.

To cost Contact Lens, simply take the estimated number of minutes used for the base calculation and multiply that by the $0.015 rate. Using our original example for Connect voice charges of 20,833 minutes per month, the cost for Contact Lens would be $312.495. Given the capabilities that Contact Lens gives you in identifying and resolving your customers' issues, it provides fantastic value. To implement that level of technology yourself in a conventional on-premises system would cost you tens if not hundreds of thousands of dollars.

Now that we have covered the individual services used to amplify Connect's capabilities, it's time to switch gears. We now need to discuss analytic capabilities regarding Connect, which uses several services that operate as a cohesive whole.

Analytics costing

There are several ways that you can extract analytics from Amazon Connect. You could use Elastic Stack or other third-party analytics and search tooling. You can also use AWS native services as well, and those are the ones that we are going to focus on in this book. I love serverless technologies. They are services where you don't need to worry about the size of servers, how and when to patch them, or even how to make them highly available. With serverless services, all you need to do is configure and use them. AWS handles all the messy stuff that doesn't add any value for you.

Since we are using these services, it won't be one-stop shopping. We are going to need some services to make it all work. The services are feature-rich but designed for a specific task. The movement of data from your Connect instance through a graphical interface has several subtasks. These tasks will each be performed by an individual AWS service. The services we will need to use to create analytics for Connect are as follows:

- Kinesis Firehose
- Glue
- Athena
- QuickSight

Together, these services create a powerful analytics engine and have zero systems management from your perspective. I say systems because QuickSight does have some administrative management around creating new dashboards. The needs of your business will change, and your dashboards should change with them. This evolution ensures that your metrics are measuring the right things in the long term.

Kinesis Firehose

Amazon Connect exports call center contact information using **Kinesis**. To work with this data, you need to set up Kinesis Firehose as a recipient of this data stream. Kinesis Firehose allows you to output data to many sources without having to build your receiver. The output that you will be looking for to save data for Connect analytics will be S3. S3 is an object store that is very cost-effective to use for large amounts of data, and it offers life cycle and tiering, as well as being a pay-as-you-go offering.

AWS charges per GB for Firehose data. For the first 500 TB, the per-GB charge is $0.029. The cost goes down from there based on utilization. You are working with minimal contact records that don't amount to a massive amount of data. My recommendation is to allocate a GB of data per agent in Connect. Why use this method? Well, to be honest, the time to calculate the actual message size and try to estimate volume would cost you a year's worth of Firehose charges in your effort alone. It's just not worth the effort. In this case, 1,000 agents would cost you about $29 a month. This calculator is good enough. Unfortunately, this isn't the case for the rest of the services required for analytics.

Glue

Glue is a heavy lifter when it comes to analytics and Connect. AWS Glue is a managed service that is also pay-as-you-go. Glue is essentially a managed **Extract, Transform, and Load (ETL)** engine that uses Apache Spark. This service saves you the time of deploying, configuring, patching, and maintaining a running Spark instance in your environment. Unlike Firehouse, the costs associated are slightly higher at $0.44 per **Data Processing Unit (DPU)**-hour. AWS Glue is billed per second, with a 1-minute minimum. A DPU is four vCPUs' and 16 GB of memory's worth of computing power. Also, two DPUs is the minimum that can be deployed.

For Connect, your instance isn't going to be putting out enough data to require more than the two DPUs. I guess I shouldn't say never, but it would take a massive call center to require more Glue compute power. Where costs for Glue climb is the number of times it runs when data is exported from Connect. The more up-to-date and accurate you want the information, the more often Glue will need to run. At a minimum, you will want to run it every hour. However, you might want to close that gap to 15 minutes to have a more current outlook on your dashboards.

Like with Firehose, we aren't going to get too deep into figuring out how much Glue will cost concerning Connect. Since it's static data consumption and runs at regular intervals, we will use a baseline cost of $150 per month for Glue. Using this number might be a little high, but it ensures that the cost is captured, and you might be pleasantly surprised at the end of the month to find that things run a bit cheaper than expected.

Athena

Once we have the data from Connect in S3 and have parsed it via Glue, our next step in the analytics toolchain is to query the data using Athena. **Athena** is yet another serverless service from AWS. This capability again saves you from managing the capacity and pathing of your infrastructure. It's worth mentioning that it only runs when there is work to be processed, keeping your costs low. Athena works by querying data right out of S3 as if it was in a traditional relational database. Pretty cool stuff, if you ask me. Talk about saving some cash on running a data warehouse.

For costing out Athena, we need to look at how we are going to use the data. We are going to use QuickSight to do the visualizations and create dashboards. This design is important to know about and understand, as there are some nuances to it. QuickSight uses **Super-fast Parallel In-memory, Calculation Engine (SPICE)** storage to store the data it works with rather than pulling data for each query. It won't be using Athena except to retrieve data from S3. It wouldn't be querying the S3 bucket for every query. By limiting the number of queries run by Athena, you also greatly reduce its costs. Athena charges $5.00 per TB of data scanned. A contact record is about 1 KB. It would take 1,024 records to equal 1 MB, and 1,024,000,000 records to make 1 TB of data. It is safe to say that allocating $5 for one TB of processing for a month will be sufficient. If you want to have reports span a longer period, I suggest allocating $5 for each additional month to ensure coverage.

QuickSight

Finally, we arrive at **QuickSight** for the visualization component of our analytics toolchain. QuickSight is comparable to Tableau or Domo. Quicksight has many pricing models available, but we are going to focus on the Enterprise Edition. The Enterprise Edition offers two classes of users: readers and authors. You will only need one or two author accounts to create the reports, and those are priced at $25 a month if you are paying monthly. If your call center has many departments, you might want to add more author accounts to create their reports.

The reader accounts are priced differently and are somewhat confusing. Reader accounts (accounts that only have read access and cannot create reports) are based on sessions and last 30 minutes. Each session is $0.30. However, there is an additional caveat. Reader users cap out at $5.00 per month. This capping and session cost can make estimations complicated if you let it. Let's not let it and instead just set the cost for each report user at $5. You probably don't have many of them and compared to all the other costs associated with Connect, this cost won't break the bank. Remember, this is only for report viewers, not for all the agents using your Connect instance. One or two people per department or contact queue probably make sense.

Summary

We have now covered the major components that need to be estimated for your Connect implementation. With these computed numbers, you should have a solid representation that can be added to your project plan for financial approval. Although there will be some variability with the numbers, this is expected. As we discussed before, a significant paradigm shift from on-premises conventional technology and the cloud's pay-as-you-go model. However, by reading this chapter, you should have the knowledge required to instill confidence in the financial forecast.

Now that we have the costs completed, the next phase of the process is to establish your Connect instance. In *Chapter 5, Base Connect Implementation*, we will cover the initial deployment of Connect along with any AWS account prerequisites to enable connectivity and administration.

Section 2: Implementation

Part 1 of this book is centered around gathering the intelligence required to deploy your Connect call center. Now that you have captured your business requirements, sketched out your call flows, and estimated your costs, you should be at the point in the project where you need to start implementing your Connect instance.

The rest of the book will focus on how rather than why. You have carefully crafted your why stories in Part 1. We will now take those stories and translate them into functional products. The focus will be on the technical aspects, and we will guide you through a complete implementation. Most of the benefits discussed will be covered to tell you about them and demonstrate them.

I encourage you to set up an AWS account to follow along with the next chapters. It is advised to use a sandbox account for the type of work we are doing to not disrupt any production workloads. Since we are primarily focusing on Connect, we will not cover the security and governance controls required for AWS accounts. We also won't cover any security aspects of the various AWS services we will use as part of the Connect contact flows. AWS security is a vast and deep subject and should be researched in depth before you implement Connect.

By the end of part 2, you will have a completely functional call center that you can use for demonstration purposes if you followed along. Often, it's better to show people new capabilities so they can better understand the impact they have. If you choose to follow along, you will have the ability to use your deployment during the reframing we discussed in *Chapter 4, Connect Costing*. By demonstrating, you will have a higher probability of getting your project approved. With that said, let's move on to Chapter 5, Base Connect Implementation, and deploy your first Connect instance.

This part of the book comprises the following chapters:

- *Chapter 5, Base Connect Implementation*
- *Chapter 6, Contact Flow Creation*
- *Chapter 7, Creating AI Bots*
- *Chapter 8, Interfacing Enterprise Applications*
- *Chapter 9, Implementing Callbacks*
- *Chapter 10, Implementing Voicemail*
- *Chapter 11, Implementing Call Analytics*
- *Chapter 12, Implementing Contact Lens*
- *Chapter 13, Implementing Chat*

5
Base Connect Implementation

Amazon is known for creating easy-to-deploy and easy-to-use products. Connect too is reasonably simple to get started with. The problem is that although it's easy, it's not always easy to do it right. Let's take, for example, setting up an EC2 instance. If you go to the AWS site and look up the EC2 *Getting Started* page (https://aws.amazon.com/ec2/getting-started/), you will notice that they list five steps to get started with EC2. Although you can perform these five steps and be up and running, you won't have the account governance, audit logging, federated login, and dozens of other things that you should have. This "getting started" position might work OK for marketing but it just doesn't cut it for enterprise deployment.

In this chapter, we are going to not only cover setting up your Connect instance but also the items and considerations necessary to *do it right*. The goal isn't to just get it operational and send it out the door. Unlike the *Getting Started* page, we will cover things in depth. We will also ensure that you have the necessary components for a long-term, enterprise-grade solution. In this chapter, we will cover the following:

- AWS account prerequisites
- Deploying Connect
- Picking your phone number

- Creating your call queues
- Creating security profiles
- Adding users

AWS account prerequisites

Connect is a bit unique with the prerequisites for your AWS account. Since Connect is essentially a **Software as a Service (SaaS)** offering at its core, it generally doesn't require as much account pre-work as other AWS services. There are, however, three things that we should look at before you deploy your Connect instance: **Virtual Private Cloud (VPC)**, federation, and management roles. These items should be configured before your deployment. However, they may or may not be needed depending on the capabilities you found necessary when sketching your contact flows. We will cover these details in the next sections.

VPC

When you deploy typical compute6 resources in AWS such as EC2, you need to have a VPC to house them. VPCs also need additional resources such as **Network Address Translation (NAT)** and public gateways. These services expand costs and your security blast radius, that is, the distance an attack can spread within your environment. With Connect, you may or may not need a VPC. If you don't have any integrations that would access a database or other software located in a VPC, you don't need one. Lambda, by default, isn't connected to a VPC and can access the internet. For instance, if you are interfacing your Lambda to your CRM, an internet-based SaaS product, you wouldn't require a VPC. In this instance, I would recommend you delete the default VPC from your account.

The opposing example would be that you need to interface with an API of a software package that you intend to run (or is currently running) in a VPC. In this case, your Lambda functions will need to be connected to that VPC to access that API. In this case, you would leave your VPC configuration alone or deploy a new one. I believe in reducing the security blast radius whenever possible, and that's why I recommend removing the VPC if you won't need it.

Federation

Amazon Connect allows you to use three forms of authentication: **Security Assertion Markup Language (SAML)** federation, **Active Directory (AD)** connectors, and local Connect users. Typically, I always recommend using SAML for any service where it is available. However, with Connect, I'm a bit on the fence. This wavering is due to the fact that even with SAML, you still must add users to Connect. The SAML interface only allows you to have a single sign-on experience. It doesn't allow you to control any Connect features such as call queues or even group management for access control.

The other issue with SAML authentication is that the token lasts for 10 hours. So, if you have agents pulling a double shift, they will get bounced out after 10 hours. It doesn't matter whether they are on a call or not. This issue isn't the best solution, and 10 hours isn't an unbelievable workday, especially if you are running a helpdesk. It's common for calls to run past leaving time.

You will have to decide whether having single sign-on using SAML makes sense for your organization. Not only does it provide the user with the convenience of a single password, but it also allows the easier integration of MFA. Plus, your users can find all their applications, including Connect, in one place. Sometimes these conveniences can go a long way for large organizations. If you opt for SAML authentication, you will need to create an IAM identity provider before deploying your Connect instance.

Management roles

When you deploy Connect, you need to have some way to manage it. It's not best practice to continually use admin access or root account access in AWS. It's not best practice anywhere, especially in AWS. To manage Connect, you should have a role dedicated to the function. You will need at least the ability to operate Connect, but if you plan on using any advanced services such as Lex and Lambda, you will need rights to those as well. Try and make sure that the roles conform to the least-privilege principle as much as possible to maintain a secure environment when you create the role.

Once you have deployed your Connect instance, I recommend adding an explicit deny for the `DestroyInstance` action. This modification will ensure that no administrators can inadvertently or maliciously delete a Connect instance. Remember, deny actions in AWS take precedence over allow actions. Someone else with a higher-level role will need to delete the instance instead. It's been quite a journey up to now, and we are finally at the stage where we will deploy Connect.

Deploying Connect

Now is when the real work starts:

1. The first thing you need to do is log on to your AWS account using the management role that we just discussed. How you access this role will depend on the authentication mode you are using, such as SAML. Once you are logged on with that role, you will need to find the **Amazon Connect** service. Connect is located under the **Customer Engagement** heading. It will appear as in *Figure 5.1*:

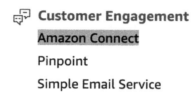

Figure 5.1 – Amazon service menu

2. Once you click on **Amazon Connect**, you will be greeted with the Connect service welcome page as shown in *Figure 5.2*. Here you will want to click on **Get started**. If you don't see **Get started**, don't worry; this just means that someone has accessed or created a Connect instance before you got here. If this is the case, you will instead see a list of deployed Connect instances:

Figure 5.2 – Getting started

3. When you click on **Get started**, you will be prompted for the authentication method you will want to use. If you are using Connect to store your users or SAML authentication, you will need to give the access URL for your Connect instance as detailed in *Figure 5.3*:

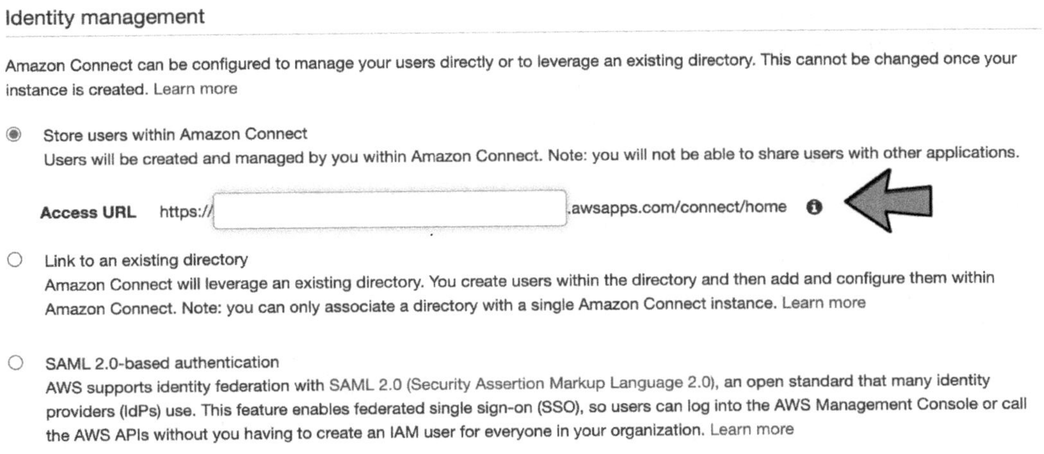

Identity management

Amazon Connect can be configured to manage your users directly or to leverage an existing directory. This cannot be changed once your instance is created. Learn more

◉ Store users within Amazon Connect
Users will be created and managed by you within Amazon Connect. Note: you will not be able to share users with other applications.

Access URL   https:// [   ] .awsapps.com/connect/home ⓘ ⬅

○ Link to an existing directory
Amazon Connect will leverage an existing directory. You create users within the directory and then add and configure them within Amazon Connect. Note: you can only associate a directory with a single Amazon Connect instance. Learn more

○ SAML 2.0-based authentication
AWS supports identity federation with SAML 2.0 (Security Assertion Markup Language 2.0), an open standard that many identity providers (IdPs) use. This feature enables federated single sign-on (SSO), so users can log into the AWS Management Console or call the AWS APIs without you having to create an IAM user for everyone in your organization. Learn more

Figure 5.3 – Identity management

4. If you select **Link to an existing directory**, you will need to choose a directory from the drop-down list shown in *Figure 5.4*. Please note that once you select an authentication method, you are unable to change it. The only way to change authentication method after deployment would be to export whatever resources can be exported from the original instance and import them into a new instance with another authentication method selected:

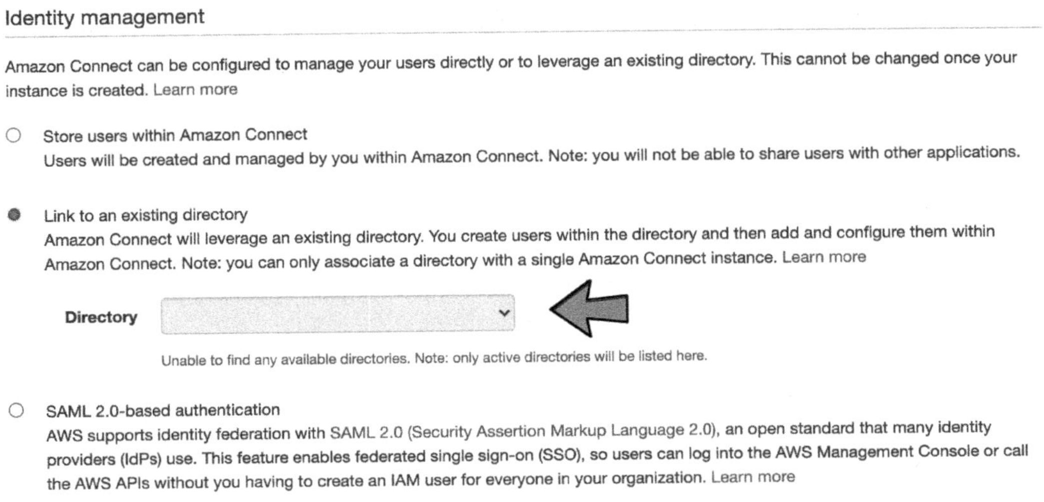

Identity management

Amazon Connect can be configured to manage your users directly or to leverage an existing directory. This cannot be changed once your instance is created. Learn more

○ Store users within Amazon Connect
Users will be created and managed by you within Amazon Connect. Note: you will not be able to share users with other applications.

● Link to an existing directory
Amazon Connect will leverage an existing directory. You create users within the directory and then add and configure them within Amazon Connect. Note: you can only associate a directory with a single Amazon Connect instance. Learn more

Directory   [⌄] ⬅
                Unable to find any available directories. Note: only active directories will be listed here.

○ SAML 2.0-based authentication
AWS supports identity federation with SAML 2.0 (Security Assertion Markup Language 2.0), an open standard that many identity providers (IdPs) use. This feature enables federated single sign-on (SSO), so users can log into the AWS Management Console or call the AWS APIs without you having to create an IAM user for everyone in your organization. Learn more

Figure 5.4 – Connect directory

5. Once you have identified your authentication mode, you will be prompted to add an admin user. If you are using SAML or a directory, you will be prompted to add a user, but it won't contain a password or email field; you will see something like what you see in *Figure 5.5*. The username you enter must match your users in your directory exactly, or you will receive an access denied error when you try to log in:

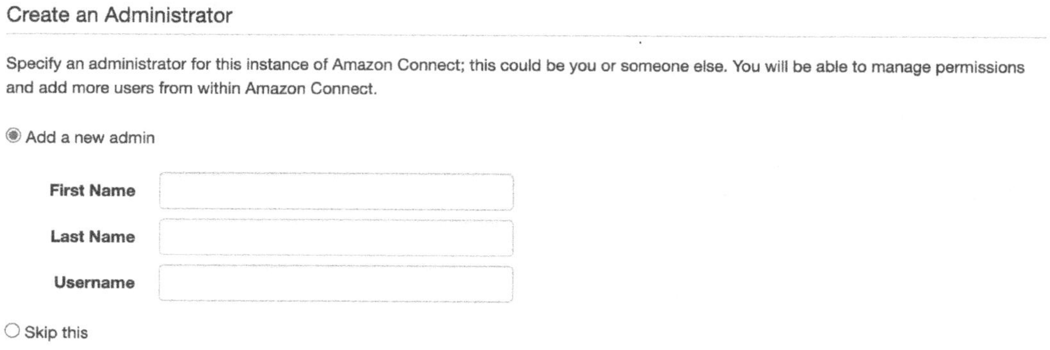

Create an Administrator

Specify an administrator for this instance of Amazon Connect; this could be you or someone else. You will be able to manage permissions and add more users from within Amazon Connect.

◉ Add a new admin

First Name

Last Name

Username

○ Skip this

Figure 5.5 – Creating an admin user

6. If you select the option for Connect to be your user store, you will get a different screen like that shown in *Figure 5.6*, where it asks you for a **Password** value and **Email Address** value to be entered. One thing that I've run into is that the **Password** field doesn't tell you about the complexity requirements until you enter a password, which is a bit odd. For your reference, you need an uppercase letter, a lowercase letter, and a number for the password to be valid. Passwords must also be at least eight characters long with a maximum of 64 characters:

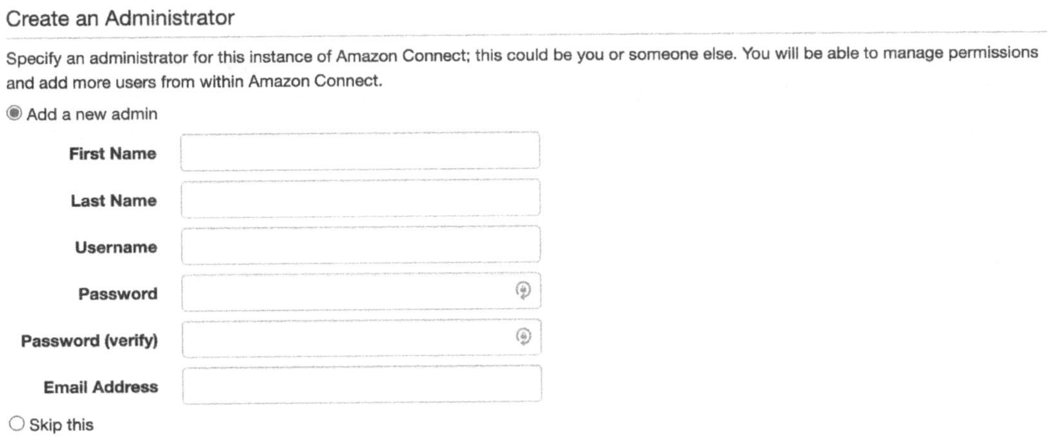

Create an Administrator

Specify an administrator for this instance of Amazon Connect; this could be you or someone else. You will be able to manage permissions and add more users from within Amazon Connect.

◉ Add a new admin

First Name	
Last Name	
Username	
Password	
Password (verify)	
Email Address	

○ Skip this

Figure 5.6 – Local Connect administrator

7. Next, the deployment will ask you whether you want to allow inbound and outbound calls. You will see a screen like *Figure 5.7*. For most deployments, you will want to choose both options. One thing to keep in mind later is that you might want to limit who can make outbound calls. In my experience, you might be surprised by calls to Puerto Rico when you don't do business there. You wouldn't control that here, though, since this is for the entire Connect instance:

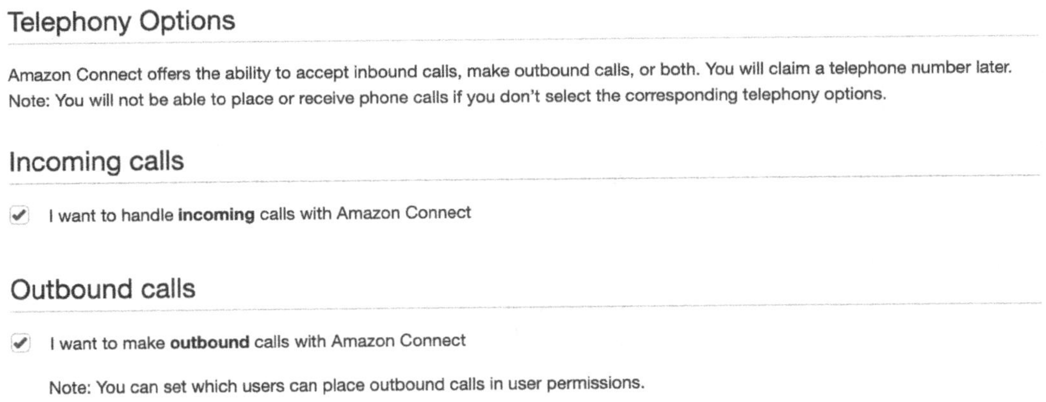

Telephony Options

Amazon Connect offers the ability to accept inbound calls, make outbound calls, or both. You will claim a telephone number later.
Note: You will not be able to place or receive phone calls if you don't select the corresponding telephony options.

Incoming calls

☑ I want to handle **incoming** calls with Amazon Connect

Outbound calls

☑ I want to make **outbound** calls with Amazon Connect

Note: You can set which users can place outbound calls in user permissions.

Figure 5.7 – Telephony Options

8. Once you select your call options, you will be prompted for where you want to store your data for Connect, as in *Figure 5.8*. By default, Connect will create a CloudWatch log group and an encrypted S3 bucket to store this data. If you are a stickler for using IaC to deploy your resources, you will want to create these items before deploying Connect and selecting the customize option. Otherwise, you can let Connect create them for you:

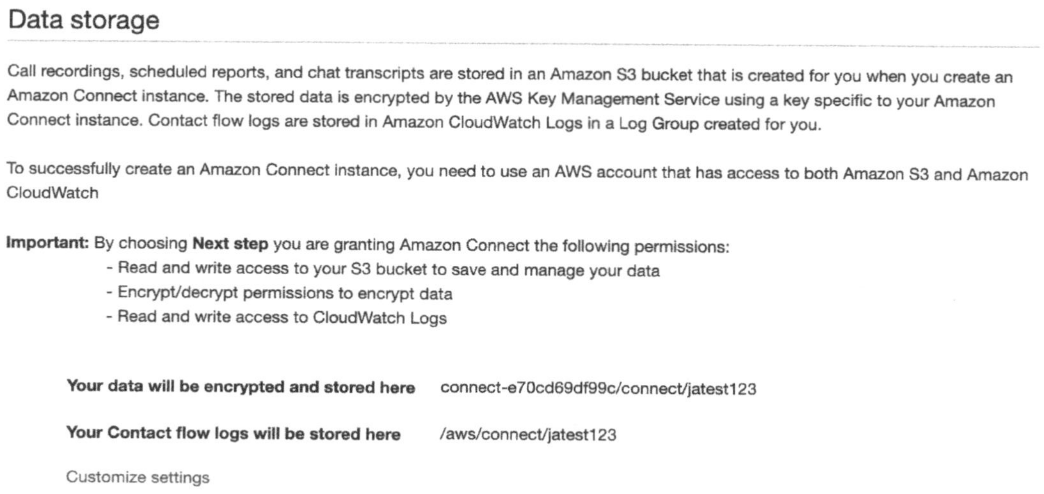

Data storage

Call recordings, scheduled reports, and chat transcripts are stored in an Amazon S3 bucket that is created for you when you create an Amazon Connect instance. The stored data is encrypted by the AWS Key Management Service using a key specific to your Amazon Connect instance. Contact flow logs are stored in Amazon CloudWatch Logs in a Log Group created for you.

To successfully create an Amazon Connect instance, you need to use an AWS account that has access to both Amazon S3 and Amazon CloudWatch

Important: By choosing **Next step** you are granting Amazon Connect the following permissions:
-   Read and write access to your S3 bucket to save and manage your data
-   Encrypt/decrypt permissions to encrypt data
-   Read and write access to CloudWatch Logs

Your data will be encrypted and stored here   connect-e70cd69df99c/connect/jatest123

Your Contact flow logs will be stored here   /aws/connect/jatest123

Customize settings

Figure 5.8 – Data storage

The last screen that you will see will show you all your options to review. At this point, you will want to recheck all the settings to ensure that everything is configured correctly. Once you are satisfied, click the **Create Instance** button to complete the process. Congratulations! You have just deployed your first Amazon Connect instance.

Logging in to your instance

The next time you click on the **Amazon Connect** service in the console, you will be presented with a list (*Figure 5.9*) of instances rather than the *Get Started* greeting. In this case, I named my instance `jatest123`. I know, very creative. You will notice that there are two clickable locations on the list. The first column, with the heading **Instance Alias**, takes you to a menu to change your instance settings. We will cover these items later. The second column, with the heading **Access URL**, is the link you will use to administer your instance and how your users will log on:

Amazon Connect virtual contact center instances

Select a virtual contact center instance to manage its directory, administrator(s), telephony options, data storage, and advanced features.

	Add an instance	Remove				⟳
Instance Alias		**Access URL**	**Channels**	**Create Date**	**Status**	
☐ jatest123		https://jatest123.awsapps.com/conn...	Inbound, outbound telephony	11/2/2020	Active	

Figure 5.9 – Connect instance list

When you click the second column link, you will be presented with a login screen as shown in *Figure 5.10*. This screen is where you would input your admin user and password that was created during your deployment. You will use this console for the next few sections:

Figure 5.10 – Connect URL login screen

When you log in to your Connect instance for the first time, you will be prompted with a welcome screen that walks you through all the settings you need to configure to get your instance online. These instructions (*Figure 5.11*) are great for a quick start to see how Connect works and build a proof of concept. Unfortunately, they aren't geared for anything more complicated than that. We will operate a more complex instance, so we will not follow this predetermined path, but we will cover the items listed:

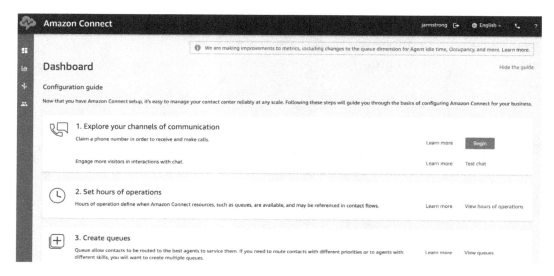

Figure 5.11 – Connect configuration guide

You now have an operating Amazon Connect instance. Next, we will configure some basic settings, starting with selecting your phone number.

Picking or transferring your phone number

Amazon Connect gives you the option of selecting a new phone number or porting an existing number over. For this exercise, we are going to choose a new number. I recommend setting up a new number even if you are going to port over your existing one. Whenever someone migrates from a current system to Connect, it is advised to set up a new number and temporarily forward your existing number during a preliminary testing phase. This method allows you to fall back to the old system if something was missed. If you were to port your number over and then cut over, you would have no fallback. I'm not saying that you will make a mistake, but I like to err on the side of caution. Once you have done the preliminary soft launch of your call center, you can start the number porting process.

When it is time to port your number, you will need to open a support ticket to port the number. There are a couple of hoops you need to jump through to get the process rolling, one of which is a **Letter of Authorization** (**LOA**) that the support team will supply you with when you initiate the process. Also, note that not all numbers can be ported. When you open the support ticket, the team will verify whether your number can be ported over. Depending on the carrier, some numbers cannot be ported.

Let's get started with selecting our new number:

1. Before we start the process, let's first dismiss the getting started guide. You can do this by selecting the **Hide the guide** link in the top right. Once you have done that, you will want to click on the menu on the left on the icon that looks a bit like the USB logo. See *Figure 5.12* for reference:

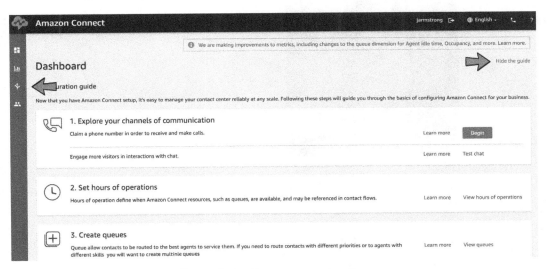

Figure 5.12 – Connect menu location

2. When you click there, a sub-menu will appear with several options (*Figure 5.13*). From this menu, you want to select **Phone numbers**:

Figure 5.13 – Routing menu

3. You will now be taken to a screen that will list your allocated phone numbers if you have any. However, at this time, the list will be empty. We now want to claim a number by selecting the **Claim a number** button.

On the claim phone number screen, there are a couple of options that we want to configure. First, we need to choose whether we wish for a toll-free or a DID number. You can select this option by clicking the headings at the top of the page as shown in *Figure 5.14*. From there, we need to select a country. For my demonstration, I will pick the US, which is denoted by the +1 country code. The page offers a prefix as an optional item. The prefix allows you to list numbers that are available that match the prefix. Since I am choosing to use a toll-free number, I will pick the first available number.

You can enter any description that you like. If your call center has multiple numbers, it will make sense to use the description field to document what the number will be used for. For instance, you might have one number for the helpdesk and another for sales.

Finally, we arrive at the contact flow field. At this time, we haven't built any contact flows, so you will only choose the canned option that ships with Connect. It doesn't matter which you prefer at this point. We are going to change the setting later when the flows are ready. When you have all your options selected, click on the **Save** button:

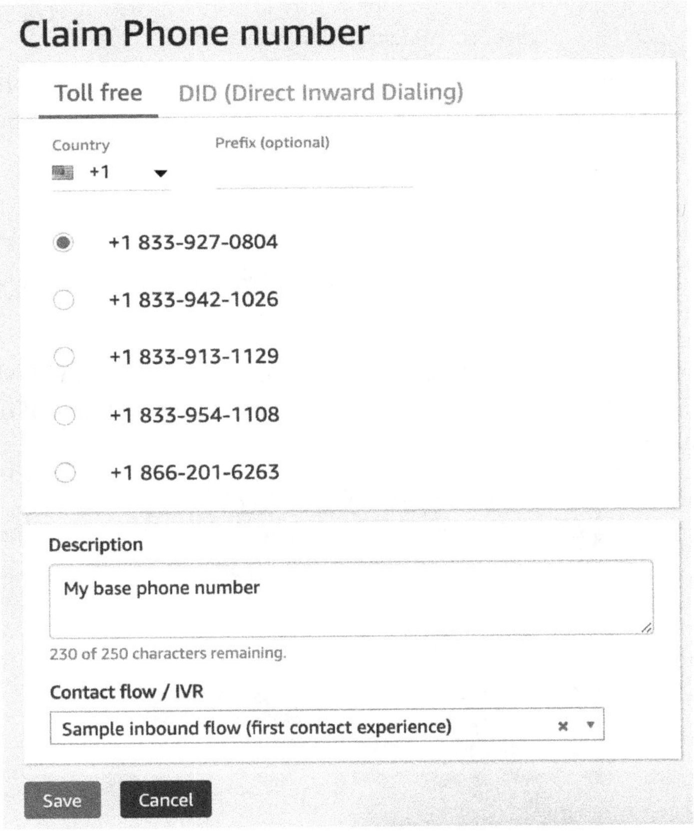

Claim Phone number

Toll free   DID (Direct Inward Dialing)

Country
+1 ▼

Prefix (optional)

● +1 833-927-0804

○ +1 833-942-1026

○ +1 833-913-1129

○ +1 833-954-1108

○ +1 866-201-6263

Description

My base phone number

230 of 250 characters remaining.

Contact flow / IVR

Sample inbound flow (first contact experience)   ✕ ▾

Save   Cancel

Figure 5.14 – Claim Phone number

4. If everything went as expected, you should be taken back to the phone number list populated with the number you just selected (*Figure 5.15*):

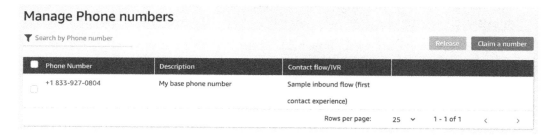

Figure 5.15 – Manage Phone numbers

Congratulations, you have your first call center phone number. Repeat the process for any other numbers you may need. Often, departments will have their own numbers to dial directly without having to go through the main contact flow.

Setting your hours of operation

Now that we have a phone number set up, we need to tell Connect when we will have staff available to handle calls:

1. To do this, we need to go back to the menu on the left and click the USB looking icon again. From this sub-menu, we are now going to select **Hours of operation** as shown in *Figure 5.16*:

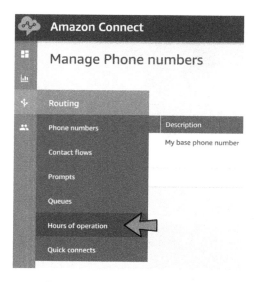

Figure 5.16 – Hours of operation

2. Like the phone numbers page, you will now be directed to a list. However, this list will be prepopulated with a single item called **Basic hours** with a description of *Always open* hours. Typically, I leave this item as is. You can use this setting for testing your contact flows when your regular hours are closed. We wouldn't want to have to edit those hours directly. To create new hours of operation, click the **Hours of operation** button in the window's top-right corner. The first hours setting we want to add is an always closed option. We can use this later to test our contact flows for after-hours operation.

    When you reach the **Hours of operation** screen (*Figure 5.17*), you can enter your name and description. You also need to choose a time zone for your call center hours. Since this setting is for testing after-hours, we need to check the first check box on the first column to select all current-day options. Then, click the **Remove** button on the right. The days should be removed from the screen, leaving no hours of operation. When finished, click the **Save** button:

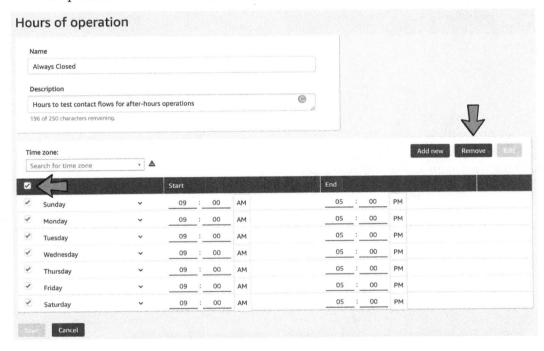

Figure 5.17 – Editing Hours of operation

3. Now that there are testing options for all hours and no hours, it's time to create a new setting for your actual hours. Start by clicking the **Add new hours** button again. However, instead of deleting all the days, select the checkboxes in front of the days you want to remove and click the **Remove** button. You can adjust the individual hours by editing the data in each of the time fields. When you are satisfied with the setup, click on the **Save** button. Remember to select your time zone; I seem always to forget this field, and it won't let you save without it. For my demonstration, I've left the hours from 9 am to 5 pm:

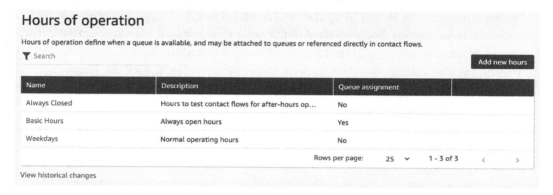

Figure 5.18 – Hours of operation list

When you return to the list of the **Hours of operation** page (*Figure 5.18*), you may notice that your new settings have a **No** in the queue assignment column. Don't worry; you didn't miss anything. This setting is covered in queue settings. If you have other hours of operation, such as an after-hours helpdesk, enter them now.

Creating your call queues

Connect comes with a default queue called basicQueue. Follow these steps to create your queue:

1. You can get to a queue list by selecting the USB looking icon to bring up the menu and select the **Queues** option as shown in *Figure 5.19*:

Figure 5.19 – Queues menu

2. An interesting thing about Connect is that you can't delete queues. I'm not sure why this is, but it's something to keep in mind. Don't go around creating queues like it's a free for all. You won't be able to get rid of them. I recommend taking a BasicQueue instance and repurposing it from the start. When you get to the list of queues as noted in *Figure 5.20*, click on the **BasicQueue** instance to edit it:

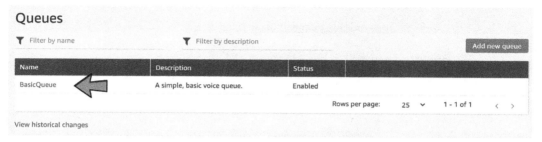

Figure 5.20 – Queue list

3. The queue editing screen (*Figure 5.21*) has several options for you to configure. I've changed the name of the basic queue to the primary queue and changed the description. On this page, you can select the **Hours of operation** setting that you created in the last section. I've selected my **Weekdays** hours. The queues are also where you define your caller ID settings. Connect allows you to select what your outbound number will be. The list is pre-populated with the numbers that you created beforehand. There is also an option to set the outbound caller ID name. I've set mine to **Jeff's test**. Honestly, with cellphones' proliferation today, this setting probably doesn't matter all that much as the names are not displayed, but I set it anyway. Finally, we have the **Outbound whisper flow**. This flow is the flow that outbound calls will play to the client receiving the call. Since we haven't created any yet, we will leave this blank. Once we create one, we can come back later and update the queue configuration:

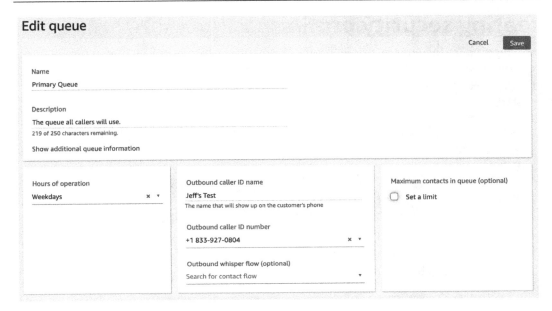

Figure 5.21 – Editing the queue

The last setting that I want to bring up is the quick connects. These are also optional. Quick connects are what you will use to allow agents to transfer calls to other queues and agents. Again, we will leave this setting for later. When you are done with your changes, click the **Save** button in the top right. If you have any more queues for other departments or purposes, you identified during your stakeholder sessions, create them now by clicking the **Add new queue** button.

Creating security profiles

After wrapping up the queues, we now come to creating security profiles. If you recall, I mentioned before that the default security profiles are OK, but I like to create a few more with greater granularity. To edit and create security profiles, you need to follow these steps:

1. Select the people icon on the left menu bar and select **Security profiles** as shown in *Figure 5.22*:

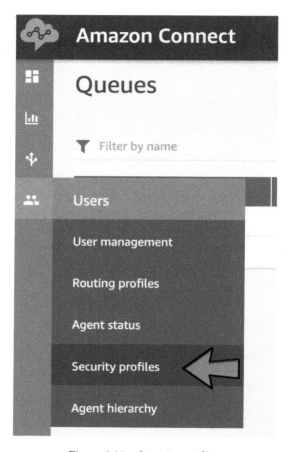

Figure 5.22 – Security profiles

2. Connect comes with four profiles: admin, agent, call center manager, and quality analyst. Typically, I like to add other security profiles that are like the call center manager. I feel that the call center manager has too many permissions for general administration. I create a new security profile for a user administrator and another profile for flow administration to address this. These two groups combined give me the same capabilities but allow for separate people to perform them.

The first method we will use to create a security profile is to copy an existing one. To do this, you need to hover over an existing profile. In this instance, I am using the CallCenterManager profile. When you hover, an icon with two sheets of paper will appear. Click this icon to copy the profile (*Figure 5.23*). When you click the icon, a pop-up window will appear:

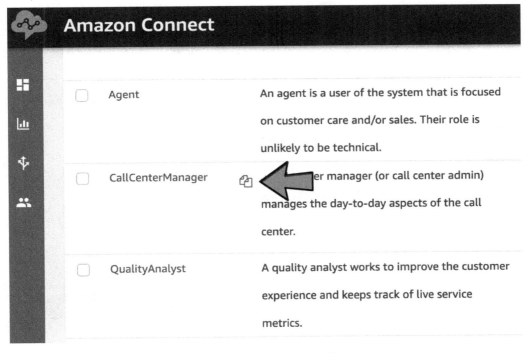

Figure 5.23 – Copy the profile

3. This pop-up window (*Figure 5.24*) will list all the capabilities of the profile being copied. Once you enter a name for your new profile at the bottom, the **Duplicate** button will activate. I have called my new profile Contact Flow Admin:

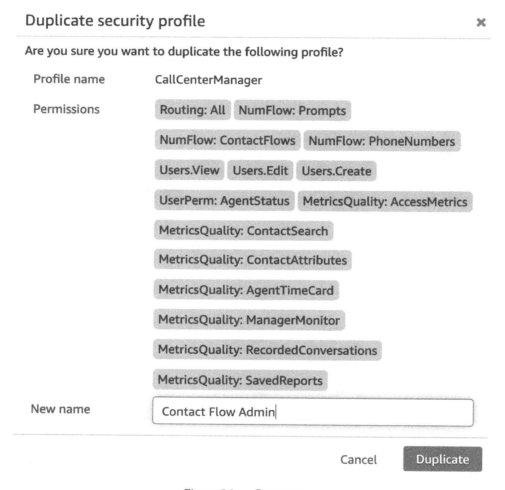

Figure 5.24 – Copy popup

4. I want to be able to assign this security profile to administrators to manage the flows, but I don't want them to be able to see any of the metrics or listen to conversations. These permissions are why the standard `CallCenterManager` profile won't work. When you click the **Duplicate** button, the profile will be added to the list. To edit this profile, click on the name in the left-most column. You will now be presented with a new screen that lists all the permissions categories discussed in *Chapter 3, Sketching Your Contact Flows*:

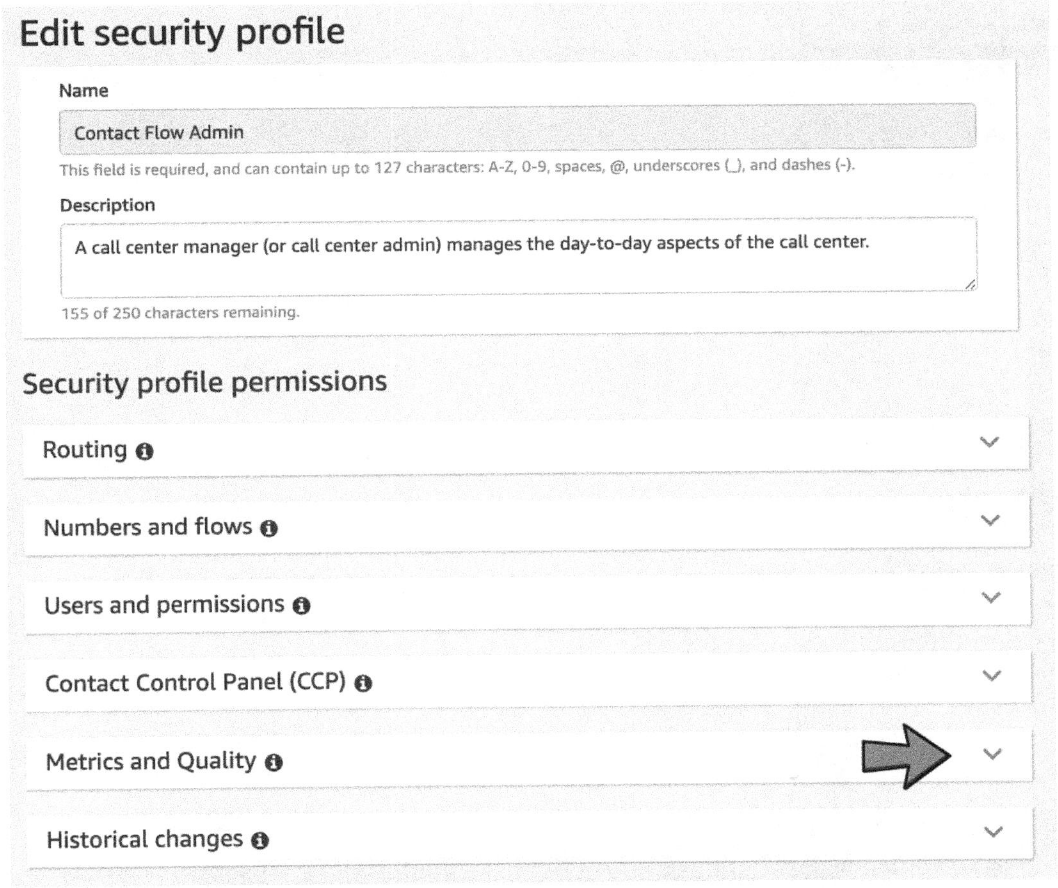

Edit security profile

Name

> Contact Flow Admin

This field is required, and can contain up to 127 characters: A-Z, 0-9, spaces, @, underscores (_), and dashes (-).

Description

> A call center manager (or call center admin) manages the day-to-day aspects of the call center.

155 of 250 characters remaining.

Security profile permissions

Routing ❶   ⌄

Numbers and flows ❶   ⌄

Users and permissions ❶   ⌄

Contact Control Panel (CCP) ❶   ⌄

Metrics and Quality ❶   ⌄

Historical changes ❶   ⌄

Figure 5.25 – Edit security profile

5. We want to click the down arrow on the permissions bar's far-right to modify the permissions noted in *Figure 5.25*. Then, select **Metrics and Quality** permissions. The bar will expand and show you all the options available (*Figure 5.26*). Since I don't want the **Contact Flow Admin** group to access any of this information, I will uncheck all the boxes. Some of the items are mandatory based on other settings. You may need to turn off some of the settings before you can uncheck all of them. Usually, you need to start unchecking from the right and move to the left:

Metrics and Quality ⓘ										∧
Type	**All**	**Access**	**View**	**Edit**	**Create**	**Enable/Disable**	**Enable download button**	**Delete**	**Publish**	**Schedule**
Access metrics	☐	☐	☐	☐	☐	☐	☐	☐	☐	☐
Contact search	☐	☐	☐	☐	☐	☐	☐	☐	☐	☐
Search contacts by conversation characteristics	☐	☐	☐	☐	☐	☐	☐	☐	☐	☐
Search contacts by keywords	☐	☐	☐	☐	☐	☐	☐	☐	☐	☐
Restrict contact access ⓘ	☐	☐	☐	☐	☐	☐	☐	☐	☐	☐
Contact attributes	☐	☐	☐	☐	☐	☐	☐	☐	☐	☐
Contact Lens - speech analytics ⓘ	☐	☐	☐	☐	☐	☐	☐	☐	☐	☐
Rules	☐	☐	☐	☐	☐	☐	☐	☐	☐	☐
Recorded conversations (redacted) ⓘ	☐	☐	☐	☐	☐	☐	☐	☐	☐	☐
Login/Logout report	☐	☐	☐	☐	☐	☐	☐	☐	☐	☐
Manager monitor	☐	☐	☐	☐	☐	☐	☐	☐	☐	☐
Recorded conversations (unredacted)	☐	☐	☐	☐	☐	☐	☐	☐	☐	☐
Saved reports	☐	☐	☐	☐	☐	☐	☐	☐	☐	☐

Figure 5.26 – Metrics access controls

6. Once all those permissions are removed, you can click the up arrow to close the bar back down. Since we want to segment the user administration component, click on the down arrow on the **Users and permissions** bar. The bar will expand and look as shown in *Figure 5.27*. Repeat the process of removing the permissions in this category as well. When you are done, scroll to the bottom and click the **Save** button:

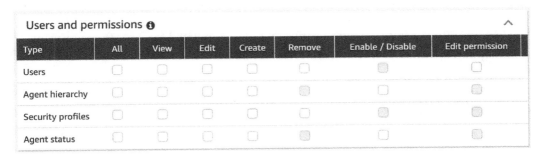

Figure 5.27 – User access controls

7. For the user admin profile, we will start with a new profile rather than making a copy. From the security profile, click on the **Add new security profile** button (*Figure 5.28*) on the main screen. You won't be prompted with a pop-up window this time. You will go straight to the profile window:

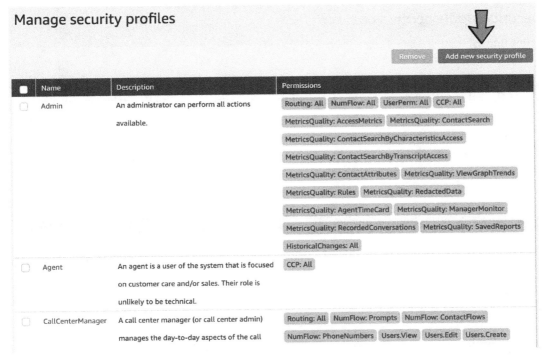

Figure 5.28 – Security profiles list

8. The first thing you need to do is fill out the details box at the top of the window (*Figure 5.29*). When you copy a profile, these are populated for you. Then, we want to expand the users and permissions bar so that we can set those permissions properly:

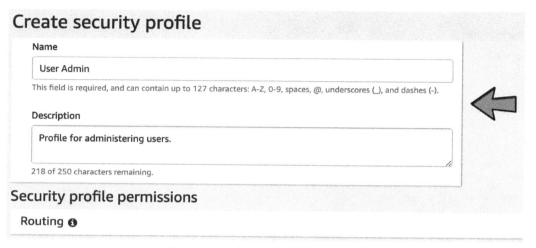

Figure 5.29 – Creating a security profile

9. Select the **All** column checkbox for all the rows except for the **Security profiles** row. You don't want to choose these settings because that would allow the user admin to change their security profile and give themselves elevated rights. Your configuration should look as shown in *Figure 5.30*. At this time, you can repeat the process for any additional security profiles that you will need for your deployment:

Figure 5.30 – User admin settings

Now that we have the security profiles set up the way we would like, we can begin adding users.

Adding users

Next, we will configure some users so that we have a way to test functionality later:

1. You get to the user management screen by clicking the left menu bar on the people icon and then selecting the **User management** menu option as shown in *Figure 5.31*:

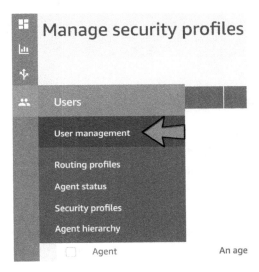

Figure 5.31 – User management menu

2. The user management screen is the same format as the other screens in Connect. You will see a list of the users in your Connect instance and their permissions and routing profiles. To create new users, click the **Add new users** (*Figure 5.32*) button in the top right:

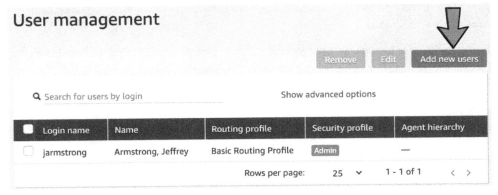

Figure 5.32 – User list

3.   Remember, if you are using domain or SAML login, you will have to match the usernames exactly and won't have a password field. The process will essentially be the same, no matter your authentication method. In this demonstration, I'm using Connect based users so that I will be entering password data. When you click the **Add new users** button, you will be presented with a wizard screen as shown in *Figure 5.33*:

Figure 5.33 – Add new users

4.   The first step in the process gives you two options for adding users. You can manually enter users using the **Create and set up a new user** option or upload a list of users in the form of a CSV file. For the CSV file option, you can download a template using the **template** link. The CSV option is great when you are getting ready to complete your installation and add many users. The process is straightforward: fill out the file, then upload and complete the process after the file has been imported. A special note for the CSV import: make sure that your password generator doesn't use single- or double-quotes as special characters. It messes up the upload.

For this step, we are just going to create a new user manually. That option is selected by default, so just click the **Next** button to continue to the next step:

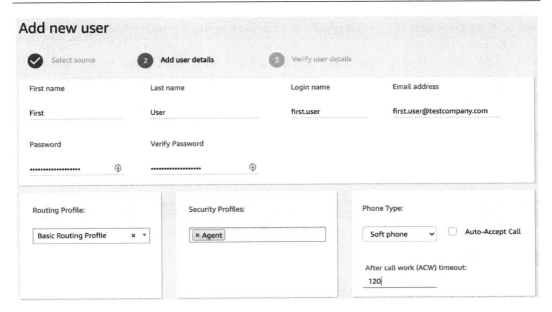

Figure 5.34 – User details

Most of the fields for creating a user are self-explanatory. You can see the values I used in *Figure 5.34*. The ones that need attention are **Routing Profile**, **Security Profile**, and **After call work (ACW) timeout**. We haven't talked about routing profiles before. Routing profiles are where you control the channels and queues an agent is assigned to. By channels, I mean voice calls or chat. Routing profiles also let you control the priority of queues. We haven't created a routing profile at this time, so just select **Basic Routing Profile** with the default Connect deployment.

The **Security Profiles** field allows you to add security profiles to a user. A single user can have multiple profiles if they have various roles. To add a profile, click in the text box. When you do this, Connect will populate a list of available options for you to choose from. For this user, I selected the **Agent** profile. We will be using this user later for testing purposes from the agent's perspective.

The final setting that needs attention on this page is **After call work (ACW) timeout**. After an agent takes a call, yous typically don't want them to get calls back-to-back. There is usually some amount of work that needs to be done before the next call. They might need to update some customer records or finish some notes about the call in your CRM system. The ACW field is where you set this timeout, so the agent has time to complete the work without a phone ringing and a potentially missed call. I've set mine to 120 seconds, or 2 minutes. This time is not fixed. If an agent completes the work sooner, they can click the **Complete** button and transition back to an available status to take the next call.

When all the settings are to your satisfaction, click **Save** at the bottom of the page. You will then be directed back to a page listing your new user. If you had imported a CSV file, you would see a list of users at this point rather than just one. Click the **Create users** (*Figure 5.35*) button to create your user. If you were to navigate away at this point, your user wouldn't be saved, so make sure to click the button:

Figure 5.35 – Create users

Adding users is a vital function for any application and Connect isn't any different. It's unfortunate that you still must create users in the Connect system even if you use federation. Maybe in the future they will add the ability to capture groups from the SAML assertion and use that to control users' capabilities rather than adding them.

Summary

We now have a somewhat operational Connect instance. There are still many missing pieces, but you should be able to call your new phone number at this point. If you try your number, you will be prompted with several options that demonstrate some of the Connect capabilities.

It is highly probable that you will come back to some of the items discussed in this chapter several times during your call center's deployment. Picking phone numbers, creating call queues and security profiles, and adding users are all common actions.

The next step in the process is to start creating our contact flows. As we discussed before, contact flows allow you to control the experience for your customers. In *Chapter 6, Contact Flow Creation*, we will cover creating those contact flows. We will rely on the features we created in this chapter, such as the testing user and operating hours, to test those flows.

6
Contact Flow Creation

Now that we have created the Connect instance, it's time to complete the contact flows that form the user experience. The bulk of the work that is done in Connect is performed in contact flows. We will walk through creating several contact flows, using a couple of the types that we discussed in *Chapter 3, Sketching Your Contact Flows*. The reason for multiple flows is that we can demonstrate the connectivity between them. Understanding this connectivity is vitally important if you want to be able to segment your flows properly. Remember, proper flow segmentation reduces long-term risk by lowering individual flow complexity.

In addition to introducing you to creating a few types of contact flows, we will also cover many of the flow components we also discussed in *Chapter 3, Sketching Your Contact Flows*. A contact flow cannot perform any function and needs the flow components nested inside of it to operate. By following along in this chapter, your Connect instance that you have deployed will start to take shape and will be able to accept calls and perform actions. This chapter will demonstrate the following topics:

- Creating a contact flow
- Copying contact flows
- Exporting and importing contact flows
- Putting it all together

Creating a contact flow

Since we are getting deeper into call center deployment, it would probably be an excellent time to set the stage a bit more about what my demonstration call center will look like. To do this, we will need to cover some of the business objectives to be accomplished. These objectives will be some of the items that would be uncovered by the processes we discussed in *Chapter 2, Reviewing Stakeholder Objectives*.

In my scenario, I'm creating a call center for a hospital. It has been a common theme so far, so it seems fitting to continue with it. We will not work with any advanced features such as integrations or sentiment analysis for this phase of the implementation, but will add those features as we progress through the book. For this chapter, these are the criteria that we will be working with to deploy contact flows:

Company name	Mega Mercy Hospital
Number of agents	200+
Number of departments	8
Departments	Billing
	Accounts payable
	Radiology
	Oncology
	Outpatient procedures
	Purchasing
	Intensive care unit
	Cardiology
Callback desired	Yes
Hold music desired	Yes
Outbound calling enabled	Yes
Call recording	Yes

Feel free to use these criteria or invent your own. Try to stay close to the preceding design, as a significant deviation might make it harder to follow along in later chapters. With these initial criteria defined, we can begin creating our first contact flow.

The question now is: Where to get started? Frequently, people feel inundated when getting started with their call center deployment. After all, they are—or at least can be—extremely complex systems. You might be sitting in front of dozens of business objectives and many sketched-out contact flows. You might think that it's logical to start at the beginning, with the contact flow that gets kicked off when someone calls. I would advise against this if you are new to Connect. The entry-point contact flow cascades into the entire deployment, which means it can be daunting and take a long time to feel like you have accomplished anything or can test it.

Being new to Connect, I suggest instead starting with flows that have a definite beginning and end. This is where we are going to start. The first flow that we are going to configure will be the outbound whisper. The outbound whisper has a definitive start and end, so it's a great place to get started with contact flows.

Editing an existing flow

Contact flows are one of the items in Connect that you can't delete. Not sure why— that's just the way it is. Since there is a limit to how many contact flows you can have, I recommend repurposing the default ones that come with the Connect deployment whenever possible. Plus, some of the work you need to do might already exist in these default flows anyway. For the outbound whisper, we are going to repurpose the **Default outbound** contact flow. To get started, we need to get to the **Contact flows** list in Connect, as follows:

1. We need to activate the left-side menu and select the icon that looks like a **Universal Serial Bus (USB)** symbol. Then, click on **Contact flows**, as depicted in the following screenshot:

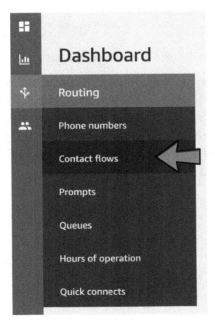

Figure 6.1 – Contact flows menu

2. Once you click the menu item, you will be presented with a list of contact flows (*Figure 6.2*), as with the other screens we learned about in *Chapter 5, Base Connect Implementation*. 19 default and sample contact flows come with Connect. Since you are limited to 100 total contact flows, you would already have decreased your capacity by 20% if you were to leave these as-is. To ensure we get the maximum capabilities of our instance, we will edit the **Default outbound** flow. To do this, select the **Default outbound** link in the leftmost column, as illustrated in the following screenshot:

Contact flows

▼ Search by name

Create contact flow ▾

Name	Type	Description	Status
Default agent hold	Agent hold	Audio played for the agent when on hold	Published
Default agent transfer	Transfer to agent	Default flow to transfer to an agent.	Published
Default agent whisper	Agent whisper	Default whisper played to the agent.	Published
Default customer hold	Customer hold	Default audio the customer hears while on hold.	Published
Default customer queue	Customer queue	Default audio played when a customer is waiting in queue.	Published
Default customer whisper	Customer whisper	Default whisper played to the customer	Published
Default outbound	Outbound whisper	Default flow for outbound calls.	Published
Default queue transfer	Transfer to queue	Default flow used to transfer to a queue.	Published

Figure 6.2 – Contact flows list

3. Once you click on the contact flow, you will be presented with a contact flow editing screen. The menu on the left side of the screen, depicted in *Figure 6.3*, holds all the connect flow components discussed in *Chapter 3, Sketching Your Contact Flows*. You will probably note that the category names look familiar. This menu lets you source the components by dragging and dropping them into the design field that looks like graph paper, as illustrated in the following screenshot:

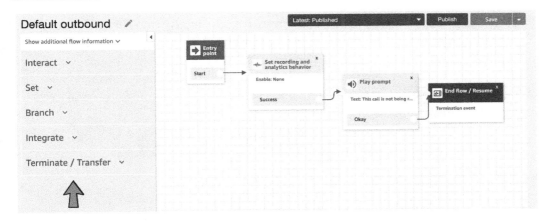

Figure 6.3 – Contact flow components

4. At the top of the screen are a couple of control options, as depicted in *Figure 6.4*. These menu options are what you use to save and publish contact flows. We haven't covered publishing yet, so let's take a second to explain that. In Connect, when you save a contact flow, it's saved but hasn't been made active yet. The Save feature allows you to work on flows and save your progress without worrying about completing all the changes first. For your contact flow to become active, it needs to be published. The Publish action commits the changes to the Connect instance and makes the live.

Another feature of Connect contact flows is that Connect stores previously saved and published versions of your contact flows. You can view the previous version by clicking the drop-down menu depicted in the following screenshot and selecting a previous version:

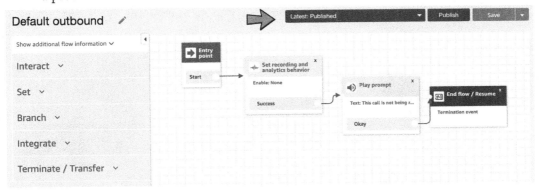

Figure 6.4 – Control menu

5. Now that we have covered the editing screen, it's time to dive into changing the **Default outbound** flow to meet our needs. The first thing we need to do is to change the name. To do this, click the pencil icon next to the name. When you do this, the name will turn into an editable field, as shown in the following screenshot. I typically preface contact flows with a company name for general items or a department name to help distinguish them long term:

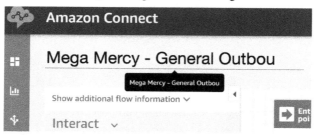

Figure 6.5 – Editing name

6. Once you rename the contact flow, we can modify it to meet our needs. Based on the Mega Mercy Hospital criteria, they want to make outbound calls—hence why we are editing this flow—but they also desire the ability to record calls. To meet these requirements with our outbound flow, we are going to have to do two things. Firstly, we will have to activate call recording, and secondly, we will have to let the person being called know that the call can be recorded, to meet state regulatory requirements.

    If you look at *Figure 6.6*, you will notice that the **Set recording and analytics behavior** contact flow component is already in our contact flow. Unfortunately, the **Enable** setting is set to **None**. We are going to have to change this setting. To change the settings within a component, click on the component name, as illustrated in the following screenshot:

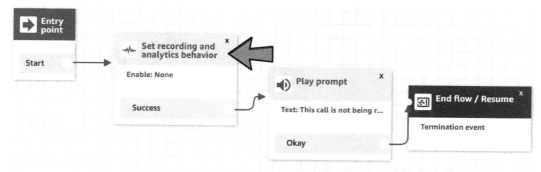

Figure 6.6 – Call recording setting

7. Upon clicking, a new screen will appear out of the right-hand side. This screen (*Figure 6.7*) will show the options for the component. In our case, we want to enable active call recording by selecting the **On** radio button. Once you do that, you will see additional options. In most cases, you will want to record both the agent and the customer. By selecting this option, we can go back later to see how the customer and the agent responded. From the agent's perspective, we see if there are issues with the service or a better way to handle certain situations. Recording the customer can be used to mitigate risks, such as a *he said/she said* problem. It will also help you to identify whether customers are displeased with your service or products.

You might also notice that there is a checkbox for **Contact Lens speech analytics** in this component. We won't turn this on now but will cover it in a later chapter, but it's important to note that you must enable call recording for it to work. When you are finished, click **Save**, as illustrated in the following screenshot:

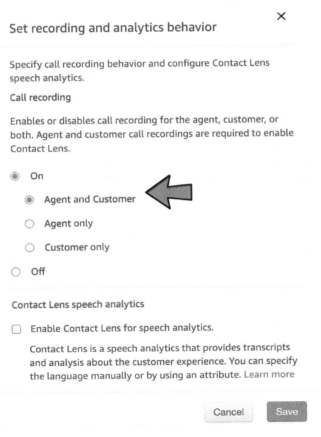

Figure 6.7 – Activating recording

8. When you return to the editing screen, the **Enable** status will now display **Agent and Customer**, noting that your changes were successful. Now we have completed that, we need to change the **Play prompt** component. As you can see in *Figure 6.8*, the component shows some text saying **This call is not being r….** Considering that we just activated call recording, we need to change that. Follow the same procedure to edit the **Play prompt** component by clicking on the heading, as illustrated in the following screenshot:

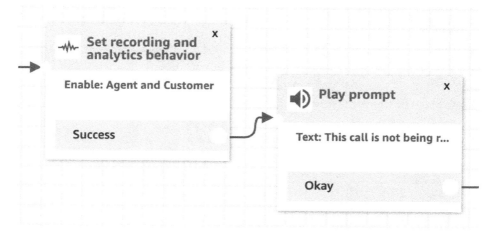

Figure 6.8 – Flow settings

9. The **Play prompt** component's editing screen will have a similar feel to the **Set recording and analytics behavior** component (*Figure 6.9*). This component has a few options. The **Play prompt** component allows you to use pre-recorded prompts. To use this feature, you would select the **Select from the prompt library (audio)** option. You would use this if you were having a professional record your prompts for you. There is also a setting under **Text-to-speech or chat text**. We will use **Text-to-speech or chat text** for this prompt. To modify, simply edit the text in the box as to what you want the prompt to say. There is another setting called **Enter dynamically**—this is a more advanced feature that can pull data based on the call. We will cover this setting in more detail later in the book, in *Chapter 8, Interfacing Enterprise Applications*.

Since this is an outbound prompt and is played before anyone talks to the person being called, I like to make some form of introduction first. For this call center, I started with the introduction of **You are receiving a call from Mega Mercy Hospital.** This prompt lets them know that they aren't being contacted by a Robo dialer or some form of a scam call, and that they should probably wait on the line. I then follow up with a prompt that the call may be recorded to meet regulatory requirements. Typically, I also follow up the prompt with a polite transition, such as *I'm now connecting you to an agent.* When you are done, click the **Save** button to save your changes, as illustrated in the following screenshot:

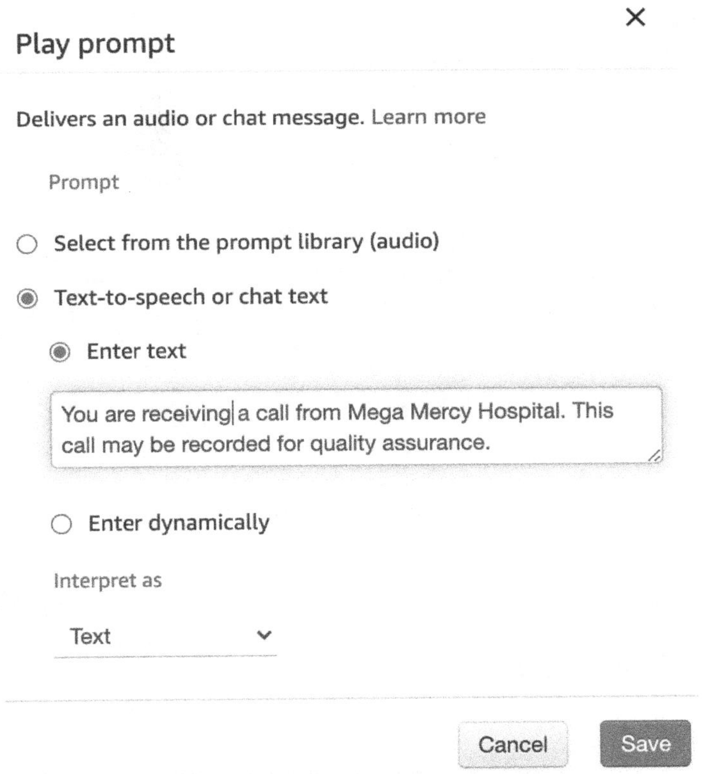

Play prompt   ✕

Delivers an audio or chat message. Learn more

Prompt

○ Select from the prompt library (audio)

◉ Text-to-speech or chat text

   ◉ Enter text

   > You are receiving|a call from Mega Mercy Hospital. This
   > call may be recorded for quality assurance.

   ○ Enter dynamically

   Interpret as

   Text   ⌄

Cancel   Save

Figure 6.9 – Play prompt editing

10. We have now completed the configuration of the first connect flow. This flow was simple and already had the components that we wanted in the default that we edited, but you should have a good idea now as to the look and feel of editing flow components. To finish up editing, we need to commit the changes to Connect. There are two options at this point: to click the **Save** button and not have it take effect, or to click **Publish** and have the changes go live. In the following screenshot, we want to publish in this instance, so we click on the **Publish** button:

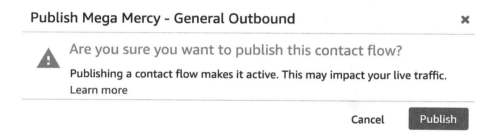

Figure 6.10 – Publishing

When you click on **Publish**, the notification in *Figure 6.10* is shown, alerting you to the fact that you are applying changes to your live traffic. Since Connect is a highly available service that spans multiple availability zones in **Amazon Web Services** (**AWS**), it takes some time for the publishing to take full effect. I'm not sure how long it takes; there isn't any information available regarding this. From anecdotal experience, I can tell you that publishing changes to existing flows take less than a minute to take effect. However, I have found that when I activate a new number and add a contact flow, this change seems to take longer, and I have had to wait a couple of minutes for the new number to become active with the contact flow.

We have now completed the first contact flow for your new call center. Even though this was a small example and didn't require a lot of editing, we have covered the process of contact flow manipulation. In the next section, we are going to cover creating a contact flow from scratch.

Creating a contact flow from scratch

Creating a contact flow from scratch is very much the same as editing an existing one. To get started, we need to navigate back to the contact flow main screen through the menu on the left. There is a button in the upper right of the screen (*Figure 6.11*) that says **Create contact flow**. You click this button to create a new contact flow. It's important to note that there is a drop-down box next to the **Create contact flow** button. This drop-down box allows you to create other types of flows.

The contact flow we are going to create now is the entry point for all the calls. I like to use the entry point to store all the settings for the call center. This design provides a single place to configure the bulk of the settings, and I follow this pattern for convenience. To get started, follow these steps:

1. Click on the **Create contact flow** button, as illustrated in the following screenshot:

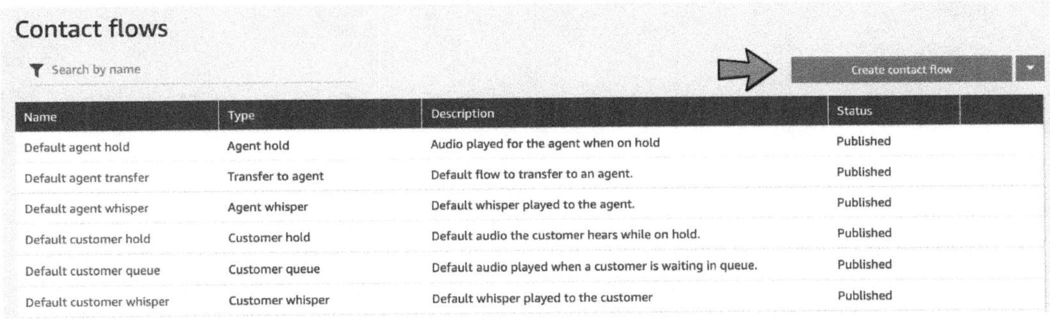
Contact flows
Search by name
Create contact flow
Name
Type
Description
Status
Default agent hold
Agent hold
Audio played for the agent when on hold
Published
Default agent transfer
Transfer to agent
Default flow to transfer to an agent.
Published
Default agent whisper
Agent whisper
Default whisper played to the agent.
Published
Default customer hold
Customer hold
Default audio the customer hears while on hold.
Published
Default customer queue
Customer queue
Default audio played when a customer is waiting in queue.
Published
Default customer whisper
Customer whisper
Default whisper played to the customer
Published

Figure 6.11 – Creating a contact flow

2. Once you click on the button, you will be presented with the same editing screen as when we repurposed a default flow, as shown in the following screenshot. The only difference is that it's completely blank. Start by giving the flow a name by clicking on the pencil icon, as before. I've named mine `Mega Mercy - Entry Point`:

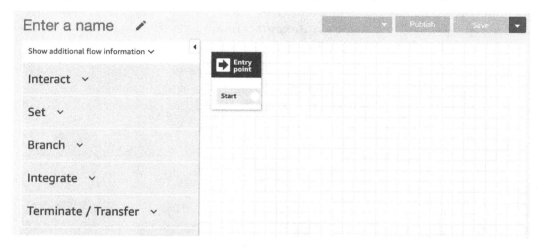

Figure 6.12 – New flow

3. The first thing that we want to add to our flow is logging. Enabling logging ensures that everything that happens in your flows is sent to CloudWatch for review. This configuration will help you diagnose if things don't work out in your flows as you would expect them to. To add the logging setting, click the down arrow next to the **Set** category, as depicted in the following screenshot:

Figure 6.13 – Expanding the Set menu

4. Once you open the **Set** menu, you will be prompted with all the flow components related to settings. Your screen should look like *Figure 6.14*. To add the logging setting to your contact flow, you need to click on **Set logging behavior** and drag it to the graph paper section, as illustrated here:

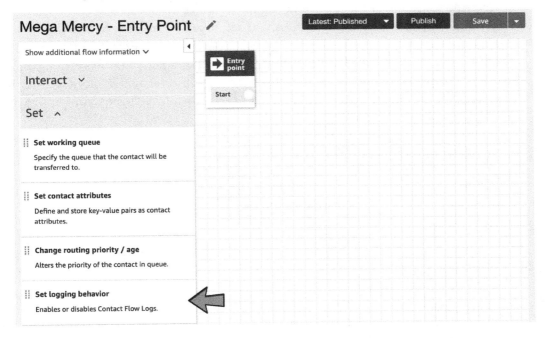

Figure 6.14 – Set menu

5. At this point, you should have something that looks like *Figure 6.15*. However, the setting still isn't usable. Right now, your **Set logging behavior** component is on its little island and isn't connected to anything. In a contact flow, everything needs to be connected so that the call can flow from one item to the next. If you look again at *Figure 6.15*, just under the red arrow, you might notice a white half-circle notch. Depending on your screen it might be hard to see, but it is there. The half-circle notch is the input for the component. Every component has one except for the exsiting Entry point included as the default in a flow. The input on the Set logging behavior component needs to be connected to an output from another block. In this case, we want the output from the entry-point block. A white circle notes outputs in the components, as illustrated here:

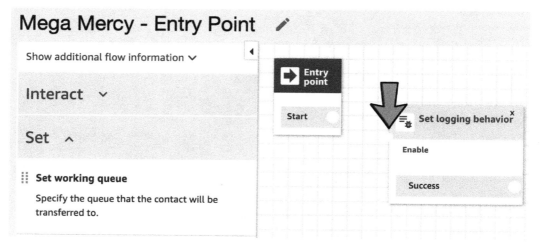

Figure 6.15 – First component

6. To connect these two components, simply click on the white circle in the **Start** box and drag to the notch in the **Set logging behavior** component. A line will appear and connect the two components, and will look like this:

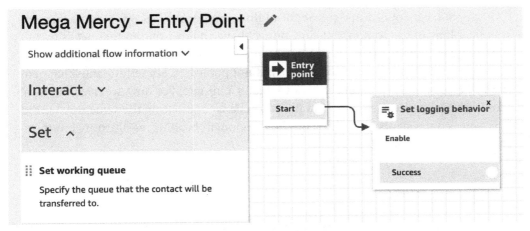

Figure 6.16 – Connected component

7. Now that a new component has been added and linked, it's time to configure the component's settings. The default setting for **Set logging behavior** is enabled, so there isn't anything for us to change on this one. Next, we want to repeat the process and configure the settings for the hold flows. As discussed in *Chapter 3, Sketching Your Contact Flows*, the **Set hold flow** component sets the flow for what happens when an agent or a customer is put on hold. Let's first add a setting for the customer. Grab the **Set hold flow** component from the menu on the left and drag it to the graph paper. Once it is there, connect the **Set logging behavior** component's **Success** output to the input notch on the new component. Your flow should now look like the one shown here:

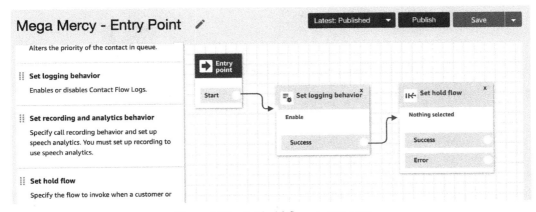

Figure 6.17 – Set hold flow component

8. You might have noticed that the **Set hold flow** component has two outputs instead of one. Many of the components in Connect have an error output that needs to be captured. What I mean by captured is that you can't just leave it disconnected. Connect will let you save it in this state but not publish it. Something must happen with the error state. We will get back to this in a minute. For now, we need to set the correct flow for the customer hold flow. We change the setting the same way we did for other components by clicking on the component heading, as illustrated in the following screenshot:

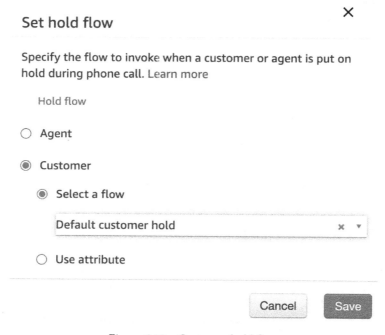

Figure 6.18 – Customer hold flow

9. Since we are configuring the customer hold flow, we select the **Customer** radio button to choose a flow. Since we haven't created any flows for holds yet, we will also choose the **Default customer hold** flow. When done, click the **Save** button.

    We now need to repeat the process to set the agent hold flow by dragging another hold flow component onto the design field. Then, connect the success of the previous component to the new component and configure it. Your contact flow should now look like this:

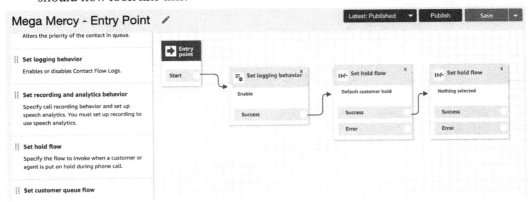

Figure 6.19 – Hold flows

10. Now that we have these components in, we are going to need some error handling. Errors typically get directed to a Disconnect component. However, it's important to include a prompt first. You might have been on the phone before when something went wrong in a call center you were connected with and received the dreaded *Something went wrong—goodbye* message. I like to include a more friendly message that includes an error code to relay to an agent. Using this code, you can diagnose issues more readily.

To create this error-handling functionality, you need to drag a **Play prompt** component from the **Interact** menu and a **Disconnect** component from the **Terminate / Transfer** menu. Connect the error outputs from the **Set hold flow** components to the **Play prompt** input. Finally, connect the **Okay** output from the **Play prompt** component to the **Disconnect** component. When you are done, your flow should look like the one shown here:

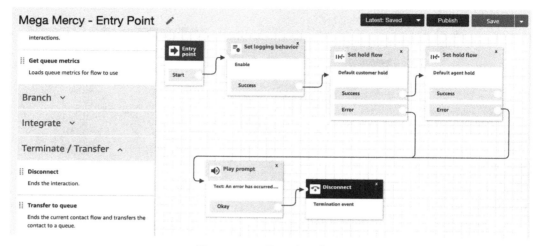

Figure 6.20 – Error handling

11. To round out this flow, we need to add a setting for our prompts for the voice we wish to use. The default is **Johanna**. I'd like to set mine to **Matthew** to be different. To set the voice, we use the **Set voice** component located under the **Set** menu. Drag that onto the design field now. We are playing a prompt in this flow, so we want to set the voice before that prompt. In this flow, the **Set hold flow** components output the errors that move onto the prompt. We will have to put the **Set voice** component in front of those to properly control the voice if an error occurs.

To do this, we need to break the link between the **Set logging** and **Set hold** components. If you hover over the line, a red **X** will appear, as depicted in the following screenshot. Click on this **X** to remove the line. Once you complete this, you can re-attach the **Set logging behavior** component to the **Set voice** component and the **Set voice** component back to the **Set hold flow** component:

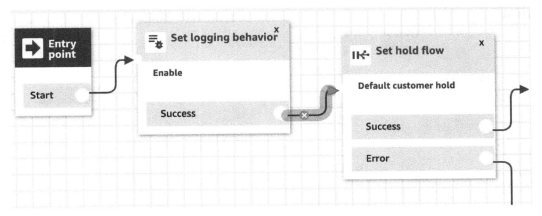

Figure 6.21 – Breaking a link

12. Finally, we want to edit the **Set voice** component to set the voice to **Matthew**. Now that we have completed all the settings we want to include in this flow, we can finish it off. We need this flow to connect to anotherflow so that we can handle calls. This flow was just for settings, so there isn't any work happening regarding calls.

Before we get to that, I wanted to point out that we didn't include any call recording settings in this flow. This flow would be a good location to put a setting such as that. However, since this is a large hospital with many departments, not all departments would want to have recording activated. In this scenario, we will set call recording for each department in a separate flow. You might have a similar situation with your call center.

The last component we need to add to tie this flow to another is the **Transfer to flow** component under the **Terminate / Transfer** menu. Drag this component to the design field and connect to the **Set hold flow** component. Connect its error to the **Play prompt** input. We don't have another flow to send it to, so we won't configure it at this time. Your completed flow should look like the one shown here:

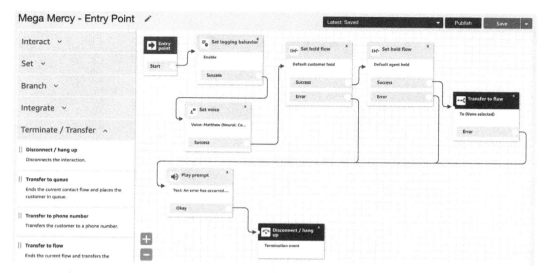

Figure 6.22 – Completed flow

13. With your flow completed, we can now save it. We won't be able to publish it at this time. Connect validates the flow when it publishes it. Since we don't have a flow to transfer to this time, it would throw an error. If you do try to publish a flow that isn't configured correctly, you will receive an error such as the one shown in the following screenshot:

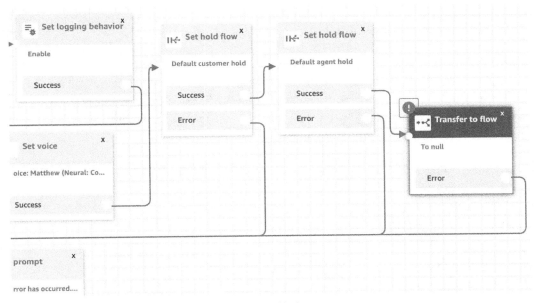

Figure 6.23 – Publishing error

Now that we have completed this flow, it's time to move on with rounding out the experience. The next flow we are going to create is the first flow that interacts with the caller.

Copying contact flows

We modified our first flow using one of the default flows that come with Connect. Then, we created our entry point from scratch by creating our flow. This time, we are going to copy an existing flow to make our first customer interaction. As you can probably tell, we walk through each way to create a flow with each new flow we create.

For this flow, we want to create a branching flow—that is, a flow that directs users to one department or another. To do this, follow these steps:

1. We will make a copy of the existing flow called **Sample inbound flow (first contact experience)**. First, we need to replicate some steps we already performed by going to the contact flow screen and then clicking on the **Sample inbound flow (first contact experience)** link. Once we do that, we will again be presented with the editing screen, which should look like this:

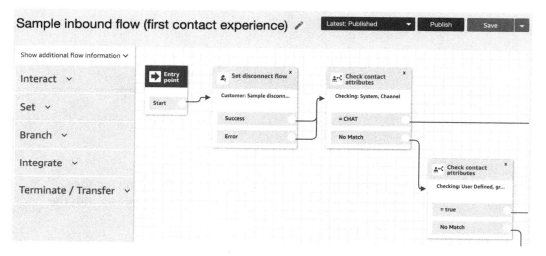

Figure 6.24 – Sample editing screen

2. At this time, we want to make a copy by saving it, but we don't want to just click the **Save** button as that would only save this sample again. Instead, we want to click the down arrow button, just next to **Save**. You will then be presented with a small drop-down list, as illustrated in the following screenshot. Click the **Save as** option to make a copy of this flow:

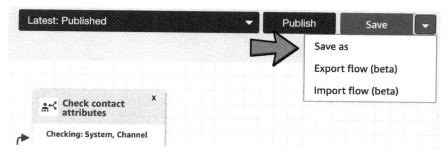

Figure 6.25 – Save as menu

3. When you click **Save as**, you will be prompted with a popup (*Figure 6.26*) that asks for a **New name** and **Description** of the flow. I have followed the naming scheme that I have been using through this chapter, prefixing the flow with `Mega Mercy` and a flow name. The **Description** field can be filled out to your liking, to help you remember what the flow is for. When finished, click **Save as**, and the screen should refresh with the new name you entered. Making copies of existing flows is a great way to save time on repetitive processes. The **Save as** popup can be seen in the following screenshot:

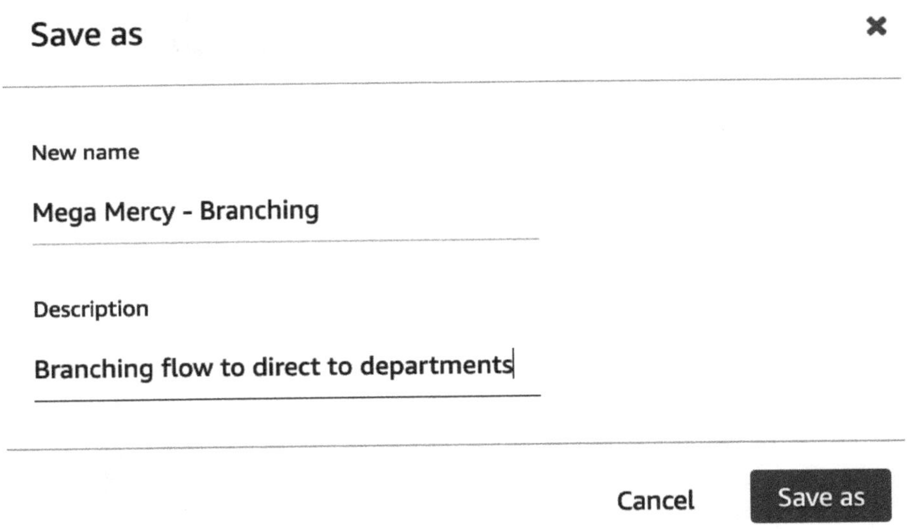

Save as   ✖

New name

Mega Mercy - Branching

Description

Branching flow to direct to departments

Cancel   Save as

Figure 6.26 – Save as popup

4. The sample flow that we copied has a few extra components for demonstration purposes that we don't need for our flow. We will want to do some cleanup and remove these at this time. Firstly, we want to remove the **Set disconnect flow** block component. This setting will be dependent on the department, so we don't want it there. We want to remove the **Check attributes** component, which checks whether it's a chat or a voice call. We will cover chat later, in *Chapter 13, Implementing Chat*. From there, we want to remove the prompt that was attached to the **Check attributes for chat** component. Finally, we want to remove the remaining **Check and set attributes** components from the flow.

Currently, there is a lot of space in our flow. Let's clean that up now. First, let's zoom out so that we can get a better look at the whole flow. You can do that by clicking on the zoom controls in the lower left of the design field, as illustrated in the following screenshot:

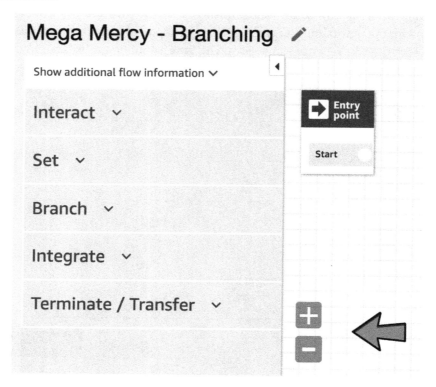

Figure 6.27 – Zoom controls

5. Zoom out and organize the flow so that it's a bit more compact. At this point, your flow should look like the one shown in *Figure 6.28*. Next, we will want to fix error handling to meet our standard by putting a polite message and an error code to help with diagnostics into the **Play prompt** component. The following screenshot provides an overview of the flow:

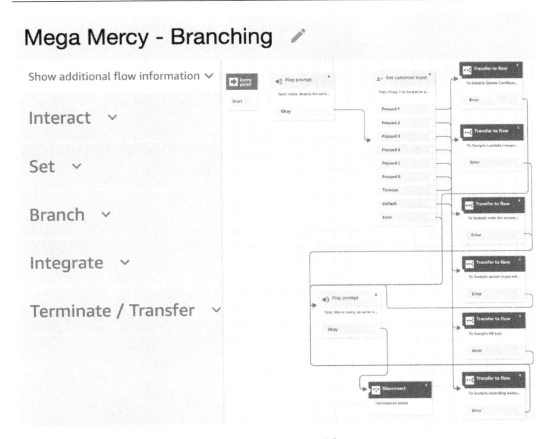

Figure 6.28 – Organized flow

6. Now, we need to do some final cleanup on this flow. The entry point is not currently connected to the rest of the flow, so let's make that connection now. We also need to change the **Play prompt** component, to give a greeting that matches our call center. I've updated mine to reflect that they are calling the Mega Mercy Hospital.

This branching flow is based on an **Interactive Voice Response** (**IVR**) system. It will play a prompt, asking the user to input a number to progress through the flow. This location would be a great place to use a Lex bot and **artificial intelligence** (**AI**) to determine where the user wants to go, instead of a legacy IVR system. We will cover this in *Chapter 7, Creating AI Bots*. For now, let's just leave it as-is. The menu doesn't have the correct options, though, so we will need to update those by editing the **Get customer input** component.

The **Get customer input** component has several options that need to be set. The top of the settings block looks the same as the **Play prompt** settings (*Figure 6.29*). The text needs to be edited to reflect the departments that we will be working with. Update all eight of them. You will need to add two, as the original only had six. The **Get customer input** component is shown in the following screenshot:

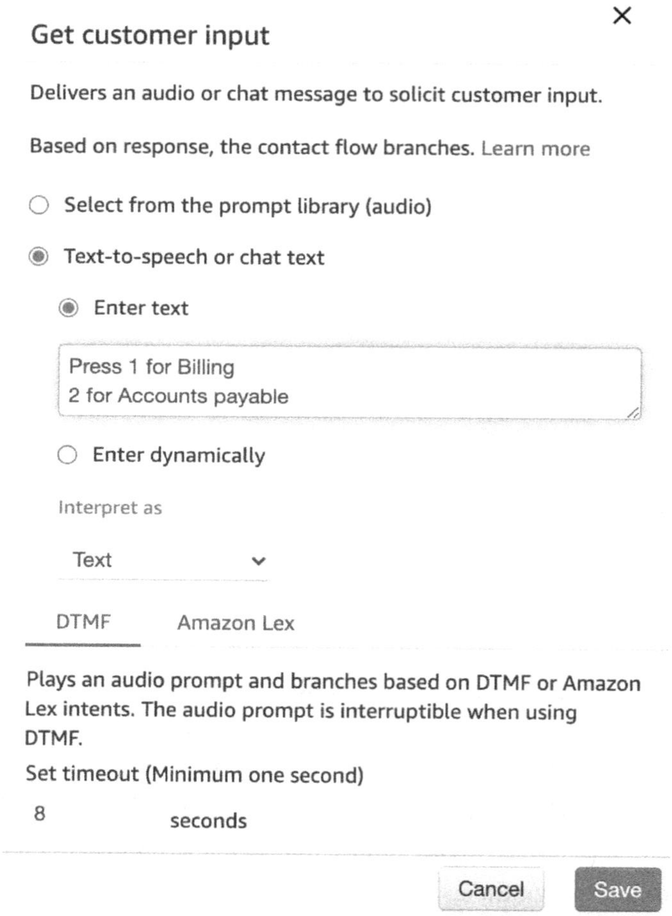

Get customer input   ✕

Delivers an audio or chat message to solicit customer input.

Based on response, the contact flow branches. Learn more

○ Select from the prompt library (audio)

◉ Text-to-speech or chat text

   ◉ Enter text

        Press 1 for Billing
        2 for Accounts payable

   ○ Enter dynamically

   Interpret as

   Text   ⌄

   DTMF   Amazon Lex
   _____

Plays an audio prompt and branches based on DTMF or Amazon Lex intents. The audio prompt is interruptible when using DTMF.

Set timeout (Minimum one second)

8   seconds

                              Cancel   Save

Figure 6.29 – Get customer input

You won't want to click **Save** at this point, as there are other options we need to configure.

7. Since the **Get customer input** component is receiving input, we need to tell it what input it will receive and how long it should wait. If you scroll down the settings window, you will see that there is a **DTMF** section. This component will wait for users' input and then time out based on the timeout setting (*Figure 6.30*). You can control what happens, specifically when a timeout occurs through the outputs. I feel 8 seconds is a bit long for a timeout, so I'm going to set mine to 5 seconds instead, as illustrated in the following screenshot:

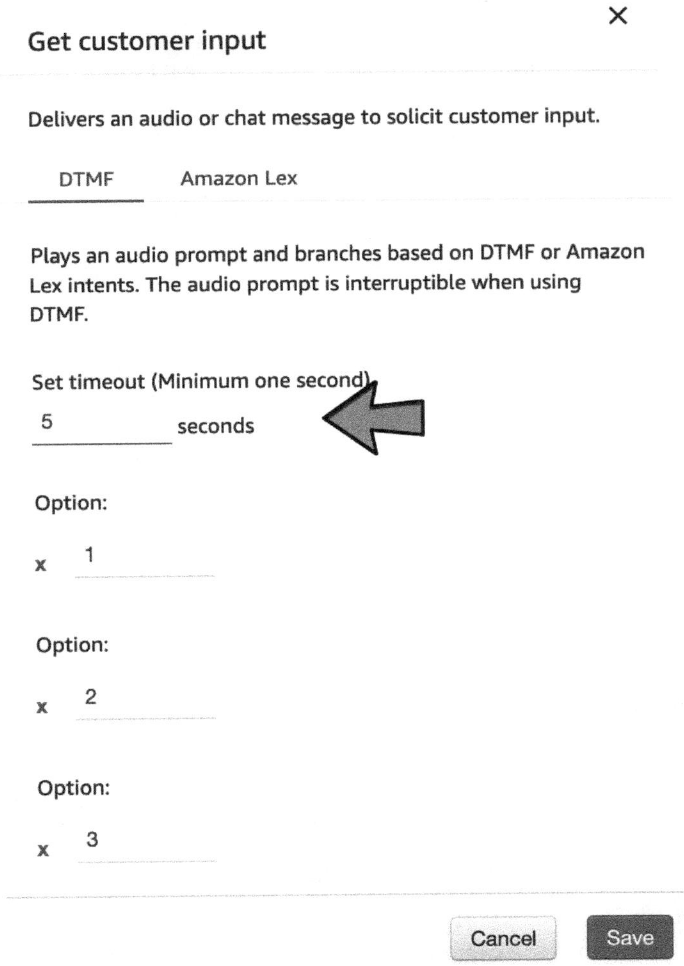

Figure 6.30 – Timeout

8.   The last piece to configure on this component is the options. The flow initially had six options, and we want eight. Continue scrolling the settings window to the bottom and select **Add another condition** (*Figure 6.31*). Add two more conditions for 7 and 8, and click **Save** when you are done. At this point, the component block will expand, adding the two options you created, as depicted in the following screenshot:

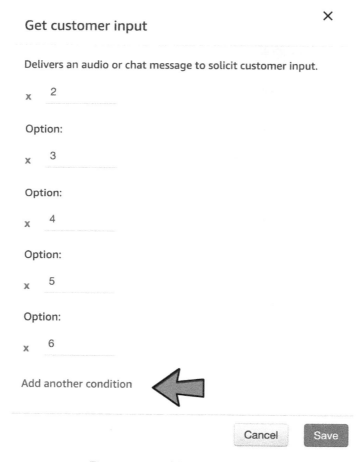

Figure 6.31 – Add another condition

Since we added two options, we will need to add two more transfers to the flow components. Drag them onto the design field and connect them to options 7 and 8. You might need to move some of the components around so that the flow is more readable.

The last change we are going to make to the flow is to change the behavior of the default and timeout outputs. The default output is used when someone enters a number that isn't 1-8, such as zero. We want both actions to go back to the input for the **Play prompt** component. This change would allow the user to be prompted repeatedly if they made a mistake or took too long to enter a response.

As a side note, you might want to have the Default ouput transfer to another flow where it's answered by a person directly, just in case the customer is having some sort of issue.

The department flows haven't been configured yet, so we will leave them be for now. We will create those in the next section. Your flow should look like the one in the following screenshot. Click **Save** to save the flow at this time:

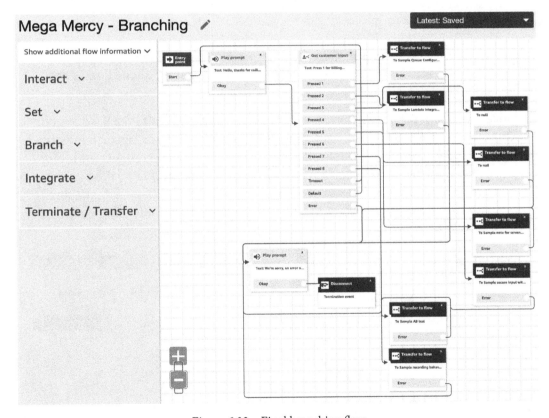

Figure 6.32 – Final branching flow

We still can't update the entry-point flow to point to the branching flow, as it's not yet published. I mentioned before how many of these flows cascade, and this is a good example. We will have to complete the department flows before we can finish any of the connections between them. In the next section, we will create the department flows.

Exporting and importing contact flows

The final way of creating a contact flow that we will cover is via exporting and importing. This capability is advantageous if you have more than one Connect instance. You might have this situation if your company is operating on more than one continent. Importing and exporting allows you to migrate work you have done in one instance to another instance, with minimal effort. There will be some changes that need to be made to make the flows work once imported, and we will discuss them as we work through the flows.

> **Important note**
> Before we can begin working on the department flows, we need to create the departments' queues. Refer to *Chapter 3, Sketching Your Contact Flows,* on how to create the necessary queues.

Since we haven't created any department flows yet, we will have to pick an existing flow to export as our baseline. I have chosen to use the **Sample customer queue** flow as the baseline for the departments. To begin, edit this flow, as follows:

1. Once you are on the editing screen, select the down arrow next to the **Save** button. This time, we are going to choose **Export flow** instead of **Save as**. You can look at *Figure 6.33* for reference. You may notice that the menu item says **beta**. The import/ export function has been in beta for some time (since 2017, actually). I have never run into an issue using it, but your mileage may vary since it's in beta. Make sure to verify your flows upon import to ensure everything is copacetic. The process is illustrated here:

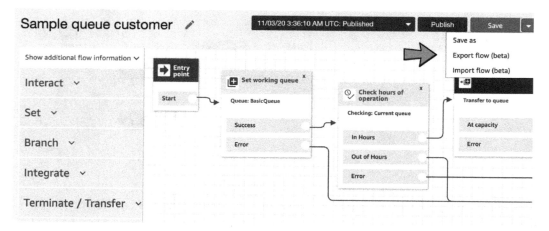

Figure 6.33 – Export flow

2. When you select **Export flow (beta)**, a popup will appear, as in *Figure 6.34*. You can name the exported file in this popup if you choose, but it's not entirely necessary. The filename has no bearing on the imported data, and the name of the flow when imported will not change from its current value. When you are satisfied, click the **Export** button, as illustrated in the following screenshot:

Export flow (beta)   ✖

When you export a flow, the most recently saved version is exported. Any unsaved changes to the flow will not be exported. If you modify the exported file it may not import correctly. Learn more about Contact Flow Import/Export.

Name your exported file

Sample queue customer

Cancel   Export

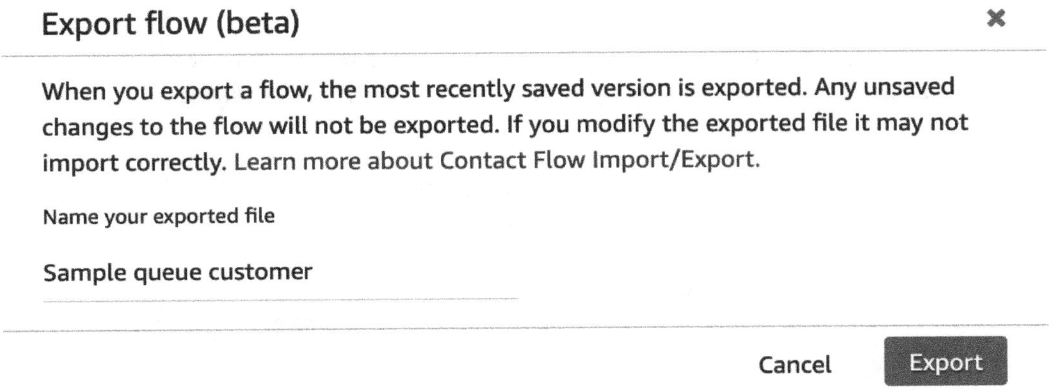

Figure 6.34 – Export flow (beta) popup

3. Once the flow has been exported, the next step is to create a new flow using the procedure we performed previously. However, once the flow is created, we can begin the importing process. From the editing screen, select the down arrow next to the **Save** button. The menu now displayed only shows **Import flow (beta)**, as in the following screenshot. Select this option:

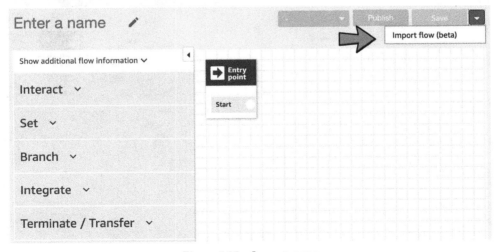

Figure 6.35 – Import menu

4.   Upon selecting **Import flow (beta),** you will again be prompted for a filename. Instead of entering a filename, click the **Select** button to navigate to your downloaded export file. Once you have selected that file, click the **Import** button to import the file, as illustrated in the following screenshot:

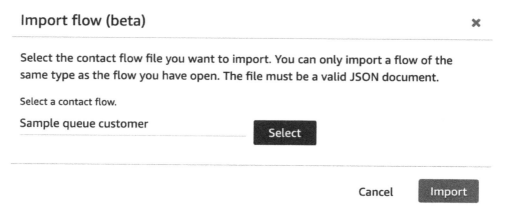

Figure 6.36 – Import flow (beta) popup

5.   When the file imports, your screen will be refreshed and will look like the one shown in *Figure 6.37*. You will now see the flow, including the old name of the flow that was exported. The first thing we want to do is change that name. In this case, I will use `Mega Mercy - Billing` as my flow name, as illustrated in the following screenshot:

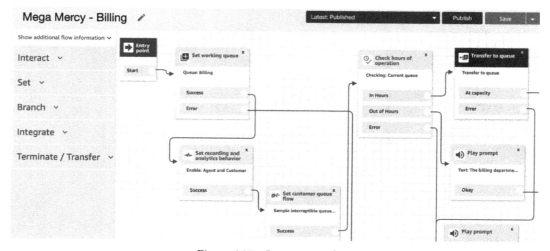

Figure 6.37 – Import complete

6. Now that we have imported this flow, it's time to configure it for our needs. The first thing we need to do is to set the working queue. Edit the **Set working queue** component and change the queue to the billing department.

We need to add some components to this flow to make it operate as we want. We discussed earlier in the *Copying contact flows* section that we were holding off on some settings to control them at a departmental level. This flow is where we will now put those settings. We will want to break the connection between the **Set working queue** and **Check hours of operation** components. In between these two components, we want to add a **Set recording behavior** component. If you remember, we saved this component to control the recording based on the department. The billing department wants call recording to be in place, in case of customer issues.

The second component we want to add here is the **Set customer queue flow** component. Since the **Set customer queue flow** component controls what a customer hears when they get transferred into a queue, you might want to control this by department. We didn't create one of these flows. If you wish, you can use the copy procedure we covered to make a copy of the **Sample interruptible queue flow with callback** component to customize your own. The settings for the **Set customer queue flow** component look like those shown in the following screenshot. When you have added these two components, connect them in line back into the flow:

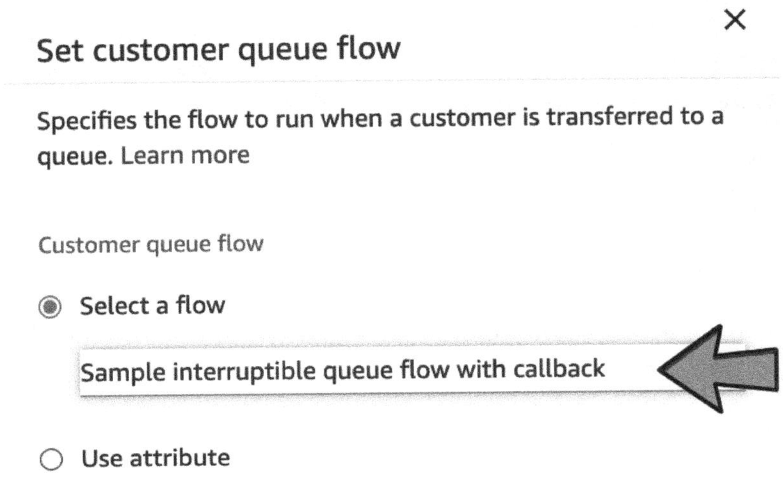

Figure 6.38 – Set customer queue

This flow should also match our pattern for error handling. Edit the error handling in this flow using a **Revised play prompt** component, including a new error code. When that is complete, remove the connector from the **Out of Hours** output component to the **Play prompt** component. We won't want people hearing an error message if the call center is closed. We also want to remove the connection from the **At capacity** output of the **Transfer to queue** component. This component will send calls to the **At capacity** output when there are too many customers in the queue. We wouldn't want an error message to play here either, as that would be a poor customer experience.

To repair the **Out of hours output** component, we need to add a new **Play prompt** component. In this prompt, we want to let the customer know that the department is closed and to call during business hours. The billing department is open between 8 A.M. and 5 P.M. Monday through Friday, so those are the hours I've used. Connect this new component to the **Out of hours output** component. Then, connect the **Play prompt** component to the **Disconnect** component to end the call.

To repair the **Transfer to queue** component, we want to create another new **Play prompt** component. Later in this book, we will change this to a callback flow but will leave a prompt in here, for now, to publish the flow without errors. The prompt should say something about the call center being at maximum capacity and to try again later. I know this isn't the best customer experience, but it will have to work for now. Leaving it to transfer to a flow will prevent publishing and create yet another cascading blocker. When you complete the prompt, connect its output to the **Disconnect** component and the input from the **Transfer to queue** component. When you are done, your flow should look like this:

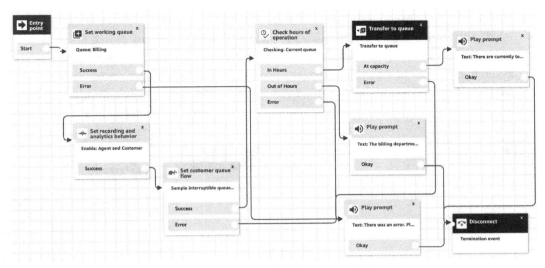

Figure 6.39 – Completed departmental flow

7.   At this point, we want to publish the flow to make it active. We now can use the copy procedure to replicate this flow seven more times, once for each department. When you make the copy, edit the **Set working queue** and **Play prompt** components connected to the **Out of Hours** component for each department. You will then publish each of these flows to make them active on Connect.

When you get to the intensive care unit, the flow will need two changes. If you recall, the intensive care unit was always open and didn't have any closed hours. In this instance, you don't need to check for in hours or have a prompt to let them know to call back when the department is open. Remove these two components from the flow before publishing. Your flow for the intensive care unit should look like this:

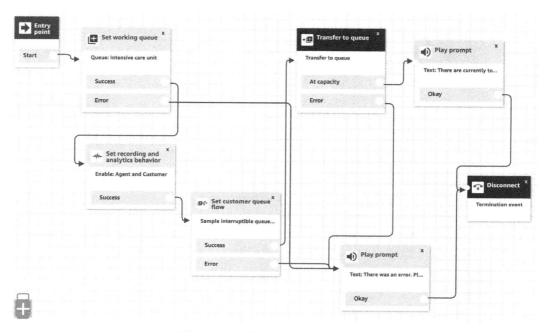

Figure 6.40 – Intensive care unit flow

You now have the design for all your department flows and you can see how you make modifications based on the individual requirements of the department. Next, we will move on to tying all of these departmental flows together to round out the system.

Putting it all together

With the departmental flows completed, we can go back to the branching flow and finish the **Transfer to flow** components, which currently send the callers to sample flows. When you edit the branching flow and edit an individual **Transfer to flow** component, the flow list will now show all your new department flows, as in the following screenshot. If you have some missing, you might have saved them instead of publishing them. They will not show up until they are published:

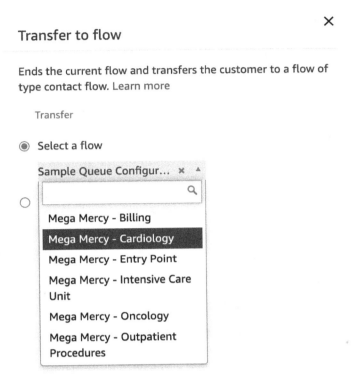

Figure 6.41 – Departmental flows list

When you have saved the component settings, continue editing the seven other transfer components for the correct departmental flows. When you have completed all of them, you can publish the flow, and it shouldn't error out. Remember that if you did make a mistake, Connect will highlight the error.

Once the branching flow is published, we can finally finish the entry-point flow. Edit the entry-point flow and modify the **Transfer to flow** component. The branching flow will also show in the list now that it has been published. Save the component and publish the entry-point flow. At this time, your call center is now operational. You should be able to call in and test all your call branching. However, you don't have anyone logged in as an agent, so calls won't be successful once you pass the IVR.

If you would like to test hours of operation, change the department queue hours to **Always closed**. When you call in and choose that department, you will receive a message that the department is closed. We will continue rounding out the flows through the next chapter, as we add more functionality. However, you have an operating call center.

We created several flows and tied them together. It was mentioned before how trying to fit too much into a single flow can increase your risk when you are editing your flows. Hopefully, walking through these demonstrations has shown you how combining them into a more central design would have made the overall design complex and unmanageable.

Summary

There has been a lot of work to get your call center to this position in the book. This chapter covered some of the heaviest lifting from a technology perspective. The ability to create, copy, and import contact flows are central knowledge points for operating Connect. We touched on how to configure many of the most common components in contact flows as well.

By completing this chapter and the exercises, you are well on your way to understanding how you can operate Connect for base functionality. In truth, if you don't have a complex call-center need, this chapter might be all you need to make it operational. However, even if that is the case, I hope you continue to follow along and increase your skillset.

In the remainder of the book, we will create the more advanced features that provide many of the benefits we discussed in *Chapter 1, Benefits of Amazon Connect*. In the next chapter, we will start by creating Lex bots that allow us to capture human speech and convert it to intents to drive the contact flows forward.

7
Creating AI Bots

For me, using Lex **artificial intelligence (AI)** bots is a game changer for the call center world. **Interactive voice response (IVR)** gets the job done, but it just doesn't mimic the human experience enough to make you feel like you're not talking to a machine. With IVR, the system can only understand a few options that you configure, and the response has to be in the form of a button press. Lex can change all of that and give your call center a more human feel without burdening your staff.

The recent COVID pandemic has caused an unseen burden on clients using IVR systems. Everyone was, and may still be, wearing masks. These masks prevent a facial recognition system from unlocking your phone. Imagine how annoying it is for your callers to enter their unlock code when their screen locks by typing a number rather than speaking their answer. Using AI, you can eliminate not only the machine-like feeling but also the customer's wasted time.

This chapter will focus on the implementation of Lex with Amazon Connect. We will replace the IVR of the department list that we created in *Chapter 5, Base Connect Implementation,* with a Lex bot. This implementation will improve our example's customer experience and provide you with a blueprint for using bots in your implementation.

In this chapter, we will cover the following topics:

- Amazon Lex capabilities crash course
- Creating your first bot

- Connecting to Amazon Connect
- Modifying the bridging contact flow

Amazon Lex capabilities crash course

Amazon Lex became generally available in April 2017, and the world has never been the same since. Lex has been used in countless ways, from chatbots on websites and mobile applications to, of course, Amazon Connect. Lex works with both voice and text and uses a combination of **automatic speech recognition (ASR)** and **natural language understanding** (NLU) to listen to and understand what your customer wants to do.

ASR isn't something new. Siri and Alexa are probably two of the most well-known systems that use ASR. When you use dictation on your phone or other systems, you are also using the same ASR technology. ASR uses AI to determine the words that are being spoken. This technology works very well for dictation, but alone it isn't super useful for chatbots. Words alone don't easily convey meaning. The original speech recognition systems were rule-based, which has its limitations. Eventually, the ruleset gets so large that it's unmanageable. This situation is where NLU comes in.

Lex uses AI to interpret the words used and uses NLU to understand what is being said. Lex calls these *intents*, which is fitting. After all, we are trying to find out what our callers intend to do. NLU is the same technology that Siri and Alexa use to figure out that you want to turn on your living-room lights or update your shopping list. For our example, our intents will be which department our callers are looking to speak to.

Lex is a powerful tool, but it does have a drawback that I would like to call out. Suppose you are used to working in **Amazon Web Services (AWS)** with other services, such as **Elastic Compute Cloud (EC2)** or **Simple Storage Service (S3)**. If so, you are most likely well versed in CloudFormation. CloudFormation is AWS's **infrastructure as code (IAC)** tooling. Unfortunately, Lex does not support CloudFormation, so all configuration has to be performed in the console. We will be using the console method in this book. A **software development kit (SDK)** is available for creating Lex bots programmatically, but this is outside the scope of this book and requires a more specialized skill set. Next, we are going to create our bot so that we can utilize it in Connect.

Creating your first bot

To begin creating our bot, we need to access Lex via the AWS console. In *Chapter 5, Base Connect Implementation*, we covered that you would need a role with rights to access Lex. You should be using that role at this time. The following steps will walk you through creating the bot:

1. You can access Lex via the AWS console under the **Machine Learning** heading, as illustrated in the following screenshot:

> Machine Learning
> Amazon SageMaker
> Amazon Augmented AI
> Amazon CodeGuru
> Amazon Comprehend
> Amazon Forecast
> Amazon Fraud Detector
> Amazon Kendra
> Amazon Lex
> Amazon Personalize

Figure 7.1 – AWS console

2. Once you click on **Amazon Lex**, the next screen you will be presented with will be the **get started** screen shown in *Figure 7.2*. If you don't see this screen, don't worry. The change in the screen just means that someone has already set up a Lex bot previously. In this case, you will only be presented with a list of bots. To get started, click the **Get Started** button, as illustrated here:

Figure 7.2 – Getting Started

3. The next screen you will be presented with will be a wizard for creating bots that look like those shown in *Figure 7.3*. We need to configure a few settings on this screen. The first thing we need to do is choose the **Custom bot** box, highlighted here:

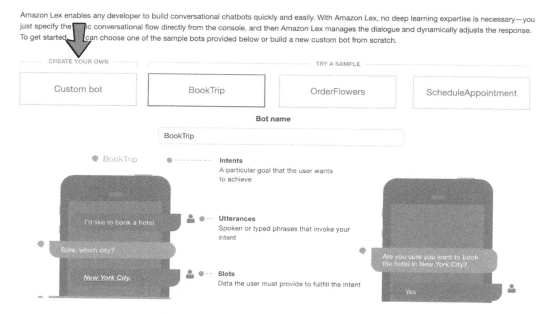

Figure 7.3 – Wizard

4. Upon selecting this, the screen will change and request several inputs for our bot's configuration. We need to set most of the settings, otherwise the page won't let us continue forward. For our demonstration, I've called my bot `DepartmentBot`. We also need to set the language and output voice. I live in the US, so I'm using **English (US)** as the language. Thinking back to *Chapter 6, Contact Flow Creation*, you might remember that I chose to use the **Matthew** voice for my call center. To match that and provide consistency, I'm selecting **Matthew** as my output voice here as well. When it comes to setting the session timeout, I use a low number. 1 minute should be sufficient to capture the department from a caller. When you are done with your settings, this section of configuration should look like *Figure 7.4*.

You can leave the **IAM role** with the default setting as AWS will create the role for you automatically. You can also leave off **Sentiment analysis** and **Contact Lens**, which we will cover in *Chapter 12, Implementing Contact Lens*. These initial settings are shown here:

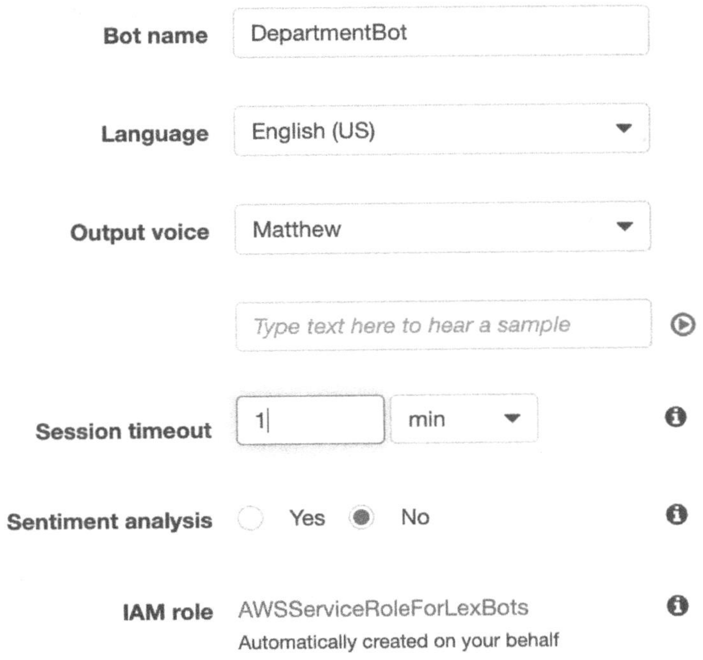

Bot name	DepartmentBot
Language	English (US)
Output voice	Matthew
	Type text here to hear a sample
Session timeout	1 min
Sentiment analysis	○ Yes ● No
IAM role	AWSServiceRoleForLexBots Automatically created on your behalf

Figure 7.4 – Settings Part 1

5. For the rest of the settings, we need to select the **COPPA** setting (**COPPA** is an acronym for the **Children's Online Privacy Protection Act**). Since this call center is for a hospital, we won't be expecting any calls from children. We will set this setting to **No**. The **COPPA** setting is more for websites or applications that could interact with children, not call centers.

Once you select **No** for **COPPA**, the **Create** button will activate. When you are done with your configuration, the rest of the page should match *Figure 7.5*. We don't need to configure any more options, so feel free to click the **Create** button, as shown here:

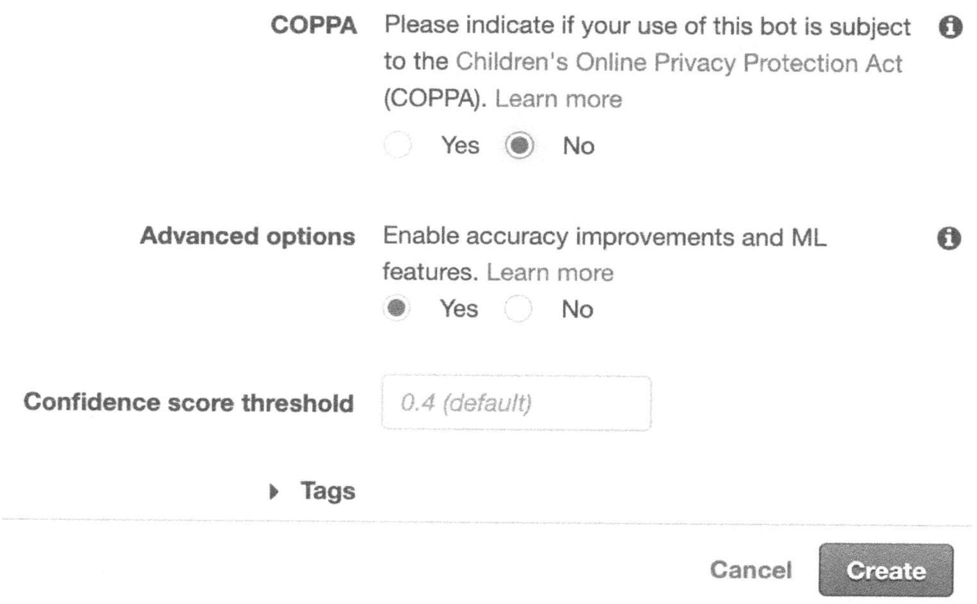

COPPA   Please indicate if your use of this bot is subject 🛈
            to the Children's Online Privacy Protection Act
            (COPPA). Learn more

            ○   Yes   ◉   No

Advanced options   Enable accuracy improvements and ML   🛈
                       features. Learn more

            ◉   Yes   ○   No

Confidence score threshold   [0.4 (default)]

            ▶ **Tags**

                                    Cancel   Create

Figure 7.5 – Settings Part 2

6. When you click **Create**, the wizard will progress forward and show you a new screen for more configuration. At this point, we need to create intents. To create a new intent, click the **Create Intent** button, as noted in the following screenshot:

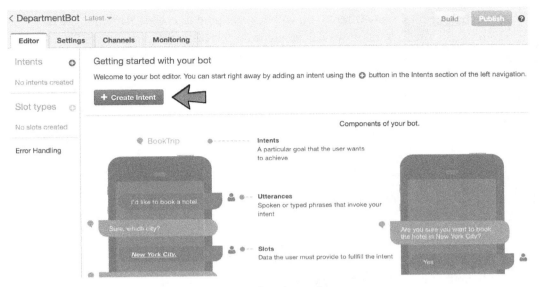

Figure 7.6 – Creating an intent

7. When you click the button, a new popup will appear. This popup (*Figure 7.7*) will display three options for adding an intent. Since we don't have any intents to import, we can't choose that option. Click the **Create intent** button to continue the process, as illustrated here:

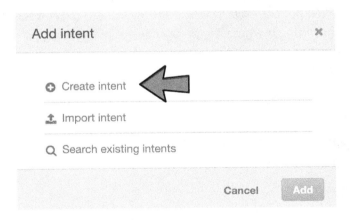

Figure 7.7 – Adding an intent

8. After clicking on **Create intent**, you will be prompted to enter a name for the intent (*Figure 7.8*). The first intent we will create is for the **billing** department. When you enter the department name, click the **Add** button, as illustrated here:

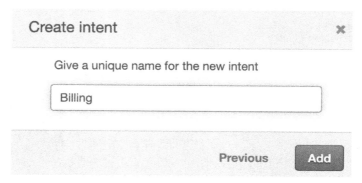

Figure 7.8 – Intent name

9. The benefit of using Lex is that we can move away from having callers enter a number to contact a department. When we create our intent, we can include multiple ways in which a caller may communicate that. Many people might just say *billing*, but what if they ask about an invoice or want to make a payment? The power of AI allows you to expand on the language that your call center can understand.

    When you click the **Add** button, you will be presented with a new configuration screen, as depicted in *Figure 7.9*. The first setting we need to set is **Sample utterances**. This setting is where we will put the options of what callers might say when attempting to reach the billing department. These are the utterances that I have put into the **billing** intent:

    a) **Make a payment**

    b) **Dispute a charge**

    c) **I want to speak to the billing department**

    d) **I have a bill to pay**

    e) **Billing department**

    Enter these into the **settings** page on your bot configuration. When you're done, your settings should mirror the data shown here:

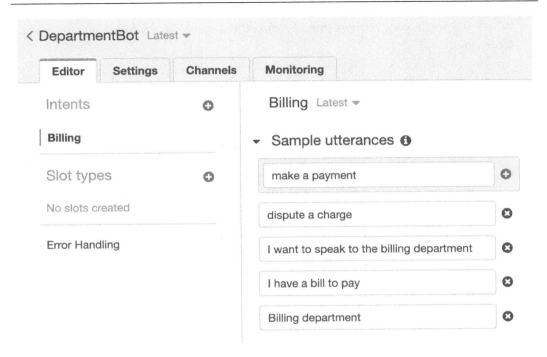

Figure 7.9 – Settings page

10. The next item that we need to configure for our intent is the response setting. The response setting allows you to tell Lex how you would like to respond when the intent is triggered. I like to enter more than one response—this makes the bot feel more human. When you call and speak to an agent, do they always say the same thing in the same way? No—there is variability in the responses. I've added these three responses:

a) **Sure! I'll transfer you to billing now.**

b) **I'll connect you to the billing department now.**

c) **Absolutely, let me connect you to billing.**

When you finish, your settings should match those shown in the following screenshot:

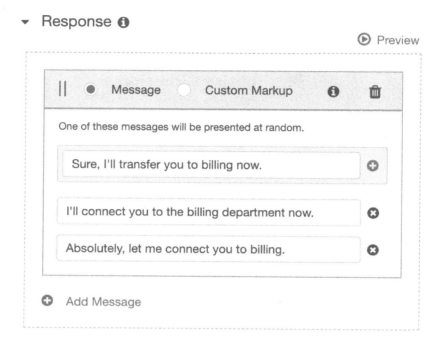

Figure 7.10 – Responses

11. After entering the responses, click the **Save Intent** button at the bottom of the page, as noted in the following screenshot:

Figure 7.11 – Saving an intent

12. The next step in the process is to build your bot. You will be unable to test the bot until the build is complete. Let's get the process started by clicking on the **Build** button in the upper right of the screen. This button is shown in the following screenshot:

Figure 7.12 – Build button

13. When you click the **Build** button, a new popup will appear (*Figure 7.13*), letting you know that you can continue editing your bot as it builds. Click the **Build** button again to continue, as illustrated in the following screenshot:

Figure 7.13 – Build popup

14. When the build completes, we can now test our bot to make sure that it functions properly. You can access the test console by clicking the **Test Chatbot** sidebar located on the screen's right-hand side. You can see what this menu looks like in the following screenshot:

Figure 7.14 – Test chatbot sidebar

15. The test window will expand out from the right side of the page (*Figure 7.15*). The test feature is a way to evaluate your bot configuration to ensure that it operates in the way you want, without publishing it and connecting it to Connect. Lex, like Connect, has a **Save** and a **Publish** function. With the segmentation of functions, you can save, build, and test your Lex changes without impacting your production workloads. The test feature can be seen in the following screenshot:

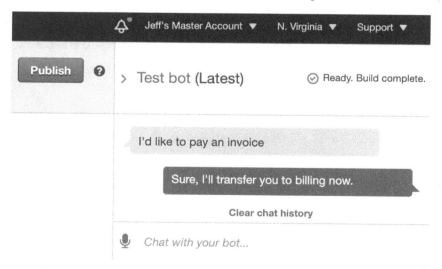

Figure 7.15 – Testing

Creating your first bot 151

16. In the test box, type something that will correlate to the billing department. If you look at what I entered in *Figure 7.15*, you will notice that I didn't type any of the utterances we entered into our bot's intents. Since Lex is AI-powered, it can identify my intent even without having an exact utterance. If it needed to be exact, it would have been a rules engine. As you can see, even though I asked to pay an invoice, it was still able to identify that I wanted the billing department.

After a successful test, we need to add intents for all of the other departments. This procedure is slightly different from the one we just performed. We don't want to create a new bot; we want to add more intents to this one. To do that, we will need to click on the plus sign (+) next to **Intents** on the upper left of the screen. Reference the following screenshot to see where to locate this button:

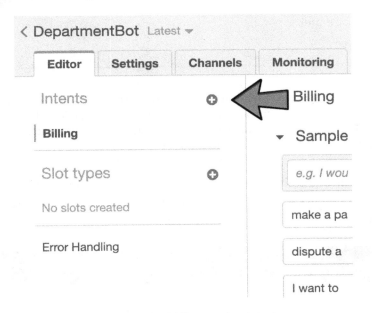

Figure 7.16 – Adding another intent

17. When the button is clicked, it will display the **Add intent** popup that we saw previously. You can refer to *Figure 7.7* for a reminder of what it looks like. Add the next department's intent, adding utterances that make sense for the department, along with several responses. Just as before, you will want to save your settings when complete by clicking on the **Save Intent** button.

At this point, we need to go and add all of the other intents to this bot for all of the departments. Remember to save each intent so that you don't lose your work if something were to go wrong during the process. As a reminder, these are the departments we added before:

a) Billing

b) Accounts payable

c) Radiology

d) Oncology

e) Outpatient procedures

f) Purchasing

g) Intensive care unit

h) Cardiology

> **Important note**
> You cannot have spaces in the name of an intent. I have replaced the space in multi-word departments with an _ to resolve that issue for simplicity. If you replace the spaces or remove them, make a note of the names. You will need this information later when we connect the bot to the contact flow.

18. When all of the intents have been added, it's time to publish the bot (after testing, of course). To publish the bot, click the **Publish** button in the upper right of the screen, as noted in the following screenshot:

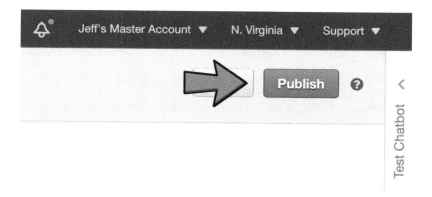

Figure 7.17 – Publish button

19. When you publish, you will be prompted for an alias for your bot, as in *Figure 7.18*. I've used the name **Departments** for this version of the bot. When you have entered the name, click the **Publish** button, as illustrated here:

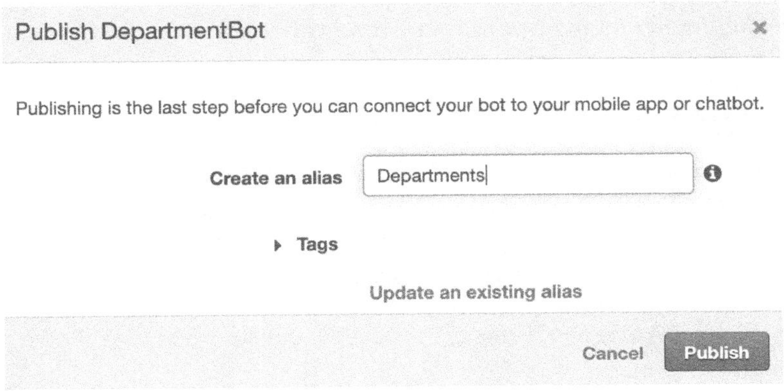

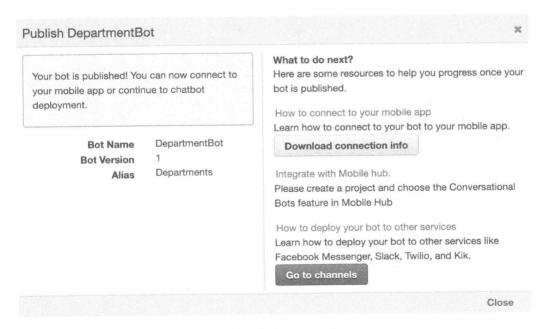

Figure 7.18 – Alias

The bot might take a minute or two to publish. When publishing is finished, you will be prompted with another popup, like the one shown in the following screenshot, letting you know that publishing is completed. Feel free to close this window after you have reviewed the information:

Figure 7.19 – Publishing finished

With the publishing completed, we can now move on to adding the bot into Amazon Connect. We will cover this process in the next section. The bot we have created is rather simplistic, but it performs the actions we need at this point in the deployment. We will get deeper into bots with more advanced functionality when covering enterprise application integrations in *Chapter 8, Interfacing Enterprise Applications*.

Connecting to Amazon Connect

By default, Connect cannot just use Lex bots after they are created—they need to be attached first. To make this connection, we will have to enter the AWS Management Console and edit the instance. This function isn't performed in the Connect Administration Console. Let's use the following steps to build this connection:

1. To begin, click on **Amazon Connect** in the AWS console. See the following screenshot for reference:

Customer Engagement
Amazon Connect
Pinpoint
Simple Email Service

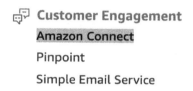

Figure 7.20 – Amazon Connect

2. You will be presented with a list of your Connect instances. Find the instance that you deployed as part of *Chapter 5, Base Connection implementation*. You will want to click the link in the leftmost column (*Figure 7.21*) to access the AWS Management Console for this instance. If you click the **Uniform Resource Locator (URL)** in the second column, you will be taken to the Connect Management Console. We will get to those configurations in the next section. The instance list is shown here:

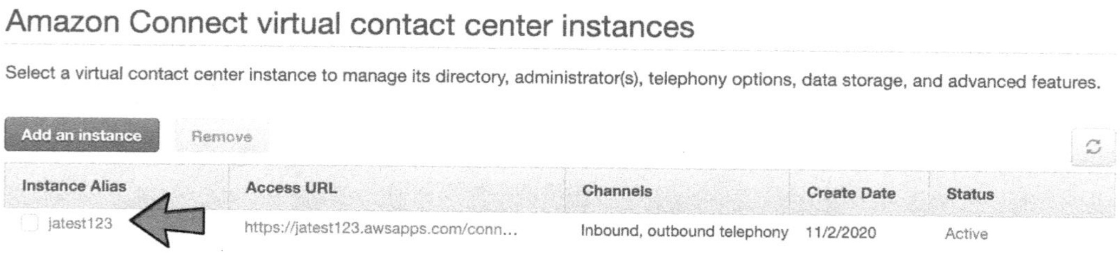

Amazon Connect virtual contact center instances
Select a virtual contact center instance to manage its directory, administrator(s), telephony options, data storage, and advanced features.
Add an instance
Remove
Instance Alias
Access URL
Channels
Create Date
Status
jatest123
https://jatest123.awsapps.com/conn...
Inbound, outbound telephony
11/2/2020
Active

Figure 7.21 – Connect instance list

3. You will now be taken to a screen to edit your Connect instance. The menu on the left-hand side of the screen is not intuitive about where the Lex settings might be located. You can find these in the **Contact flows** menu item, highlighted in the following screenshot:

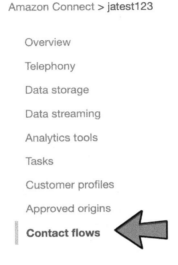

Figure 7.22 – Editing Connect menu

4. The **Contact flows** menu will show several settings. We are only interested in the ones under the **Amazon Lex** heading (*Figure 7.23*). Select the drop-down box on the right and find the bot that you just created, as illustrated here:

Amazon Lex

Integrate Amazon Lex bots into your contact flows to take advantage of the same speech recognition and natural language understanding technology that powers Alexa.

Note: By adding Lex bots, you are granting Amazon Connect permission to interact with them Create a new Lex bot ☐

Region   US East: N. Virginia   ▼   Bot   *Select*   ▼   ⬅ x Bot

                                                        DepartmentBot

Lex bots

                                                                                    DepartmentBot

Figure 7.23 – Amazon Lex Connect settings

5. At this point, you might think that your bot is added, but it's not. This interface isn't super intuitive, in my opinion. To add your bot, you need to click on the **Add Lex Bot** link noted in the following screenshot. It's not a button, nor does it follow the pattern of having the plus sign (+) be a button:

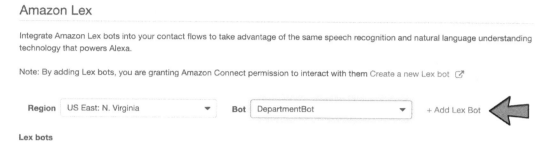

Figure 7.24 – Adding a bot

6. Once you click the button, you will see the bot in the **Add Lex bot** list in the lower left of the section, as illustrated in the following screenshot:

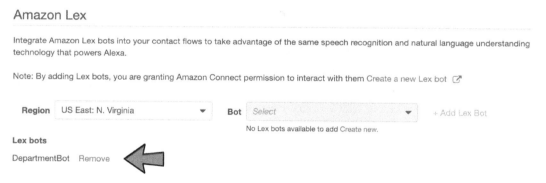

Figure 7.25 – Bot added

Your Lex bot is now attached to the Connect instance. Now, we can update the bridging contact flow to remove the existing IVR that we created in *Chapter 6, Contact Flow Creation,* with this bot.

Modifying the bridging contact flow

To modify contact flows, we need to log in to the Connect instance's management site. You can do this by clicking the link located in the center column (*Figure 7.21*) on the Connect service screen in the AWS console. Follow these steps once you are on the management site:

1. When you access the console, we need to select **Contact flows** from the left menu under the icon that looks like a **Universal Serial Bus (USB)**. You can look at the following screenshot for a refresher:

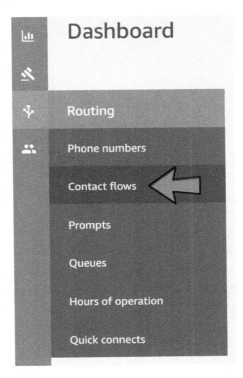

Figure 7.26 – Contact flows

2. Thankfully, there isn't a tremendous amount of work to convert our IVR menu to a Lex bot system. Select the **Mega Mercy – Branching** flow to edit it. Amazon Lex interfaces with the **Get customer input** component. Looking at our contact flow, we already have that component in this flow, highlighted in the following screenshot:

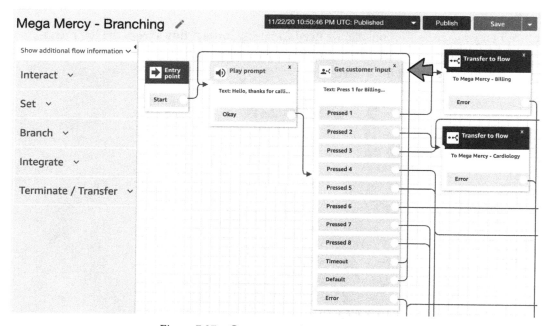

Figure 7.27 – Get customer input component

Click on the **Get customer input** title to edit the component. First, we want to change what the text-to-speech setting says. We wouldn't want it to be talking about pressing numbers now, would we? I've changed mine to say: **Please let me know how I can help you. For instance, you can ask for a department, or tasks such as pay a bill or schedule an appointment.**

In this component, we also need to change from the **DTMF** setting, which has all of the button presses, to the **Amazon Lex** bot setting. Select the heading to make the switch. *Figure 7.28* will highlight the location. Once you make the change, you can select the bot that we just created using the **Name** parameter's drop-down menu.

We have an alias assigned to our Lex bot. You may notice that the alias listed doesn't match the alias that we used. We aliased ours as **Departments**. However, our version of the bot is also flagged with $LATEST. The alias allows us to set up more than one version in Lex and then change them in our contact flows. This functionality allows us to test and revert versions of the Lex bot without major complications. For instance, if we published a new version that had an issue, we could change $LATEST in this field, as displayed in the following screenshot, to the older version's alias, thus reverting to the working version:

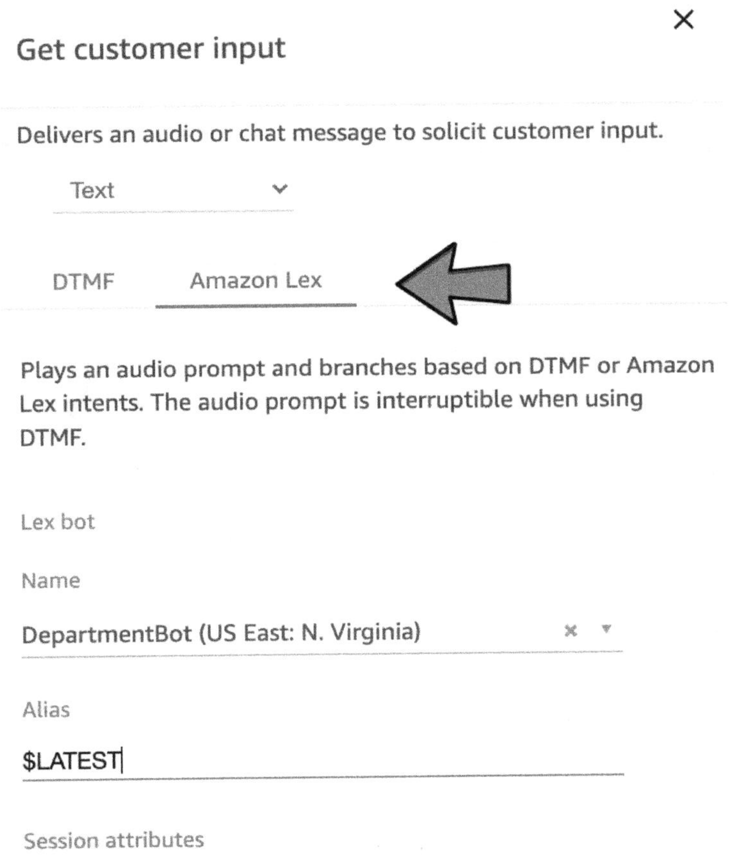

Get customer input

×

Delivers an audio or chat message to solicit customer input.

Text ⌄

DTMF   Amazon Lex

Plays an audio prompt and branches based on DTMF or Amazon Lex intents. The audio prompt is interruptible when using DTMF.

Lex bot

Name

DepartmentBot (US East: N. Virginia)   × ▾

Alias

$LATEST

Session attributes

Figure 7.28 – Converting to Lex

3. Once this part of the configuration is complete, we need to scroll down to configure the intents. Click on the **Add intent** link at the bottom and add the departments' Lex bot intents. When you are done, your settings should match those shown in the following screenshot:

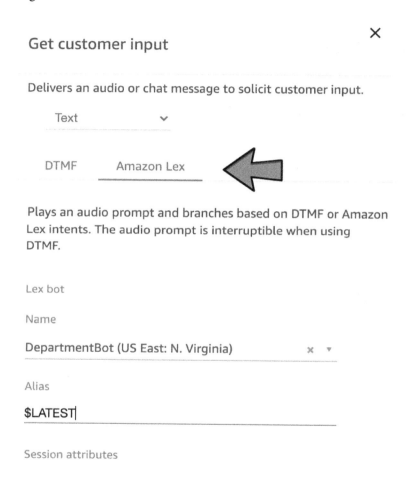

Figure 7.29 – Lex intents

4. Your settings should look like the ones in the following screenshot. Ensure that all of the departments are listed in the list and that none are missing. When you are done, you can save your settings:

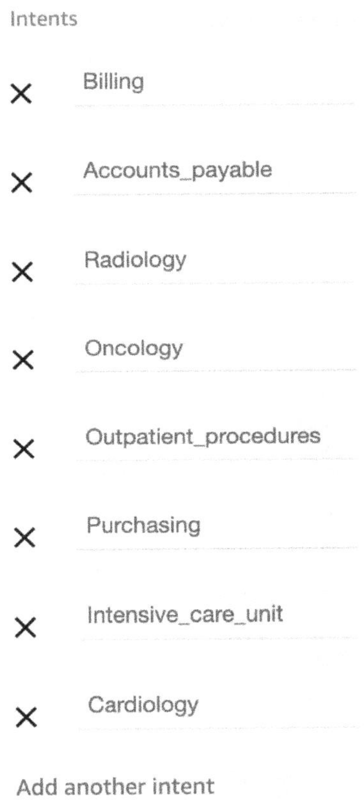

Intents

×   Billing

×   Accounts_payable

×   Radiology

×   Oncology

×   Outpatient_procedures

×   Purchasing

×   Intensive_care_unit

×   Cardiology

Add another intent

Figure 7.30 – Completed intents

5.   When you click **Save**, the component will drastically change. All of the previous button presses will be gone and will be replaced with the intents that we entered. Connect these new component outputs with the **Transfer to flow** components that correspond to the correct departments. When you are done, your revised **Get customer input** component should resemble the one shown in the following screenshot. Click on **Publish** at this time to commit your changes to Connect:

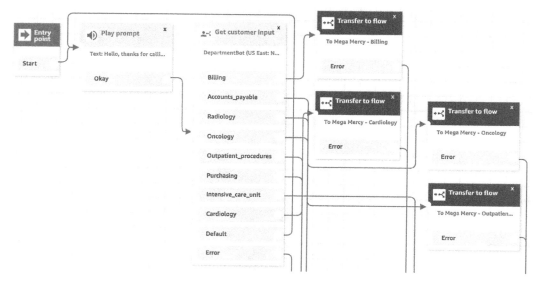

Figure 7.31 – Revised Get customer input component

Congratulations! You have just completed your first Amazon Lex bot integration with Connect. Feel free to call in to your call center to test out the new capabilities. You should now be prompted with the new customer input using your bot.

Summary

Your call center is starting to take shape now. This chapter is the first that dives into the new capabilities that Connect has to offer over existing on-premises systems. We covered the Connect contact flow modifications and the creation of the bot itself through the AWS console. You can use this same knowledge to create bots for other applications and websites—it's not just Connect-specific.

We will be creating more advanced bots later when we talk about enterprise application integrations in the next chapter. These will play a key role in how those integrations operate. This chapter lays a great foundation to build upon as we progress through the book.

8
Interfacing Enterprise Applications

Of all the features that Connect brings to an organization, the ability to interface with enterprise applications is by far the most impactful. By interfacing with your applications, you can create interactive solutions that significantly reduce your costs. Let's face it, employing people is expensive, and any way to reduce the amount of manual human effort your work requires has a significant impact on your bottom line.

There is a basically limitless selection of applications to choose from and an infinite number of ways to integrate with these applications. The landscape is so vast that it may seem that there is no way to decide which application to use. In this chapter, we will interface with a simple application that I have created to demonstrate how you can interface with an application. We will be using a simple and easy-to-follow recipe but we'll highlight the key points of the integration. You should be able to take what you learn in this chapter and apply it to your company's use case.

This chapter will cover the following:

- Learning about your API capabilities
- Understanding Lambda's capabilities
- Solution overview
- Retrieving required information
- Deploying a solution via CloudFormation
- Connecting Lambda to Connect
- Creating a contact flow
- Testing the solution
- Other potential types of integrations

Learning about your API capabilities

The basic concept of how Connect interfaces with your application is that an AWS service, such as Lambda, communicates with it via an API to send and receive data. How this communication takes place can vary. Common communication methods include REST, SOAP, GraphQL, and gRPC, to name a few. I would say that REST is the most common today. For our example, Lambda will mimic an API request. This simplicity limits the number of moving parts and ensures that the test will be successful.

To learn about your specific application's API capabilities in your environment, you will have to review its documentation. Not all applications publish this information readily, and you might have to contact the support department to get the required information to make your interface work.

> **Note**
>
> For API write operations, it's important to have some form of authorization in place, such as entering a customer number, order number, or birth date. If you don't, you leave the door open for a malicious actor to cause issues in your environment by inserting tainted data into your application. Always have some form of authorization in front of any write operations.

Our sample application will be a lab results system that Mega Mercy Hospital uses for patient labs across the entire organization. The API for this application simulates the ability to make read (GET) API calls from the application to retrieve results based on a user's patient ID number. It has no capabilities to write or store information.

Our intent with this chapter is to create a contact flow that customers will interact with that asks them to enter their patient ID number. It will then prompt the caller for which test result they would like using IVR. Connect will use Lambda to access the data and retrieve the results based on the caller's inputs. In the next section, we will cover some of the basics of Lambda, so you understand its capabilities.

Just to be clear, you're not going to create a custom integration if you don't have (either personally or at your disposal in your organization) programming skills. Since everything about integration is custom, so is the code. Several systems integrators such as Deloitte and Cognizant have experience with Connect that would assist if you don't have the skills internally. However, hiring external actors is going to drive up the project costs. Keep that in mind and make sure that the ROI for the integration is there.

Understanding Lambda's capabilities

Lambda is probably my favorite AWS service. Lambda allows you to run code without worrying about the underlying infrastructure. This service allows you to focus on what matters most: your code. After all, who wants to worry about things like how much CPU your application needs? Additionally, without running instances in EC2, your costs for running code are significantly reduced. This feature makes Lambda an excellent choice for our integration with Amazon Connect. We wouldn't want to use an entire EC2 instance to run our integration code. It wouldn't be utilized enough to warrant the expense.

Lambda is an event-driven service. What I mean by that is that code is executed based on an event or trigger. A trigger could be a scheduled event, or a file put into an S3 bucket, or a trigger from Connect, for instance. This functionality makes Lambda an excellent choice for our integration as there is an easy way to interface between the Connect and Lambda services.

When AWS triggers a Lambda function, it passes data in the form of an event. This JSON-formatted document has information about how the event was triggered and custom properties passed from the calling entity. In our case, Connect will pass important details about the call, including parameters. The parameters section is where our information that we collected from the caller will be located, specifically, their patient ID and the type of lab they want the results for. Here is a sample of an event from Connect to Lambda:

```
{
  "Name": "ContactFlowEvent",
  "Details": {
    "ContactData": {
      "Attributes": {},
```

```
    "Channel": "VOICE",
    "ContactId": "5ca32fbd-8f92-abcd-92a5-6b0f970f0efe",
    "CustomerEndpoint": {
      "Address": "+11234567890",
      "Type": "TELEPHONE_NUMBER"
    },
    "InitialContactId": "5ca32fbd-abcd-46af-92a5-
6b0f970f0efe",
    "InitiationMethod": "API",
    "InstanceARN": "arn:aws:connect:us-east-
1:123456789012:instance/9308c2a1-abcd-4cea-8290-6c0b4a6d38fa",
    "MediaStreams": {
      "Customer": {
        "Audio": {
          "StartFragmentNumber": "913438523331814323926820626
22220590765191907586",
          "StartTimestamp": "1565781909613",
          "StreamARN": "arn:aws:kinesisvideo:us-east-
1:123456789012:stream/connect-contact-a3d73b84-ce0e-479a-a9dc-
5637c9d30ac9/1565272947806"
        }
      }
    },
    "PreviousContactId": "5ca32fbd-abc-46af-92a5-
6b0f970f0efe",
    "Queue": null,
    "SystemEndpoint": {
      "Address": "+1125555555",
      "Type": "TELEPHONE_NUMBER"
    }
  },
  "Parameters": {}
}
}
```

You can see that in this code example, there were no parameters passed from Connect, noted by the line `"Parameters": {}`. In our deployment, this section will be populated. We will get into more detail later when we work on the contact flow for our solution. Now that we have a bit of background on Lambda, let's look at our solution in depth.

Solution overview

The solution we will be deploying consists of a CloudFormation template and a Connect contact flow. We will deploy the CloudFormation template first and then follow it up to create the contact flow in Connect.

CloudFormation deploys the required components to operate the Lambda function and the function itself. The Lambda function will access an internal datastore and retrieve the lab results for the identified patient. The Lambda function is written in Python.

The flow of the solution is detailed in *Figure 8.1*:

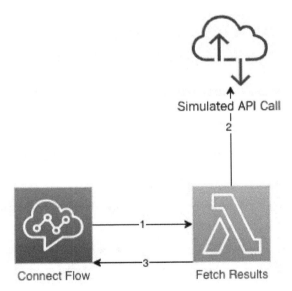

Figure 8.1 – Solution flow

Everything originates from your Connect flow, which makes sense, as Connect is aware when the call originates, it would be impossible for your application to originate the request as it wouldn't know what data to send. Once your connected flow reaches the Lambda component, it begins the flow in the solution. These are the steps as they occur:

1. Connect reaches out and launches the Lambda function, passing `patientID`.

2. The Lambda function reaches out to the API and queries the results based on the ID.

3. The Lambda function returns the results to Connect.

Once Connect receives the data back from Lambda, it will be stored in a special variable called `External`. This variable is separate from the system variables that we have touched on in other implmentation sections up to this point. The Lambda function is going to return a single variable with the requested result. We will cover that in greater detail when we create our contact flow.

Retrieving required information

The solution requires our Connect instance ID. This ID is needed to grant access to the Lambda functions from Connect. Otherwise, it won't execute the function. If you recall, we have captured the instance ID for Connect before. If you don't have it handy, you can get it from the **Overview** section in the AWS console for Connect.

Access the Connect console in AWS. Locate your instance in the list of Connect deployments. Click on the link in the first column as shown in *Figure 8.2*:

Amazon Connect virtual contact center instances

Select a virtual contact center instance to manage its directory, administrator(s), telephony options, data storage, and advanced features.

| Add an instance | Remove | | | | ↻ |

Instance Alias	Access URL	Channels	Create Date	Status
☐ jatest123	https://jatest123.awsapps.com/conn...	Inbound, outbound telephony	11/2/2020	Active

Figure 8.2 – Connect instances

You can see in *Figure 8.3* the ARN for your instance. The instance ID is the UID located after the /. Save this information for use later:

Overview

Instance ARN	arn:aws:connect:us-east-1:993613994443:instance/8a41b405-9770-409b-ad21-4981c4ae1471
Directory	jatest123
Service-linked role ❶	AWSServiceRoleForAmazonConnect_nkNn0XOqb6PjupIuApph Learn more
Login URL	https://jatest123.awsapps.com/connect/login
Emergency access	⚠ Warning: This login method will give you full permission within the Amazon Connect instance and should not be used for day-to-day operations. Log in for emergency access. ☑

Figure 8.3 – Instance ID

In this sample integration solution, all we need is the instance ID. I've hardcoded everything else into the template that would be necessary. However, if this were a homegrown solution, you would need more information. You would need the API endpoint URL and access information as well. It might use an API key or have some form of username and password combination. There are multiple ways to accomplish authorization with APIs.

If you are accessing a database directly instead of an API, there will also be more requirements that need to be identified, such as database server DNS names, user names, passwords, and maybe table names. All of these requirements will be set by you or your development team as you craft the integration. I'm just highlighting these items here, so you have a baseline as to what you need to identify for your application.

Now that we have the information we need, let's move on to deploying the solution.

Deploying the solution via CloudFormation

With our instance ID in hand, we can now begin the process of deploying the solution. I've chosen CloudFormation here because users of AWS widely understand it. You might opt for another **Infrastructure as Code (IaC)** tool such as Terraform for your integration in your organization. It's important to understand the pros and cons of your IaC tooling before you start programming your integration.

To begin the deployment, access CloudFormation via the AWS console. CloudFormation is located under the **Management & Governance** section, as shown in *Figure 8.4*:

Figure 8.4 – CloudFormation

Download the template file from `https://connect-up-and-running.info/files/connect_lambda.yaml`. When you access the CloudFormation console, click the **Create stack** button in the screen's upper right noted in *Figure 8.5*:

Figure 8.5 – Create stack

A dropdown will appear; since we haven't created any resources that we need to import, select **With new resources (standard)** (*Figure 8.6*):

Figure 8.6 – Stack type

On the next screen, we want to select the option to upload a template file. Click the **Choose file** button and upload the file that we just downloaded named connect_lambda.YAML. When you are done, click **Next**. You can refer to *Figure 8.7* to verify your settings:

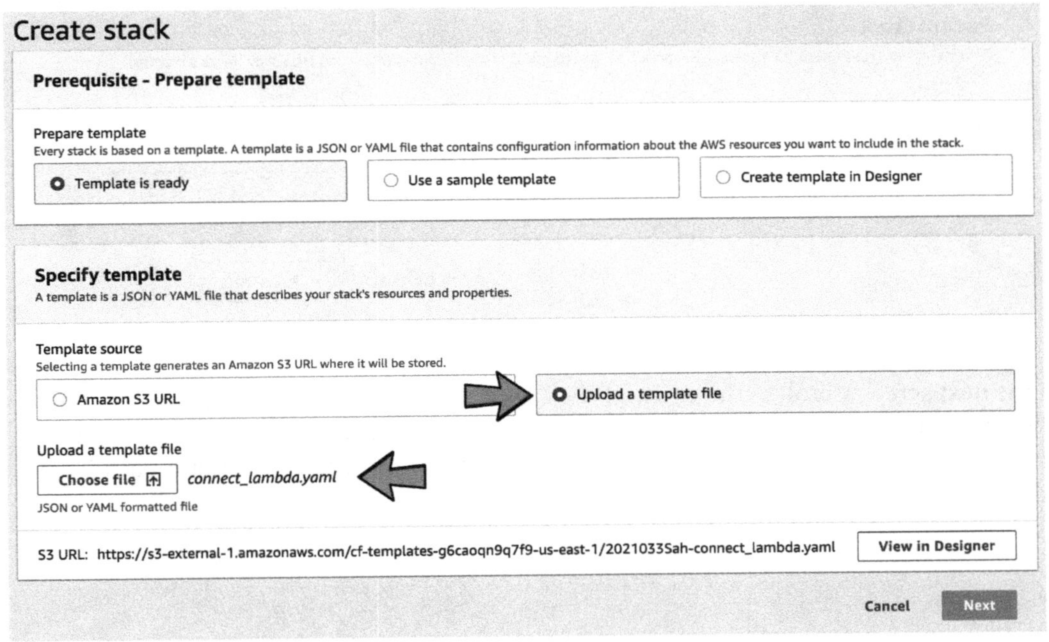

Create stack

Prerequisite - Prepare template

Prepare template
Every stack is based on a template. A template is a JSON or YAML file that contains configuration information about the AWS resources you want to include in the stack.

- ● **Template is ready**
- ○ **Use a sample template**
- ○ **Create template in Designer**

Specify template
A template is a JSON or YAML file that describes your stack's resources and properties.

Template source
Selecting a template generates an Amazon S3 URL where it will be stored.

- ○ **Amazon S3 URL**
- ● **Upload a template file**

Upload a template file

Choose file   *connect_lambda.yaml*

JSON or YAML formatted file

S3 URL: https://s3-external-1.amazonaws.com/cf-templates-g6caoqn9q7f9-us-east-1/2021033Sah-connect_lambda.yaml   **View in Designer**

Cancel   **Next**

Figure 8.7 – Create stack

On the stack details page, enter the name of the stack. I've used the name CONNECT-LAMBDA-EXAMPLE to align with the convention we use in this book. This screen is also where you will enter your Connect instance ID (*Figure 8.8*), which we captured earlier. When you have entered all the required information, click **Next**:

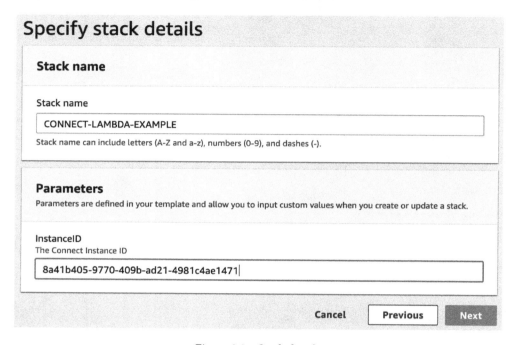

Figure 8.8 – Stack details

On the next screen, scroll to the end and click **Next** again. There is nothing that needs to be done on this screen. On the final screen, scroll to the bottom and check the box to acknowledge that the stack will create IAM resources (*Figure 8.9*). When done, click **Next** to deploy the stack:

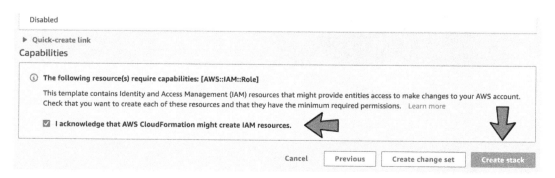

Figure 8.9 – Create stack

The stack will now deploy, creating the necessary resources. When it is done, it will show in the list of CloudFormation stacks as shown in *Figure 8.10*:

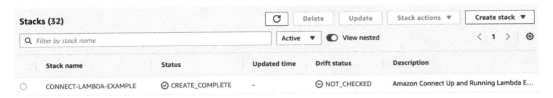

Figure 8.10 – Stack deployed

Now that we are done with the deployment of the solution, we will now work on connecting Lambda to Connect.

Connecting Lambda to Connect

To tie the Lambda function to Connect, we need to access the Connect console. Without creating the link between Lambda and your Connect instance, the contact flows won't see the available Lambda functions. When you create your contact flow and add the Lambda component, the dropdown won't be populated. If you encounter a situation where you don't see your function, you will be aware of how to resolve the issue.

First, access the console and locate your instance in the Connect console and click the link in the leftmost column (*Figure 8.11*):

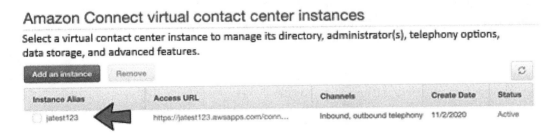

Figure 8.11 – Connect

Using the menu on the left, locate the **Contact flows** menu item indicated in *Figure 8.12*:

aws
Services
Amazon Connect > jatest123
Overview
Telephony
Data storage
Data streaming
Analytics tools
Tasks
Customer profiles
Approved origins
Contact flows

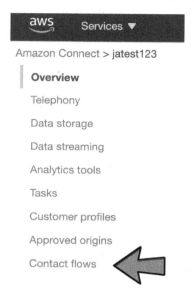

Figure 8.12 – Connect menu

Scroll down until you see the configuration for AWS Lambda on the main screen. Using the drop-down menu, locate the Lambda function called `Connect-Lambda-Example`. After selecting the function, you need to click the **Add Lambda Function** link (*Figure 8.13*). Sometimes the interface for Connect isn't straightforward; sometimes there are buttons, and sometimes there are links. This screen is one of those situations where you would expect a button but get a link:

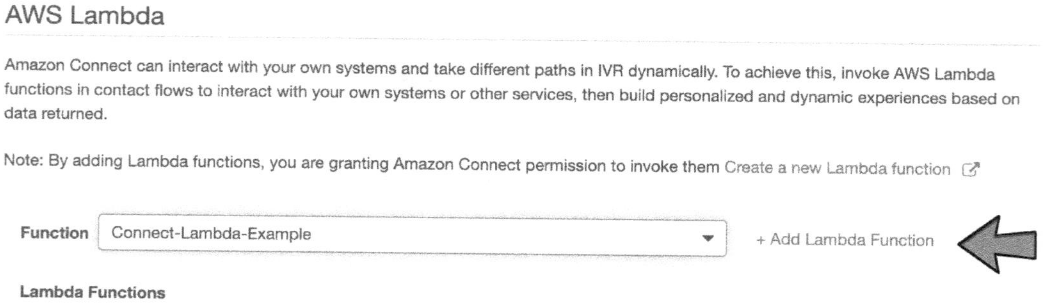

AWS Lambda
Amazon Connect can interact with your own systems and take different paths in IVR dynamically. To achieve this, invoke AWS Lambda functions in contact flows to interact with your own systems or other services, then build personalized and dynamic experiences based on data returned.
Note: By adding Lambda functions, you are granting Amazon Connect permission to invoke them Create a new Lambda function
Function
Connect-Lambda-Example
+ Add Lambda Function
Lambda Functions

Figure 8.13 – AWS Lambda

When you click the **Add Lambda Function** link, it will be added to a list that exists under the **Lambda Functions** heading. You can refer to *Figure 8.14* to see what this should look like:

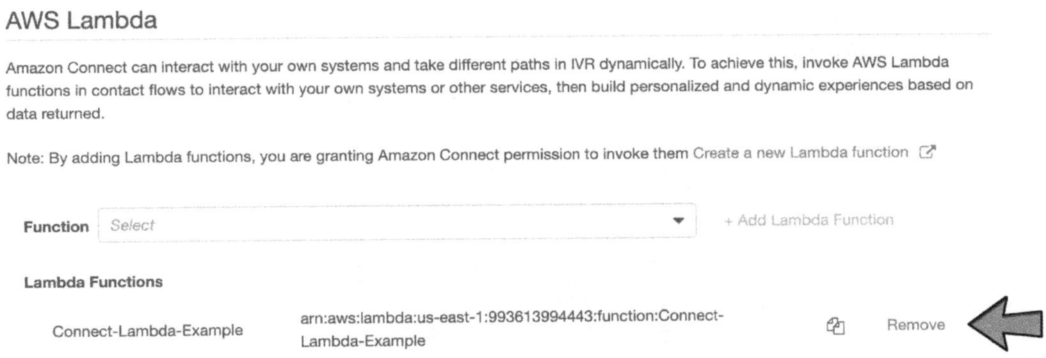

AWS Lambda

Amazon Connect can interact with your own systems and take different paths in IVR dynamically. To achieve this, invoke AWS Lambda functions in contact flows to interact with your own systems or other services, then build personalized and dynamic experiences based on data returned.

Note: By adding Lambda functions, you are granting Amazon Connect permission to invoke them Create a new Lambda function ⬀

Function [Select ▼] + Add Lambda Function

Lambda Functions

Connect-Lambda-Example   arn:aws:lambda:us-east-1:993613994443:function:Connect-Lambda-Example   ⧉ Remove ⬅

Figure 8.14 – Function added

You have now completed connecting the Lambda function to your Connect instance. At this point in the process, we have completed everything that needs to be done in the AWS console. It's now time to shift gears and use the Connect admin console to complete our interface's deployment. In the next section, we will create the contact flow.

Creating the contact flow

The contact flow is where we will do the bulk of the work for this solution. It is also where the majority of the logic is performed for the overall process. The Lambda function, after all, merely retrieves the information from the API. To get started, log in to the Connect administration console. Select your instance to view the overview page, where you will see the login URL. For a refresher, the link is highlighted in *Figure 8.15*. Log in using the administrator account:

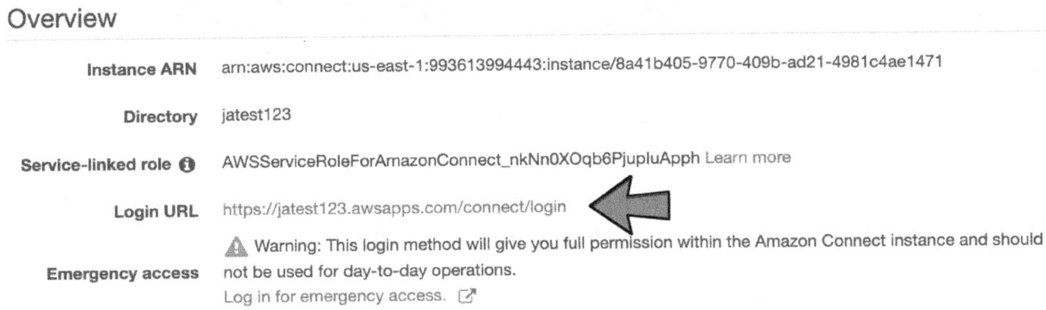

Overview

Instance ARN   arn:aws:connect:us-east-1:993613994443:instance/8a41b405-9770-409b-ad21-4981c4ae1471

Directory   jatest123

Service-linked role ❶   AWSServiceRoleForAmazonConnect_nkNn0XOqb6PjupluApph Learn more

Login URL   https://jatest123.awsapps.com/connect/login ⬅

Emergency access   ⚠ Warning: This login method will give you full permission within the Amazon Connect instance and should not be used for day-to-day operations.
Log in for emergency access. ⬀

Figure 8.15 – Login URL

Using the USB-looking menu icon on the left-hand menu, select the **Contact flows** option highlighted in *Figure 8.16*:

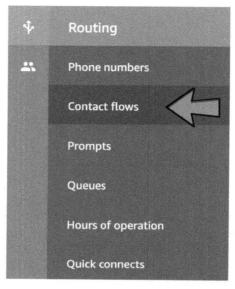

Figure 8.16 – Contact flows option

In the contact flows main screen showing a list of your flows, click on the **Create contact flow** button in the upper left-hand corner shown in *Figure 8.17*:

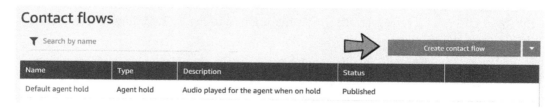

Figure 8.17 – Create contact flow

You will now be shown the contact flow editing screen. We first want to set the name of the flow. You do this by clicking the pencil in the upper left of the screen (*Figure 8.18*). I've called my flow Mega Mercy - Lab Results to align with our naming convention:

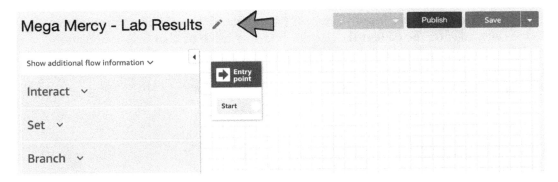

Figure 8.18 – Naming the contact flow

The first piece that we want to add to our flow is the **Store customer input** component. Add this component from the **Interact** section and connect it from the **Start** entry point. We are going to use this component to request the caller for their patient ID number. Your flow should look like *Figure 8.19* at this point:

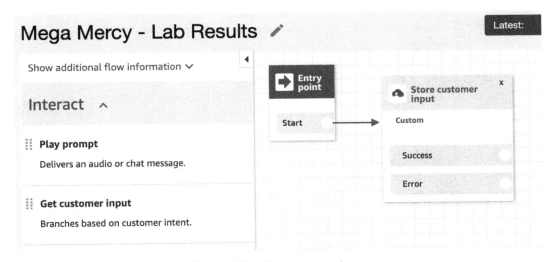

Figure 8.19 – First customer input

Click on the **Store customer input** component to edit it. We want to play a prompt that asks the caller to enter the patient ID. Use the **Text-to-speech or chat text** option and enter your prompt. I've used the phrase `Please enter your patient id to retrieve your lab results`. The editing screen will appear as pictured in *Figure 8.20*. Don't click **Save** yet. There is more configuration required:

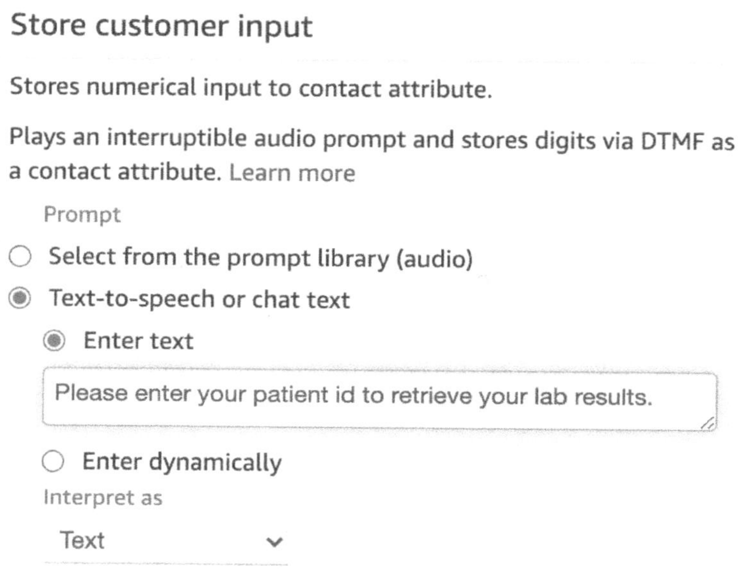

Store customer input

Stores numerical input to contact attribute.

Plays an interruptible audio prompt and stores digits via DTMF as a contact attribute. Learn more

Prompt

○ Select from the prompt library (audio)

◉ Text-to-speech or chat text

   ◉ Enter text

      | Please enter your patient id to retrieve your lab results. |

   ○ Enter dynamically

Interpret as

Text   ∨

Figure 8.20 – Store customer input

Scroll down on the **Store customer input** editing screen and locate the **Customer input** section (*Figure 8.21*). In our sample application, the patient ID only has five digits. We will set **Maximum Digits** to six, accounting for the five numbers in the patient ID plus the pound sign to signify the end. Also, select the checkbox to specify the terminating keypress, select the **Set manually** radio button, and enter # in the field. We are now done configuring this component. Click the **Save** button to finish:

Customer input

◉ Custom

Maximum Digits   Timeout before first entry

6   10

in seconds

☐ **Encrypt entry (recommended)**

☑ **Specify terminating keypress** Learn more.

◉ **Set manually**

#|

Allowed characters: 0-9, #, *

○ **Use attribute**

☐ **Disable cancel key** Learn more.

○ **Phone number**

Cancel   Save

Figure 8.21 – Addiontal store customer input settings

Now that we have the patient's ID number, we need to store it in a new variable. The reason for this is that we want to hold two pieces of information, the patient ID and the test type. Connect only allows you to keep one item in the store customer input slot. So, if we added another **Store customer input** component, it would overwrite the value of the first. Drag a **Set contact attributes** component from the **Set** menu and connect it to the **Store customer input** component. We will use this new component to store the data long term. Your flow should now resemble *Figure 8.22*:

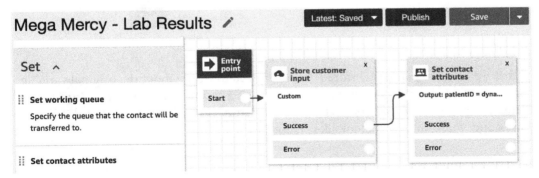

Figure 8.22 – Set contact attributes

Next, click and edit the **Set contact attributes** component. We want to store the data in the destination type of **User Defined**. Locate this setting in the **Destination type** dropdown. Since we have the patient ID number, we called the **Destination Attribute** setting `patientID`. Finally, we need to populate this variable to let the component know where the value is coming from. In our case, we will use the **Use attribute** radio button and select **System** as the type and attribute value of **Stored customer input**, which would be the value from the previous component. When you are done, validate your settings against *Figure 8.23* and click **Save**:

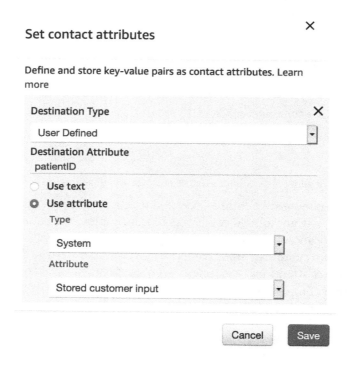

Figure 8.23 – Storing the patient ID

Now that we have the patient ID stored, we don't need to worry about the original variable being overwritten. The next component in our flow is a second **Store customer input**. Add this component now and connect it to the **Set contact attributes** component. When you are done, your flow should look like *Figure 8.24*:

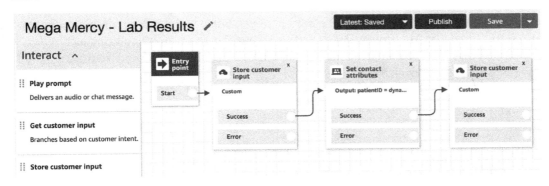

Figure 8.24 – Store customer input addition

Let's configure the **Store customer input** component. The settings will be very similar to what we had done previously. However, the prompt will be different. Our sample application is capable of returning three different test results: blood pressure and glucose and bilirubin levels. I've used this text in the `Text-to-speech` block:

```
What lab results would you like?
Press 1 for blood pressure
Press 2 for glucose levels
Press 3 for bilirubin levels
```

At this point, your settings for this component should look like *Figure 8.25*:

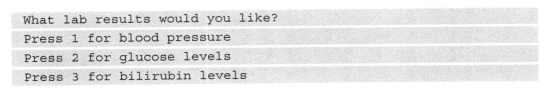

Figure 8.25 – Text-to-speech

We haven't completed configuring this component yet. Since we expect single-digit input, we need to change the **Maximum Digits** setting to one. Since we aren't entering a complex number, we don't need to configure the terminating keypress. Validate your settings against *Figure 8.26* and click **Save**:

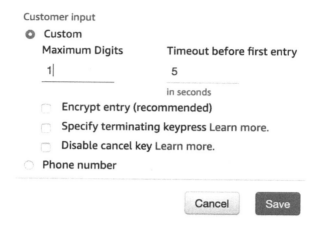

Figure 8.26 – Digit length

Now we have the test result in the flow that our caller wants. The next step is to save it like we did for **patientID** in **User Data** to preserve it long term. We will not collect any more data from the caller in our sample, as that would overwrite the **Stored user input** value. But it's good to get in the habit of saving this data so you always know you can edit and expand your flow without problems. Now, add a new **Set contact attributes** component and tie it to the previous **Store customer input**. Your flow should now match *Figure 8.27*:

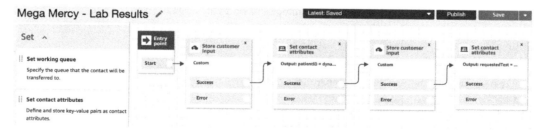

Figure 8.27 – Set contact attributes

Edit the second **Set contract attributes** component. This time, the settings will be nearly identical to the first. However, **Destination Attribute** will now state requestedTest instead of patientID. You have now ensured that you have two variables stored for later use. You can double-check your work against *Figure 8.28* before saving:

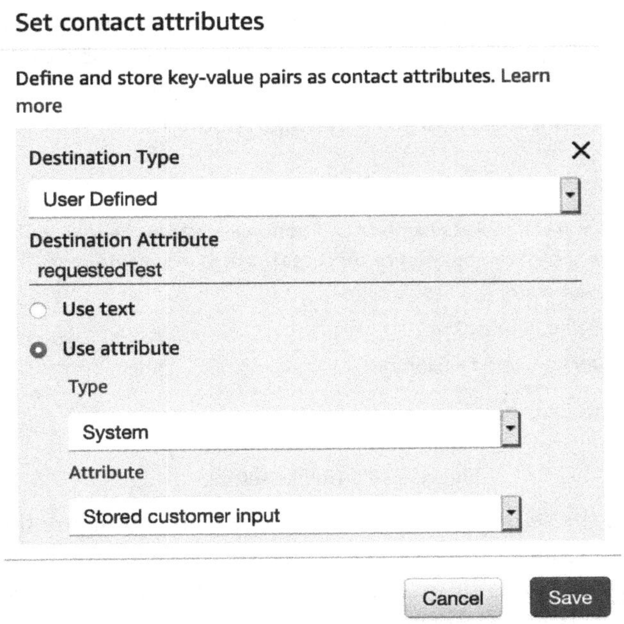

Set contact attributes

Define and store key-value pairs as contact attributes. Learn more

Destination Type   ✕

User Defined

Destination Attribute
requestedTest

○ Use text

◉ Use attribute

Type

System

Attribute

Stored customer input

Cancel   Save

Figure 8.28 – Second contact attributes settings

Alright, we now know the patient ID, so the system knows who the caller is, and we have the test type that they want the results for. Our flow is starting to take shape now. We have now come to the point where we can add in our Lambda function. Find the **Invoke AWS Lambda function** component under the **Integrate** menu and add it to your flow. Connect it to the last **Set contact attributes** block. Your flow should now look like *Figure 8.29*:

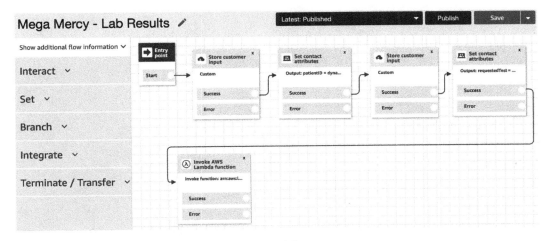

Figure 8.29 – Lambda component

We are now ready to configure our component. Click on it to edit it and select the dropdown under the **Select a Function** radio button. Find the `Connect-Lambda-Example` function in the drop-down list. If it's not there, review your configuration from the previous *Connecting Lambda to Connect* section. Your settings should match *Figure 8.30*:

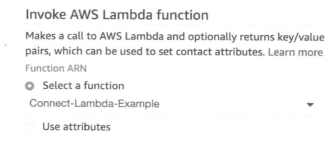

Figure 8.30 – Invoke settings

Scroll down further in the settings. This section is where you configure the parameters that you will send from Connect to Lambda. Select the **Use attribute** radio button and enter a destination key of `requestedTest`. For the **Type** field, select **User Defined** from the dropdown and enter an attribute name of `requestedText`. Validate your configuration against *Figure 8.31*. We now need to enter the second parameter. Click on the **Add another parameter** link that I've highlighted with the arrow in *Figure 8.31*:

Figure 8.31 – First parameter

The second parameter will appear after clicking the link. Configure this parameter in the same way, substituting `patientID` instead of `requestedTest` (*Figure 8.32*). There are no more settings for this component. Click the **Save** button now:

Figure 8.32 – Second parameter

If our flow were processing, we would now be at the step when the Lambda function had retrieved the patient's results. The whole point of this exercise is to get this data to the caller. Let's do that by adding a **Play prompt** component and connecting it to the Lambda component. Your flow will look like *Figure 8.33* at this point:

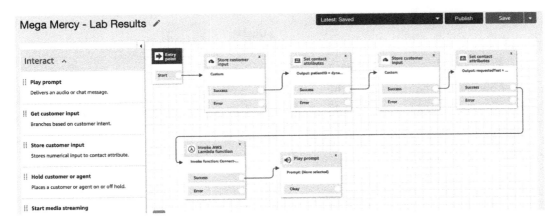

Figure 8.33 – Play prompt component

The **Play prompt** component requires a particular field this time. We will still use the text-to-speech function, but we will need to slipstream in the result from the Lambda function. Connect can do this by using internal variables. For Lambda, the returned result will be in the standard $.External variable position since we didn't define another one. In our case, Lambda returns the key of Result. To access this value, we will use the variable of $.External.Result in our text-to-speech box. I've used the phrase "Your lab results are $.External.Result, thank you, and have a great day." When you have entered your text, click on the **Save** button:

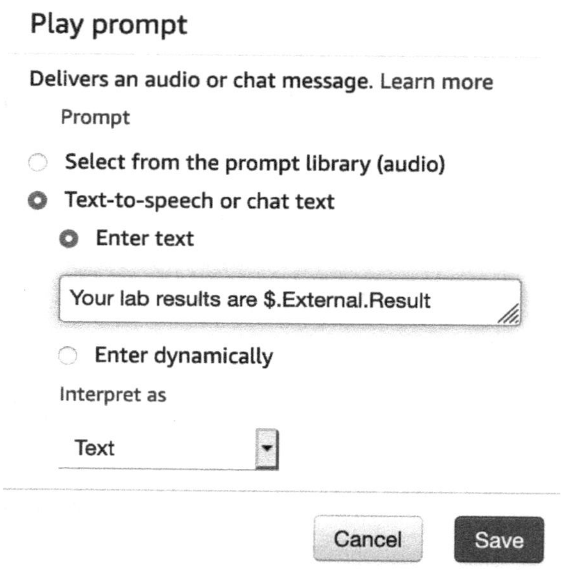

Play prompt

Delivers an audio or chat message. Learn more

Prompt

○ **Select from the prompt library (audio)**

◉ **Text-to-speech or chat text**

   ◉ **Enter text**

Your lab results are $.External.Result

   ○ **Enter dynamically**

Interpret as

Text ▾

[Cancel] [**Save**]

Figure 8.34 – Play prompt settings

We have now completed the bulk of the work for the flow. All that is left is to add error handling. Follow the same paradigm as we have for other contact flows by adding a play prompt to let the user know that something has gone wrong and a disconnect component. Tie all of the error outputs from the components to the play prompt component. When everything is done, your completed flow will look like *Figure 8.35*:

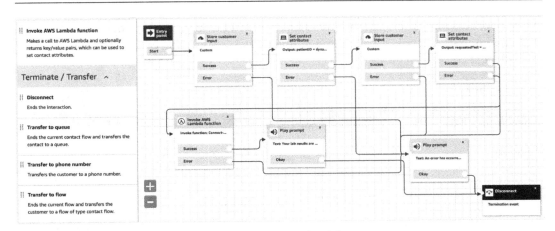

Figure 8.35 – Completed flow

Congratulations, you have now built your first integration flow. It's not very fancy and doesn't do a lot, but it will help you understand the basics. Now that the flow is complete, all we have to do is test it to ensure that everything is working the way it should.

Testing the solution

To test the solution, we aren't going to interface it with any other contact flows. Instead, we will keep it isolated and use the test number we had created to test the flow directly. Before we can try this, we need to tie this phone number to the flow.

Access the **Phone numbers** configuration page through the USB menu on the left, noted in *Figure 8.36*:

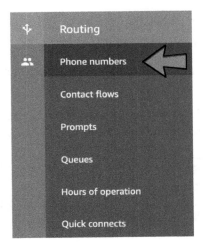

Figure 8.36 – Phone numbers menu

The Connect administration site will present you with a list of phone numbers. Select the test phone number, or claim a new number. If you select an existing one, click the number in the leftmost column (*Figure 8.37*) to edit it:

Figure 8.37 – Phone number list

When the **Edit Phone number** screen appears, select the **Contact flow / IVR** dropdown (*Figure 8.38*) and find the `Mega Mercy - Lab Results` contact flow. When you have selected the flow, click the **Save** button:

Figure 8.38 – Edit phone number

Now that we have configured the phone number, give Connect about 5 minutes to make the changes before proceeding.

I have included a couple of patients and test results in the example Lambda function. The table in *Figure 8.39* details the users and test results:

Patient ID	Patient Name	Blood Pressure	Bilirubin	Glucose
49875	Tom	120 over 82	0.6	50
39864	Samantha	180 over 94	0.8	90
98765	Bridgid	124 over 87	2.5	120
88745	Mark	156 over 78	1.1	74

Figure 8.39 – Test results table

To test the solution, select one of the patient IDs in the table and call the test number. When prompted, enter the patient ID number and select the test results you would like to hear. You should hear the expected result from Connect corresponding to the table in *Figure 8.39*. If you hear an error message, then something went wrong in your flow—double-check all of your settings to identify the problem.

The most likely cause of an issue is the misconfiguration of a variable in one of the components.

If everything checks out, congratulations, you have your first successful integration. We have concluded the deployment of the solution.

Other potential types of integrations

To highlight the power that integrations give you, I want to take some time to explain what some potential integrations might look like. After all, this example is quite limited and is purely for demonstration purposes. The integration capability of Connect and other AWS services is the real power behind connect. It would be a disservice to leave you with this one example. To demonstrate more capabilities, we will review the following scenarios:

- CRM integration
- ERP integration
- Banking integration
- In-house applications

Customer Relationship Management (CRM) integration

The first thought that most people have when discussing call center integrations is to tie it to their CRM. Connect offers built-in CRM integrations such as Salesforce. But there are many more CRM packages available on the marketplace, and you might not be running Salesforce. Using the capabilities that we covered in this chapter, you will build your integration into any CRM as long as it has an API that you have access to. Some possible things that you might do with this type of interface include the following:

- Look up the customer's name via the caller ID number and greet them personally.
- Immediately ask them identity verification questions.
- Self-service access to billing and invoice data.

The limiting factor in this integration, like most, will be how many capabilities are exposed using the API.

Information Technology Service Management (ITSM) integration

Another common request for Connect integration is to interface with ITSM, such as ServiceNow. This integration will allow you to perform actions from Connect that will speed up your overall service desk and IT operations. Connect has an interface for ZenDesk, not ServiceNow, so you need to create your interface. Here are some of the things you might do with this integration:

- Automatically create helpdesk tickets.
- Kick-off automated workflows.
- Create an automated outbound notification system.

Again, the limiting factor in this integration, like most, will be how many capabilities are exposed using the API.

In-house applications

The final scenario for integration is an internal application. For instance, let's say that you own a chain of car washes. You use custom-developed software for your customers that subscribe to monthly car wash services. Your most common customers are realtors, sales executives, and municipal services such as fire and police. The application keeps track of how many and what type of car washes your customers have and how many are left. Some of the things you can do with this type of integration are as follows:

- Look up account expiry.
- Look up remaining car washes.
- Cancel or upgrade membership.

The limiting factor for this type of integration will be if an API exists for your application at all. It's entirely possible that one does not exist. In this case, you could do something more drastic and access the database to make the changes directly. Since you have the source code for the application, you would be more suited to build this kind of hardline integration. However, I wouldn't advise it. A better solution would be to start to create an API within the application to perform the actions you require.

I hope that I have given you enough insight through these scenarios to provide you with a rounded picture of how you can integrate your specific systems with Connect. This list is by no means comprehensive. The number of integrations is limitless. The insight you have gleaned from this section should give you plenty of food for thought when communicating with your stakeholders about the potential capabilities you will have.

Summary

Although this solution's implementation was simplistic, it shows you how to interface with your enterprise application to drive value for you and your customers. The more functions you can automate, the lower your overall costs will be for operating your call center. I always recommend looking at automation whenever possible in your workflows.

This chapter covered deploying the CloudFormation template, which deployed the Lambda function and any other necessary AWS resources. From there, we created the contact flow by hand to demonstrate how to build integration and understand the pieces in play. Finally, we tested the solution to make sure that everything worked as expected. In the next chapter, we will dive deep into implementing callbacks in your call center.

9
Implementing Callbacks

No one likes waiting on the phone on hold endlessly listening to hold music. Even if you're listening on speakerphone, your time still isn't yours. You are still bound to that phone, and it tends to make callers grumpy if they are on hold for more than a few minutes. Amazon Connect allows you to offer callbacks to callers instead. This capability enables your customers to go along with their daily activities and receive a call when an agent is available to help them. Callbacks are a great way to increase customer satisfaction.

This chapter will explain how to create a callback contact flow to implement this capability in your call center. Connect offers a sample callback contact flow. However, there are ways that we can improve the customer experience above and beyond these initial capabilities.

To accomplish this, in this chapter, we will cover the following topics:

- Solution overview
- Capturing the caller's number
- Number validation
- Addressing callback concerns
- Implementing the callback contact flow

Solution overview

In this solution, we will implement a callback flow that can be used for all of our departments. We are going to start by editing the flow called **Sample interruptible queue flow with callback**. To make the flow more effective from a customer standpoint, we will automatically capture the phone number from the Connect instance. This change will allow customers to accept the number that we have captured to move on, rather than entering their number and then verifying. We will begin this process in the next section.

Before we get started on that, let's cover some callback basics so that you understand how callbacks work in depth. When a caller asks to have a callback, their information is appended to the queue that is currently assigned. When the next agent is available, this person is then called back by Connect automatically and routed to an agent.

A few critical items need to be kept in mind with callbacks. Firstly, if, for some reason, there are no agents that become active within 7 days, the calls will automatically be removed from the queue. I would anticipate that this doesn't happen often, but just in case, you now understand the limitations.

The second essential item to know is that there is no way to remove callbacks from the queue. Whether callbacks can be removed from the queue is a question that you will receive from stakeholders. This question arises when stakeholders realize that a caller can call back and potentially talk to an agent before their callback happens. However, this is rare, as they will most likely be put on hold again due to call volume.

Lastly, Connect will retry calling someone for their callback. The number of retries is set by you when you configure your flow. When Connect makes a call, if it gets a voicemail, this is considered a connection. Connect is unable to determine whether it is talking to a person or a recording, which makes sense. Again, this is a limitation that would be important to keep in mind when talking to your stakeholders about callbacks. Connect is pretty impressive, but it's not quite human (yet).

Now that we have covered all of the background information, let's start setting up the queue.

Capturing the caller's number

To get started with making our modifications, use the process we discussed in previous chapters to edit the contact flow called **Sample interruptible queue flow with callback**.

Your screen will change to the contact flow editing screen. First, let's change the name to match our naming convention since this will no longer be a sample. I've named mine `Mega Mercy - Callback`. Click on the pencil, as noted in *Figure 9.1*, to edit the name:

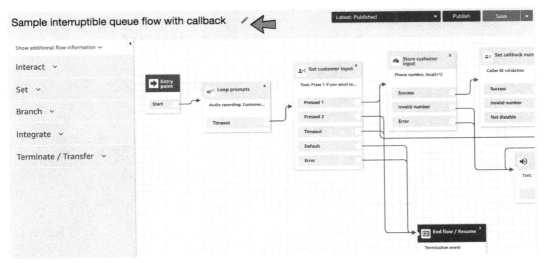

Figure 9.1 – Flow name change

We will want to change the loop prompt component settings. By default, it is set to **customerqueue.wav**. We should change this to something else so that it's more descriptive, and we can come back later and know what it's playing. I've changed mine to jazz (*Figure 9.2*); the soothing, yet not sleepy tones fit well with a call center:

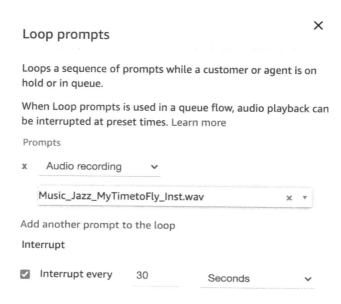

Figure 9.2 – Change loop prompt

You may also notice in this component that there is a setting to interrupt. This setting is vital for this flow. Without it, your flow will not continue to the rest of the flow as you intend.

In our call center, we want every customer interaction to be as easy as possible. Looking at this contact flow, you will see that it goes from playing a loop to asking whether the customer wants a callback. This pattern is as efficient as we could make it, but if they select 1 for yes, the flow progresses to a **Store customer input** component. This component gathers the phone number from the client. You might be asking yourself, doesn't Connect already have the phone number? The answer to that question is *absolutely*. Plus, most people use their cellphones, meaning that the number they are calling from is most likely the number they would want to be called back on.

To make our flow more user-friendly, let's break the connection from the first **Get customer input** component. Specifically, we want to break the **Pressed 1** connection. At this point, your flow should look as in *Figure 9.3*:

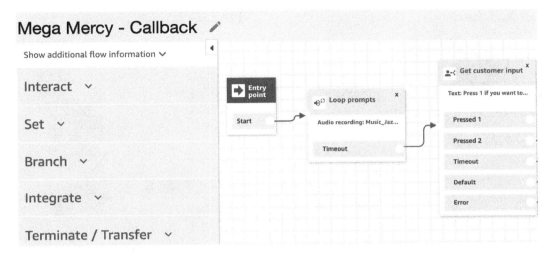

Figure 9.3 – Broken flow

Next, we want to play a message for the caller asking them whether they would like a callback on the number they are calling from. Drag a **Get customer input** component from the interaction menu on the left into the editing field. Edit the **Get customer input** settings and enter a message. I've used the message Would you like to be called back from a different number you are calling from? If yes, press one. Otherwise, we will call you back on this number.

We want to allow the caller to enter another phone number say if they call from a landline at work. Connect the **Pressed 1** output on the original **Get customer input** to the new **Get customer input**. At this point, your flow will resemble *Figure 9.4*:

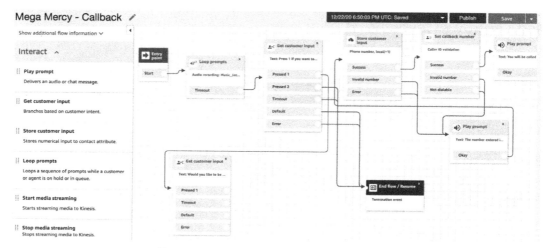

Figure 9.4 – Adding a new Get customer input

I decided to have only one button press for this input. This configuration allows the caller to do nothing if they want to keep the number that they called from as the callback number. If the caller doesn't do anything, the flow will progress out of the timeout value, which we can progress down the flow.

Let's now connect the outputs from this input component. If the caller pressed 1, we would send them to the original flow to the **Store customer input** component. This connection will allow the caller to input a callback number as the original flow had intended.

We need to determine how to handle the timeout and default outputs. Since we want the timeout value to progress to the callback, we need to create a new **Set callback number** component. The original **Set callback number** component uses the variable of stored user input. Since the user didn't input anything, we can't use this block for our timeout.

Drag a new **Set callback number** component into the editing field and connect the input to the timeout and default output for our new callback path. Finally, we need to connect the error output to the **Resume** component. If anything goes wrong, your flow will loop back to the original jazz music that we selected in the first component. Your contact flow should mirror *Figure 9.5* at this point:

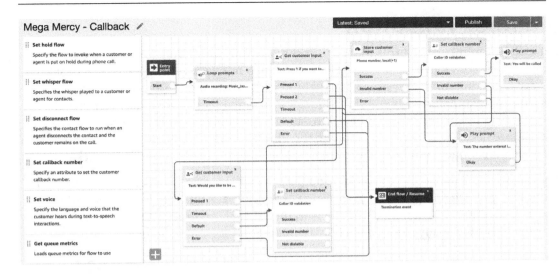

Figure 9.5 – New callback path

Since we are using the number from the system, we need to tell the **Set callback number** component to find and edit this component. Your screen should look as in *Figure 9.6*. For the type of attribute, we need to select **System**. The attribute that we are looking to use is **Customer Number**, which holds the caller ID number of the caller. When you are done selecting these fields, click on **Save**:

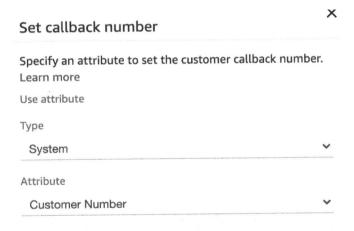

Figure 9.6 – Edit set callback

Now we can reuse the existing blocks to complete the flow.

Number validation

Set callback number performs some special functions in addition to just setting the number. This component also validates the number. Since we are using the number that the call is coming from, everything should be OK. But there may be an instance where the caller ID was not available, and therefore the system doesn't have a valid number. To account for this condition, we still need to validate the number and act accordingly. On success, we need to connect this output to the **Play prompt** component that was after the original **Set callback number**. This connection will add the callback to the callback queue.

For the invalid number and not dialable outputs, we will want to connect these to the same **Play prompt** component that the original **Set callback number** was connected to. These connections will capture any issue with the caller ID and request that the user enters a new number manually. Your contact flow should now look as in *Figure 9.7*:

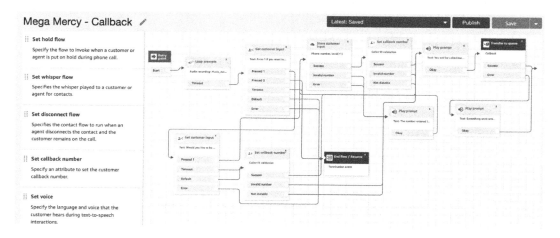

Figure 9.7 – Final flow

With the completion of the changes necessary, you can now publish the Connect flow to make the changes live within the system. Before we can use our flow, we need to make sure it's configured as a destination in any necessary flows. We will cover validating this in the next section.

Implementing the callback contact flow

Based on our original design, we opted for setting all of the queues within the departmental flows. We created specific settings for each department, such as hours of operation and hold messaging. There are two ways that we can implement our callbacks in our current design.

The first option we have is to copy the flow that we just created for each department. This option would allow us to create different messages and hold music when callers are on the phone. For instance, the billing department might want a message telling callers to pay a bill online. In contrast, the oncology department might wish to have some messaging around a cancer support group in the area.

By separating the departments, you give your stakeholders a lot more flexibility. Personally, this is the way that I would implement the system. After all, your internal stakeholders are your customers, and you want them to be satisfied just as much as an external client. A compromise to limit the amount of work you need to do is to capture hold messaging information during the initial stakeholder conversations we discussed in *Chapter 2, Reviewing Stakeholder Objectives*. With that knowledge in hand, you know what departments can use a shared flow and which you need to make copies for and customize.

Since we are creating this system for demonstration and training purposes, it's unnecessary to replicate this flow. But if you feel like it, you can; the process we are about to discuss will just need to be modified to select the correct departmental callback flows.

To start implementing the callback flow, we need to edit the first departmental flow, **Mega Mercy - Billing**. If you recall, the flow looks as in *Figure 9.8*:

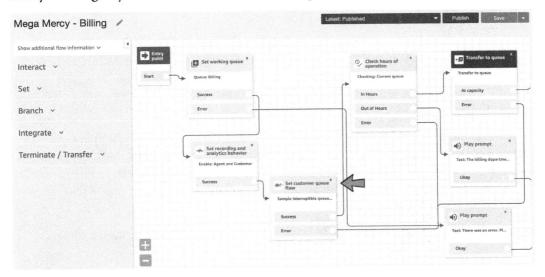

Figure 9.8 – Original billing flow

The component that we are interested in (highlighted in *Figure 9.8*) is the **Set customer queue flow** component. You can see that it's still set to the original sample that we started with at the beginning of the chapter. This name has now changed to **Mega Mercy - Callback**.

Edit this component and change the flow to the new callback flow. If you opted to create additional copies of the flow for individual departments, you would select the billing callback flow at this time. For reference, see *Figure 9.9*:

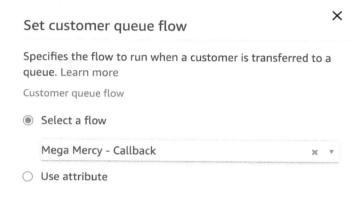

Figure 9.9 – New callback flow

Your callback flow is now complete. You can now publish your flow to make it active in your Connect instance.

Summary

The callback is great for improving your customer experience. This chapter covered how to implement this feature in your call center using the sample as a baseline. This base information on callbacks will allow you to customize your call center experience based on your stakeholders' needs.

The use of callbacks is great for your call center during business hours and can also be used for after hours. Instead of just telling your callers to call back during business hours, you can give them an option to receive a callback instead. When agents arrive for the day and log into Connect, the previous night's calls will be flushed out of the queue first. There are some cases where voicemail might make more sense.

In the next chapter, we will cover how to implement voicemail in your Connect instance.

10
Implementing Voicemail

With all the capabilities and advanced features that Amazon Connect possesses, I am quite surprised that voicemail isn't a native feature. I assume that this is primarily since the Connect service is geared toward enterprise deployments. After all, the service was created to support Amazon's own retail business. However, given the ease of use and deployment, many smaller organizations have used Connect.

In smaller organizations, the utilization of voice would be more prevalent. The possibility of there being only one person who could answer any given question is greater. Large enterprises have whole departments of people with specialized knowledge.

Amazon has partially addressed the needs of smaller organizations with a voicemail implementation. The capability itself is not a native integration but rather a bolt-on functionality. In this chapter, we will walk through the implementation and configuration of voicemail for your call center. As we do this, we will cover the following topics:

- Voicemail solution overview
- Launching the solution
- Configuring your instance

- Using the management portal
- Importing voicemail contact flows
- Testing the solution
- Other ways to integrate into contact flows

Voicemail solution overview

Amazon's solution offers a unique and completely serverless implementation of voicemail. The serverless aspect is an excellent advantage over other possible solutions on the market. Using a serverless model, you continue the model of not having to manage any servers for your call center.

In addition to being serverless, the solution offers other capabilities to increase ease of use. For instance, the solution uses Amazon Transcribe to transcribe voicemails and include the content in emails. Transcription of voicemails reduces employee overhead by removing the need to listen to long-winded or slow-speaking voicemail messages.

The voicemail solution is based on extensions that are assigned to your agents. This design doesn't seem to fit very well with a call center and sounds more like a conventional phone system. This assumption is correct. The best implementation for a full call center is callback, which would allow multiple agents to respond to clients' inquiries. However, you may have someone with very specialized knowledge, or potentially managers who need to answer specific calls. For these situations, the voicemail implementation fits well.

Amazon packages the entire solution for you, and you start the deployment using a CloudFormation template. For the most part, the implementation isn't that difficult to deploy. We will cover the implementation in the next few sections. Amazon doesn't do an excellent job of explaining other ways to integrate the voicemail solution into your call center. It's like one of those movies that keep building and building and then leave you hanging with a poor climax where you expected more. At the end of this chapter, we will cover other ways to implement the solution to give you the *The Sixth Sense* climax that you deserve. The components used in the solution and their connectivity are described in *Figure 10.1*:

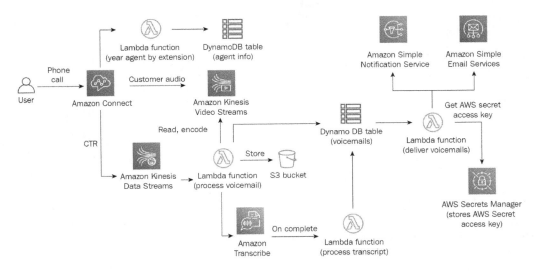

Figure 10.1 – Voicemail processing architecture (Source: https://docs.aws.amazon.com/solutions/latest/voicemail-for-amazon-connect/architecture.html)

Figure 10.1 only details the components that are deployed for the processing of voicemails. As you can see, there are a multitude of AWS services deployed by the solution, including Lambda functions, S3 buckets, Transcribe, and Secrets Manager. You can also see in the diagram the flow that process takes. An additional feature, a management portal, allows managers and admins to control the voicemail solution. The architecture of the management portal is documented in *Figure 10.2*:

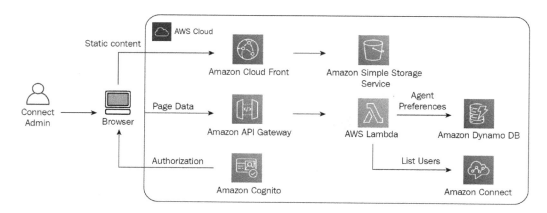

Figure 10.2 – Management portal architecture

Figure 10.2 details the services deployed as the management website. It also shows the flow of information when you access the website and store data within the solution. The designs might look complicated, but don't worry. Everything will be deployed for you. The only piece you will need to worry about is the configuration of the solution. In the next section, we will cover how to launch the solution into your account.

Launching the solution

To launch the solution, you need to download the CloudFormation template from AWS. You can download the template from this link: `https://s3.amazonaws.com/solutions-reference/voicemail-for-amazon-connect/latest/voicemail-for-amazon-connect.template`.

Before we start launching the solution via CloudFormation, you need to gather your existing Connect instance's instance ID. The solution will need to know how to access it to capture the deployed users and synchronize them to its database. The steps to gather the required information are the following:

1. To get the Connect instance ID, you will need to go to the **Amazon Connect** section of the **AWS console** and click on your instance. When you do, you will be shown the screen depicted in *Figure 10.3*. You will want to copy the instance ID, which is the part after the / in the **Instance ARN**. We will use this in a later step:

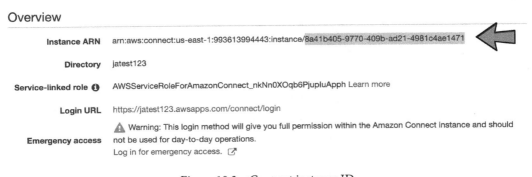

Figure 10.3 – Connect instance ID

2. Once you have that data, you can move on and start the deployment of the
    voicemail solution. To do this, you need to locate the CloudFormation service in
    AWS. CloudFormation is located under the **Management & Governance** section of
    the AWS services list. **CloudFormation** is identified in *Figure 10.4*:

Figure 10.4 – CloudFormation

3. When you get to the **CloudFormation** console, you will be presented with a screen that resembles *Figure 10.5*. The first step in the process is to click on the **Create stack** button:

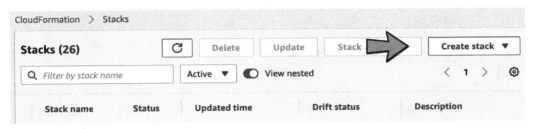

Figure 10.5 – CloudFormation console

4. When you click the **Create stack** button, a new drop-down menu will appear. With this solution, we want to deploy a new stack with new resources. To do this, select the **With new resources (standard)** option. This option is highlighted in *Figure 10.6*:

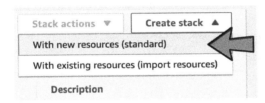

Figure 10.6 – CloudFormation Create stack

When you get to the CloudFormation **Create stack** page, you want to select the **Upload a template file** option. From there, you can click the **Choose file** button to upload the template that we downloaded earlier; when you have chosen the file, click on the **Next** button to continue. You can use *Figure 10.7* for reference:

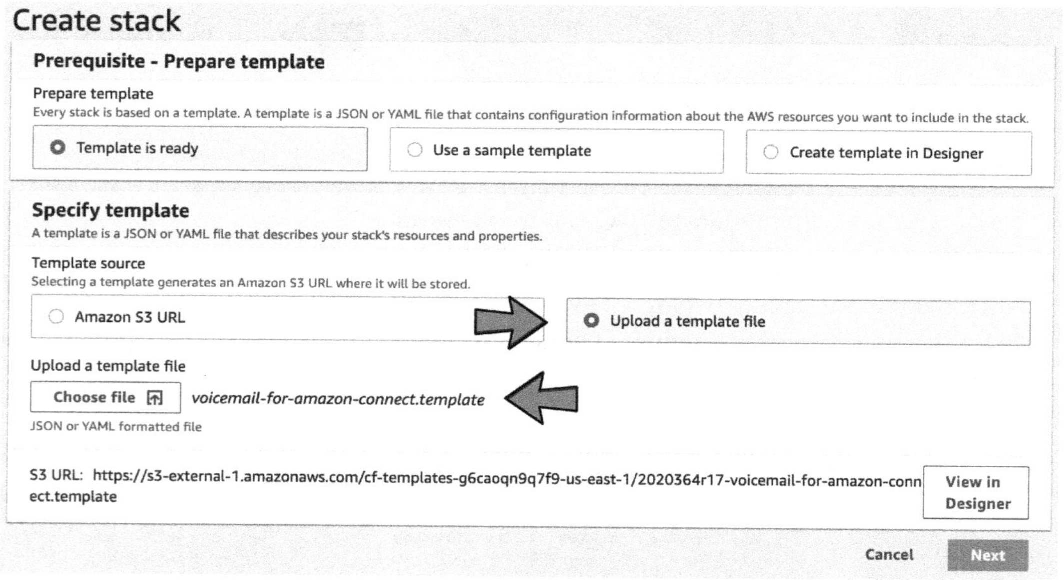

Figure 10.7 – CloudFormation setup

5. CloudFormation will then load the template, including all of the parameters that need to be entered. The next screen, depicted in *Figure 10.8*, shows all of the parameters. You need to populate these to move to the next part of the process. You can use any stack name that you wish. It just cannot have any spaces in it. Use the instance ID that we captured earlier in step 1 for the Connect instance ID. The administrator email needs to be entered next. At this point, your settings should look similar to *Figure 10.8*:

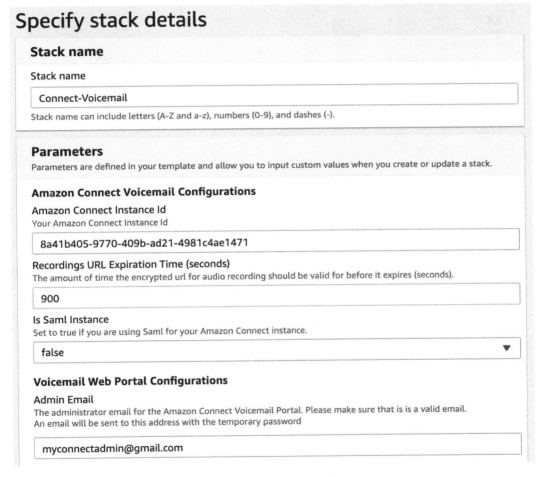

Figure 10.8 – Stack details

6.   Scroll down the screen to see more settings. The rest of the settings are for your administrator and manager configuration. These uses are used to access the management portal that will be deployed by the solution. The last setting that needs to be configured is the domain prefix. This won't be your domain name. Instead, this just represents the domain the user pool will exist in. When you are done, your settings should be similar to *Figure 10.9*. Click **Next** when you are done:

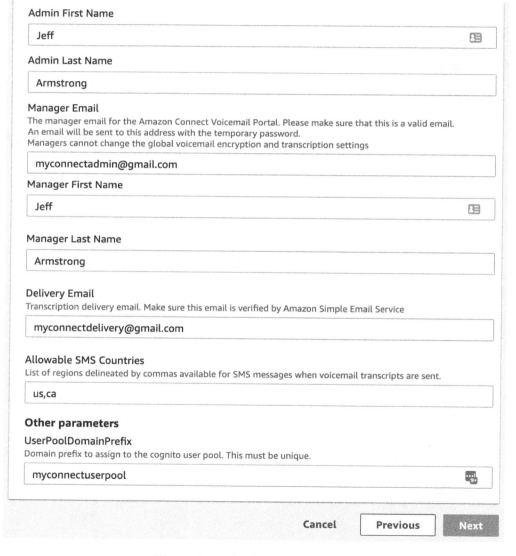

Figure 10.9 – CloudFormation settings

7. On the next screen (*Figure 10.10*), you don't need to make any changes. Simply click **Next** to continue:

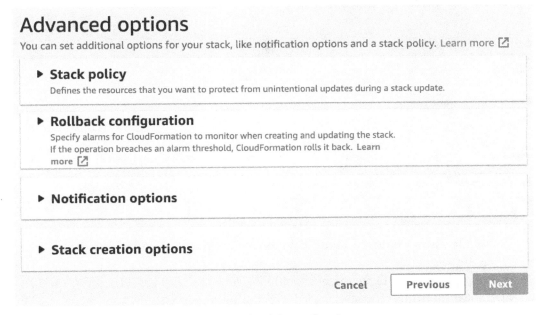

Figure 10.10 – Advanced options

8. The final CloudFormation screen (*Figure 10.11*) will have some options on the bottom that need to be checked to acknowledge the creation of unique resources and capabilities. Check both of these boxes and click **Create stack** to finish the process:

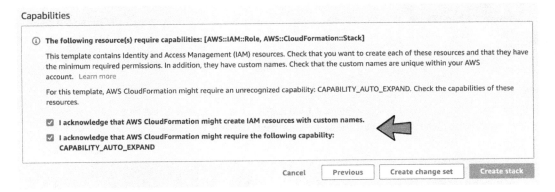

Figure 10.11 – Creating a stack

9. The CloudFormation service will now take all the inputted parameters and start deploying the voicemail infrastructure. When you return to the CloudFormation screen, you will see the stack being created, as shown in *Figure 10.12*:

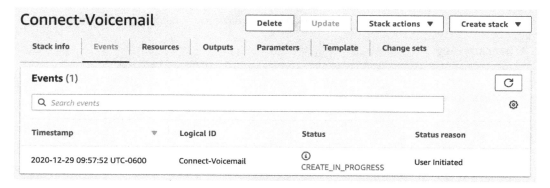

Figure 10.12 – Stack creation

10. The solution uses a unique CloudFormation feature that deploys child stacks. When the solution is fully deployed, there will be four stacks deployed in total. Your completed stack deployment should look similar to *Figure 10.13*. If you use a different stack name, your stacks will be prefixed differently:

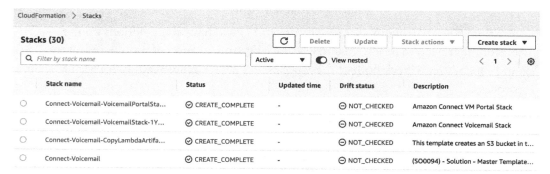

Figure 10.13 – Finished stacks

You have now completed the deployment of the solution. It's now time to move on to configuring the deployment based on your Connect deployment.

Configuring your instance

The next phase of the process requires us to configure the Connect instance so that the solution can receive the correct data. Without it, the voicemail solution won't be able to capture the voice stream to actually create a voicemail.

To begin the Connect instance configuration, perform the following steps:

1. You need to enter the AWS console for Connect as you did to get the instance ID. Once you click on your instance, you will need to locate the **Data storage** configuration in the menu on the left-hand side of the screen, as depicted in *Figure 10.14*:

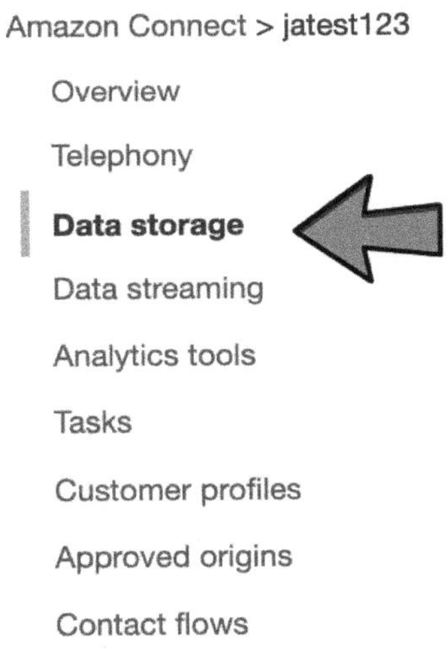

Amazon Connect > jatest123

Overview

Telephony

Data storage

Data streaming

Analytics tools

Tasks

Customer profiles

Approved origins

Contact flows

Figure 10.14 – Data storage

2. In the main section of the configuration screen, locate the **Live media streaming** configuration (*Figure 10.15*) and click the **Edit** button. This action will expand the section to make changes to the settings. Live media streaming allows the Connect instance to receive the voice stream to perform the voicemail transcription:

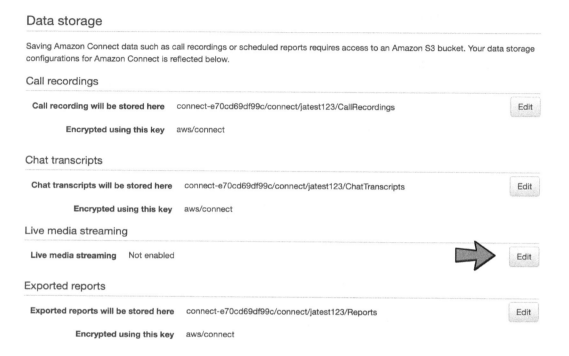

Figure 10.15 – Live media streaming

3. When the settings expand, you need to make a few changes. The changes that need to be made on this screen are the following:

    - Click the checkbox for **Enable live media streaming**.

    - Add a prefix to the Kinesis video streams.

    - Select the radio button, **Select KMS key by name,** and select the default **aws/ kinesesvideo**.

    - Set the data retention period to **1 Days**.

Once these settings are configured, you can click the **Save** button. You can check *Figure 10.16* to validate your settings:

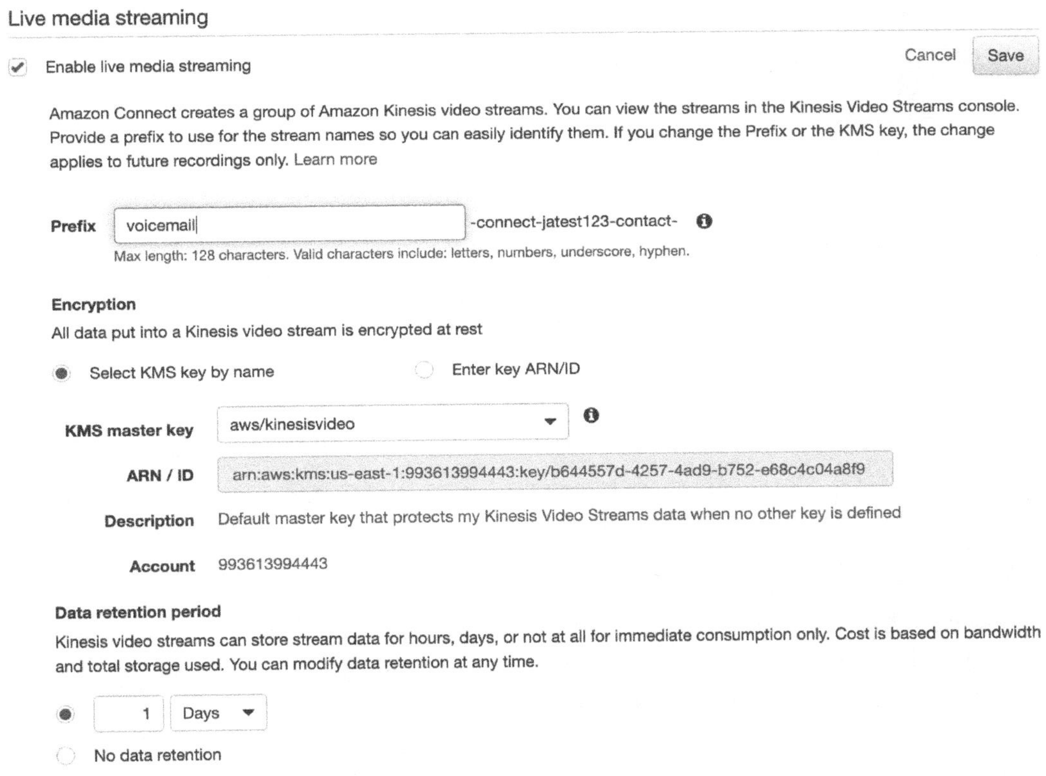

Live media streaming

☑ Enable live media streaming   Cancel   Save

Amazon Connect creates a group of Amazon Kinesis video streams. You can view the streams in the Kinesis Video Streams console. Provide a prefix to use for the stream names so you can easily identify them. If you change the Prefix or the KMS key, the change applies to future recordings only. Learn more

Prefix | voicemail | -connect-jatest123-contact- ⓘ

   Max length: 128 characters. Valid characters include: letters, numbers, underscore, hyphen.

Encryption

All data put into a Kinesis video stream is encrypted at rest

◉ Select KMS key by name   ○ Enter key ARN/ID

KMS master key | aws/kinesisvideo   ▼ | ⓘ

ARN / ID | arn:aws:kms:us-east-1:993613994443:key/b644557d-4257-4ad9-b752-e68c4c04a8f9 |

Description   Default master key that protects my Kinesis Video Streams data when no other key is defined

Account   993613994443

Data retention period

Kinesis video streams can store stream data for hours, days, or not at all for immediate consumption only. Cost is based on bandwidth and total storage used. You can modify data retention at any time.

◉ | 1 | | Days ▼ |

○ No data retention

Figure 10.16 – Live media settings

4. Next, you need to configure the **Data streaming** settings for your instance. I'm not sure why the live streaming media settings are located under the data storage settings and not the data streaming settings. It seems rather counterintuitive to me. Anyway, you can find the **Data streaming** settings in the left-hand side menu (*Figure 10.17*):

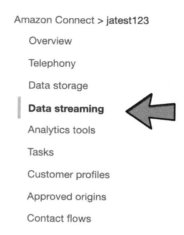

Figure 10.17 – Data streaming menu

5. You want to activate data streaming by clicking the box **Enable data streaming**. Both settings on this screen will use the same configuration. In the first setting, select the radio button for **Kinesis Stream**. In the drop-down menu, select the Kinesis the stream that was created by the solution. The name may vary depending on the stack name that you used to deploy the solution. However, it will always contain the phrase `VoicemailStack` in it.

For **Agent Events**, select the same Kinesis Stream. You can validate your settings against *Figure 10.18*. When you are satisfied with your settings, click on **Save**:

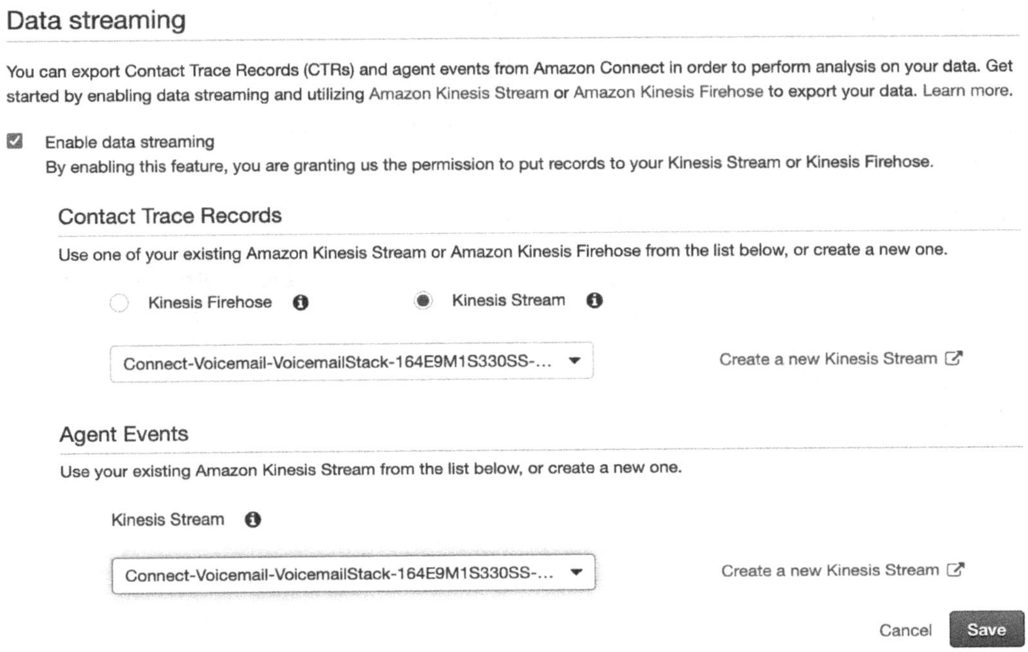

Data streaming

You can export Contact Trace Records (CTRs) and agent events from Amazon Connect in order to perform analysis on your data. Get started by enabling data streaming and utilizing Amazon Kinesis Stream or Amazon Kinesis Firehose to export your data. Learn more.

☑ Enable data streaming
   By enabling this feature, you are granting us the permission to put records to your Kinesis Stream or Kinesis Firehose.

Contact Trace Records

Use one of your existing Amazon Kinesis Stream or Amazon Kinesis Firehose from the list below, or create a new one.

◯ Kinesis Firehose ⓘ   ◉ Kinesis Stream ⓘ

[Connect-Voicemail-VoicemailStack-164E9M1S330SS-... ▼]   Create a new Kinesis Stream ☑

Agent Events

Use your existing Amazon Kinesis Stream from the list below, or create a new one.

Kinesis Stream ⓘ

[Connect-Voicemail-VoicemailStack-164E9M1S330SS-... ▼]   Create a new Kinesis Stream ☑

Cancel   **Save**

Figure 10.18 – Data streaming settings

You have now completed the configuration of the streaming of the voice data, as well as the contract records from your Connect instance. The voicemail solution will use both of these to perform its actions and provide voicemail capability. Next, we will walk through using the management portal.

Using the management portal

The management portal is used to configure your users' voicemail settings and download the preconfigured contact flows. For this part of the configuration, we are concerned with the contact flows. These flows will allow us to integrate the solution to connect as part of the call flow process.

To get started, we need to locate the URL of the management interface:

1. The management URL was created as an output to the `VoicemailPortalStack` deployed as part of the solution. To find this location, we need to access that stack's information to see its output. Locate the stack in your CloudFormation console. It should look similar to *Figure 10.19*. Click on the stack name in the left-hand column:

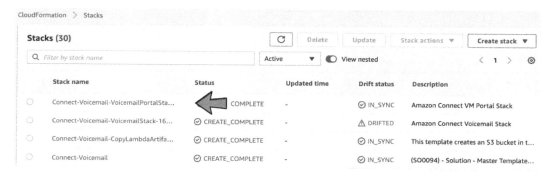

Figure 10.19 – Stacks

2. The next screen will display all of the information for the stack. We are interested in the **Outputs** tab. Click this tab to see the outputs. The output that will give you the URL you need to access is called **DistributionDomainName** (*Figure 10.20*). You might want to bookmark this URL so that you can access it in the future:

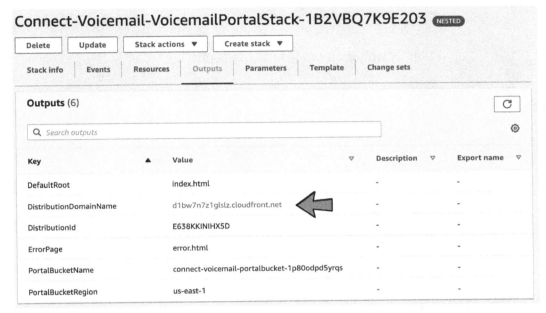

Figure 10.20 – Stack outputs

3. Click the URL to access the management portal. You will be prompted with a sign-on as shown in *Figure 10.21*. When you deployed the CloudFormation template, you received emails to the management and administrators you configured in the stack parameters. These emails contain the initial password for these users. Log on to the management portal using the administrator user and the corresponding password.

> **Important note**
> The email that you received from the system contains the password. However, it looks like it contains a period. The password is everything up to the period. The period just ends the sentence – double-check when you copy and paste the password, not to include the period.

When you log on for the first time, you will be prompted to change the password for security reasons:

Figure 10.21 – Sign-on

4. When you access the portal for the first time, you will want to click on the **SYNC AGENTS** link (*Figure 10.22*). The solution synchronizes users but only every 24 hours. Since it hasn't been online that long, the list of users will be empty:

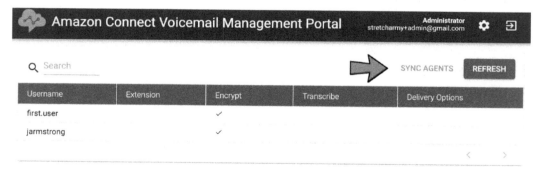

Figure 10.22 – SYNC AGENTS

5. Now that the users are synced, we need to create the contact flows. To have the management portal generate the contact flows, you need to click the gear link on the screen's upper right-hand side (*Figure 10.23*):

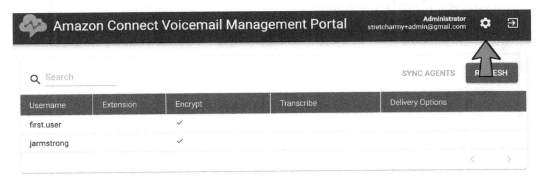

Figure 10.23 – Configuration

6. Upon clicking the gear icon, a popup will appear, as shown in *Figure 10.24*, to allow you to configure your settings. The defaults that are provided won't work. If you recall, we changed the name of the basic queue when we configured it. Change the **Fallback Queue** setting to **Primary Queue**. This name is the one that we gave it. If you don't change this setting, the Lambda program that generates the flow will error out. Unfortunately, it won't let you know this, and the download button won't do anything.

If everything is configured correctly, two files will be downloaded when you click the **DOWNLOAD** button:

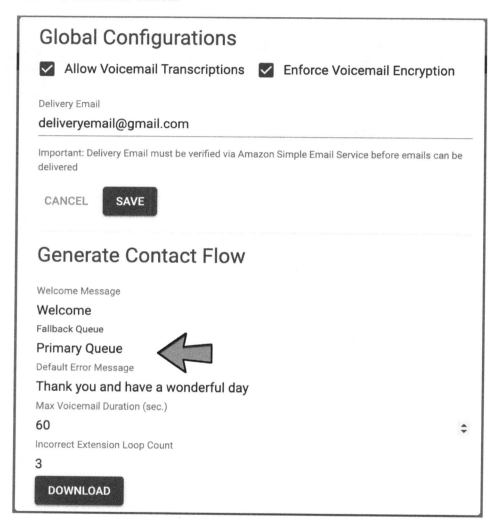

Global Configurations

☑ Allow Voicemail Transcriptions   ☑ Enforce Voicemail Encryption

Delivery Email

deliveryemail@gmail.com

Important: Delivery Email must be verified via Amazon Simple Email Service before emails can be delivered

CANCEL   **SAVE**

Generate Contact Flow

Welcome Message

Welcome

Fallback Queue

Primary Queue

Default Error Message

Thank you and have a wonderful day

Max Voicemail Duration (sec.)

60

Incorrect Extension Loop Count

3

DOWNLOAD

Figure 10.24 – Contact flow

We have now accessed and downloaded critical information so that we can continue the configuration of your Connect instance. The two flows that were downloaded need to be imported into your Connect instance. We will cover the importation in the next section.

Importing voicemail contact flows

In the previous section, we used the voicemail solution to create the instance's necessary contact flows. This process is beneficial as it saves you the time of having to create them by hand. Creating them by hand might be error-prone and require additional testing and diagnosis if you had to complete it all yourself. Now we need to import those flows so that we can complete the installation. We will follow the same process that we did in *Chapter 6, Contact Flow Creation*, to import the flows.

Since we have already covered this process in depth, we won't go through all of the steps here. We will instead just do a quick highlight recap:

1. The first flow that we want to import is the agent flow. This flow is a customer queue flow. Since this type of flow is not the default, we will need to select it from the drop-down arrow instead of clicking the **Create flow** button. Use *Figure 10.25* for a quick reference:

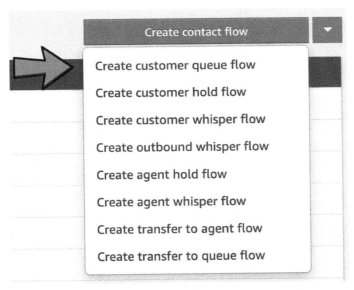

Figure 10.25 – Customer queue flow

2. When you select **Create Customer Queue Flow**, the screen will switch to the editing screen. Since we want to import the downloaded file, we need to click the down arrow next to the **Save** button to select **Import flow** (*Figure 10.26*):

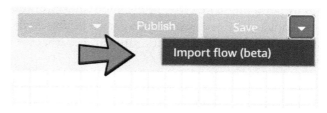

Figure 10.26 – Import flow

3. Upon selecting **Import flow**, you will be presented with a popup to select the file VM-Agent.json that was downloaded. Once you locate and choose the file, click the **Import** button:

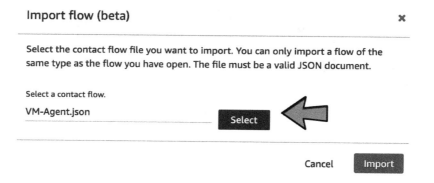

Figure 10.27 – File selection

4. After the flow is imported, your editing field will show all of the flow components and the imported connections. There are no changes that we need to make to the flows. Since the flow is completed, we can immediately publish it to commit the changes. Click the **Publish** button (*Figure 10.28*) to save the flow:

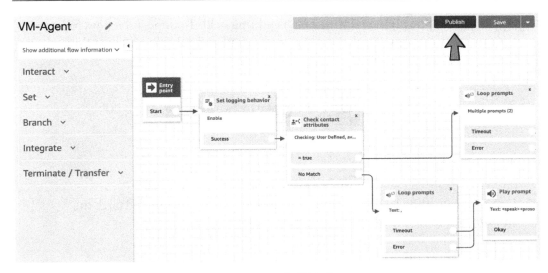

Figure 10.28 – Publish flow

5. The second flow that we need to import is the greeting flow. This flow prompts the caller for the extension of the agent they would like to leave a message for. After this flow captures the extension, it passes to the previous flow that we just imported to capture the voicemail.

    The greeting flow is a standard contact flow. To import it, we can just click the **Create contact flow** button seen in *Figure 10.29*:

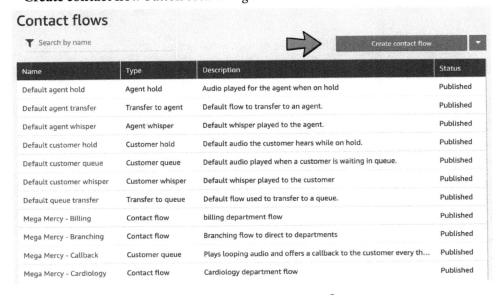

Figure 10.29 – Creating a contact flow

6. Again, you will be presented with a blank editing field. To import the flow, follow the same process again by clicking the down arrow and selecting **Import flow** (*Figure 10.30*):

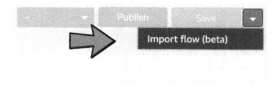

Figure 10.30 – Import flow

7. Import the greeting by selecting the file VM-Greeting.json and click the **Import** button to import the flow (*Figure 10.31*):

Figure 10.31 – Importing a greeting flow

8.   Once the flow is imported, we are in the same position as the other import. We don't need to make any changes to the flow. To complete the import, simply click on the **Publish** button seen in *Figure 10.32*:

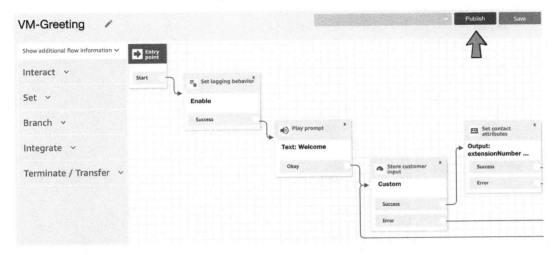

Figure 10.32 – Greeting flow

9. After both flows are imported, we have one more configuration to complete on the
    instance to allow us to test the solution. Right now, the greeting flow isn't connected
    to any other flow or phone number in the instance. For our testing purposes, we are
    going to connect this flow to our test phone number. To get started, select **Phone
    numbers** from the left-hand side menu in Connect using the icon that looks like a
    USB, seen in *Figure 10.33*:

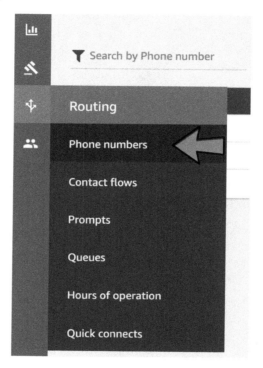

Figure 10.33 – Phone numbers

10. If you have a testing phone number already set up, enter that number. If you don't
    have a number, click the **Claim a number** button to get a new one. Click on your
    phone number in the left-hand column (*Figure 10.33*) to edit it:

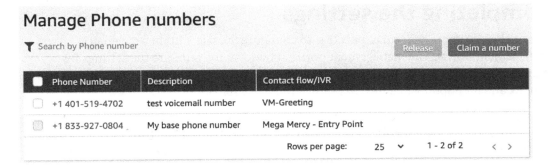

Figure 10.34 – Phone numbers

11. When you edit the phone number, change the **Contact flow** drop-down menu to VM-Greeting, as shown in *Figure 10.34*:

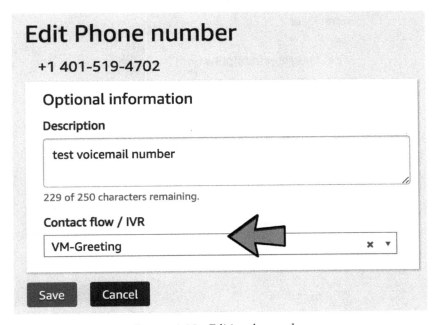

Figure 10.35 – Editing the number

This change will take the caller to the process of leaving a voicemail immediately once the call connects. We will use this phone number for testing the solution in the next section. With the completion of the configuration of the Connect instance, we can now return to the management console to finish the configuration of the voicemail solution. We will complete these settings in the next section.

Completing the settings

The final piece to our voicemail puzzle is to configure the users in the voicemail management portal. The management portal allows you to configure the settings for transcription and the user's extension. To edit a user, click on the row for the user. When you do, an edit popup will appear, as shown in *Figure 10.35*.

I used the extension based on the last four digits of the test phone number I have configured for my test user, 4702. I've also checked the **Transcribe**, **Encrypt**, and **Email** checkboxes. With these configured settings, the agent will receive a transcription of the voicemail in email. When you complete your changes, click the **SAVE** button:

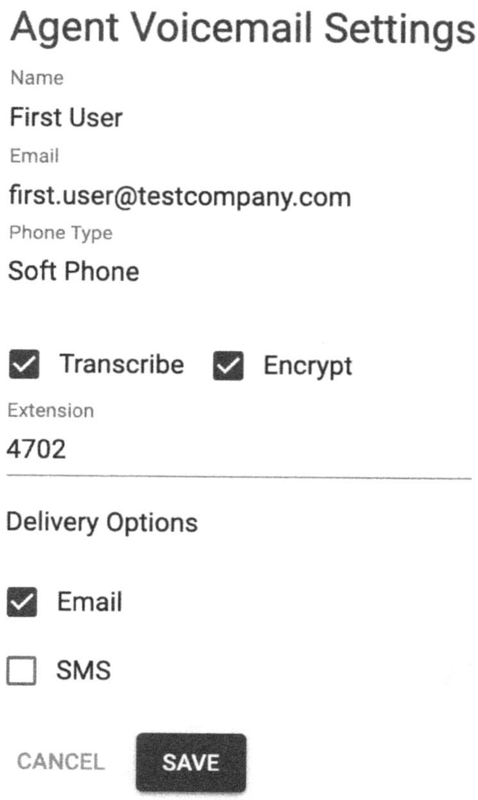

Agent Voicemail Settings

Name

First User

Email

first.user@testcompany.com

Phone Type

Soft Phone

☑ Transcribe   ☑ Encrypt

Extension

4702

Delivery Options

☑ Email

☐ SMS

CANCEL   SAVE

Figure 10.36 – Configuring user settings

When you click **SAVE**, the user list screen will display the new settings that have been saved (*Figure 10.36*). Validate that the settings you configured saved correctly. Congratulations, the configuration of the voicemail solution is now complete:

Figure 10.37 – Extension options

We now have the solution configured and, at this point, everything should be working. In the next section, we will test the solution and validate that everything is working as expected.

Testing the solution

To test the solution, make a call to the test number that you configured. When you call in, you should be prompted to enter the agent's extension that you want to leave a voicemail for. Leave a voicemail. When you are done, you can hang up the phone.

After a few minutes, you will receive an email with the voicemail's details, as shown in *Figure 10.37*. The email will contain the date and time that the call came in, the transcription, the caller's number, and a link to the voicemail recording.

To test that the S3 bucket is set up correctly, click on **Click Here** to listen to the voicemail. Note that the voicemail will expire. This expiration is based on the settings that we configured when we deployed the stack. The maximum duration that a voicemail can exist is 7 days. This limitation is based on S3 signed URLs and cannot be expanded:

Wed Dec 30 2020 16:54:33 GMT+0000 (Coordinated Universal Time)

New voicemail from +1.

Voicemail Transcript:

test voicemail.

Voicemail:

Voicemail Expiration Date: Wed Dec 30 2020 17:10:11 GMT+0000 (Coordinated Universal Time)

Click Here to listen to the voicemail

Figure 10.38 – Voicemail email

You have now completed testing of the voicemail solution, and it is now fully implemented and configured. Now that you have seen everything that the solution has to offer, you can probably see that there are some limitations on the implementation. The next section will cover some of these limitations and how you might work around them to provide a better integration in your call center. It will be essential if you have a more extensive enterprise implementation.

Other ways to integrate into contact flows

The voicemail solution is rather impressive from a technology standpoint, being completely serverless and offering transcription. Unfortunately, it doesn't provide a lot of permutations for the integration. It's up to you to create the necessary changes to make it a better fit for your implementation.

In the next section, I will demonstrate possible changes that you can make to integrate the solution better. Of course, it's highly dependent on the requirements of your individual call center's needs. This diversity is probably why the solution doesn't include any other options. However, it still would have been nice for them to at least give some ideas.

Removing the extension prompt

The first way you can improve upon the implementation is to remove the need to enter an extension to leave a voicemail. In my opinion, this would be a vital change to make. I have never had to enter an extension to leave a voicemail before. Of course, the way that voicemail is integrated would need to change to make this effective.

To remove the need to capture the extension, you would need to know where the call is being directed. For a demonstration of this change, let's use the following scenario:

Tim is a call center manager and receives all the escalations when a caller asks for a manager. Sometimes Tim is very busy when the center is taking several calls and cannot immediately accept every call. To ensure customers are satisfied, Tim wants voicemail implemented for his line. Calls are sent to him via a quick connect when the agent receives a request for a manager that sends it to a manager queue.

In this scenario, we have some pretty well-defined criteria that will allow us to know when a call is especially for Tim. In this case, Tim is working from a queue explicitly designed for him. Since the voicemail system only understands extensions and not queues, we need to assign an extension still so that the voicemail system knows how to handle it:

1. To begin the process, we need to make a copy of the VM - Greeting contact flow to modify it without disturbing the original. You can make a copy of the flow using the process from *Chapter 6, Contact Flow Creation*. Once the flow is copied, we need to remove a few components. Ultimately, we want to set the variable extensionNumber to the extension number for Tim without prompting the caller to enter it. We are primarily concerned with the first few items in the flow, noted in *Figure 10.38*:

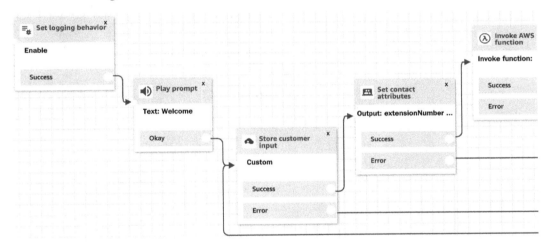

Figure 10.39 – Original greeting

2. We need to remove the play prompt and the store customer input components. Remove these from your flow. When you are done, the flow will resemble *Figure 10.39*:

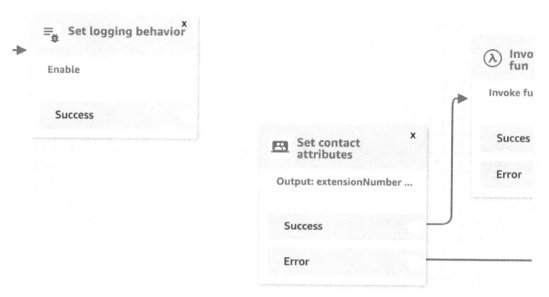

Figure 10.40 – Deleted components

3. Since we know that all these calls will be for Tim, all we have to do is set the variable to Tim's extension. For demonstration, we are using the extension of 5555. Click to edit the **Set contact attributes** component. We will want to set the extension here. The original flow used the customer input to save the value, which was variable. Since we know what it's going to be, we can set this manually. Change the radio button from attribute to text input and enter 5555 on the line – see *Figure 10.40* for details. When you are done, click **Save**:

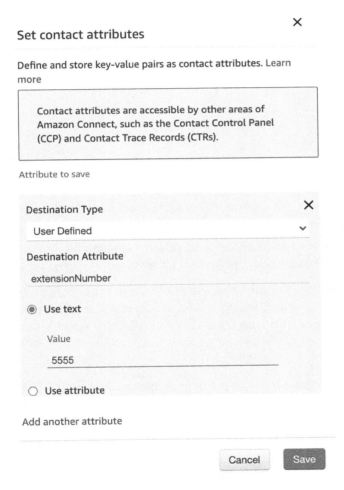

Figure 10.41 – Setting contact attributes

4. All that is left is to connect the output from the **Set logging behavior** component to the **Set contract attributes** component (*Figure 10.41*). When done, publish the flow to save the changes:

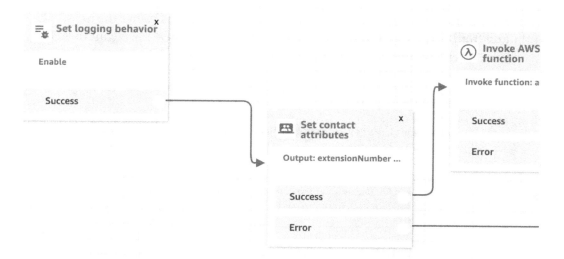

Figure 10.42 – Connecting components

With these modifications made, the overall function of the solution does not change. It will still run the necessary Lambdas and send voicemails based on the extension of the user. We just don't have to ask the user for that number, making their experience better.

The question that remains is where we would put this into the overall process to make it seamless for callers. Ultimately, I recommend that an option be added to the customer queue to allow callers to leave a voicemail. This implementation would mimic that of offering a callback to callers. However, instead of sending the call to a callback flow, the call will be transferred to a voicemail flow.

There are more possible ways that you could implement voicemail in your flows. However, the bulk of the imported contact flows will need to remain to ensure that the solution continues to work. Voicemail might take more experimentation than the rest of the items we have worked on in this book.

Summary

This chapter has worked with the first solution that needs to be manually implemented using CloudFormation. We walked through the process of deploying said CloudFormation template. Then, we covered how to complete the solution's implementation by interfacing it with Connect and the contact flows. Finally, we discussed how you might modify the solution to better fit into your call center.

This solution was the first that we will implement via CloudFormation. The second will be call analytics, which also deploys several serverless technologies. We will cover this implementation in the next chapter.

11
Implementing Call Analytics

Connect comes with built-in analytics capabilities. You can watch your call center in real time, allowing you to see how many callers are in the queue and how many agents are active. You also can view historical metrics, giving you an insight into how your call center was operating in the past.

Unfortunately, the reports that are available in the default system are a bit clumsy, and you can't customize them to your needs. You can change some of the parameters. However, for the most part, you are limited. Thankfully, Amazon has released a solution that enhances the capability of the reporting for Connect. The solution is similar in deployment to the voicemail solution.

In this chapter, we will walk through the deployment of the reporting solution and connect it to your Amazon Connect instance. We will also cover how to customize the reporting to meet your needs in the QuickSight tool. In this chapter, we will cover the following topics:

- Understanding the data flow
- Configuring the CloudFormation template
- Capturing an **Amazon Resource Name** (**ARN**) from a voicemail
- Deploying the CloudFormation template

- Setting up S3 access
- Establishing analysis
- Dashboarding with QuickSight

Understanding the data flow

Connect records everything that happens in the instance in records called **Contact Trace Records (CTRs)**. These records can be used to create reports on what has happened in your Connect instance. QuickSight can't use these reports natively. They must first be saved somewhere and processed. To do this, the solution connects your instance to S3 via Kinesis. From there, Glue and Athena are used to process the data to make it consumable for QuickSight.

The diagram in *Figure 11.1* details the pieces that make the whole process work. Thankfully, all of these components will be deployed for you using the template. Most of the work that needs to be done is within QuickSight, where you will create dashboards to monitor your call center:

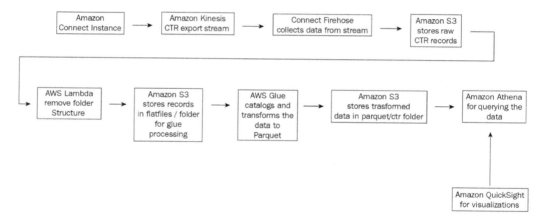

Figure 11.1 – Reporting workflow

Now that we have a basic understanding of how the selection works, let's move on to deploying it via CloudFormation.

Configuring the CloudFormation Template

AWS provides a CloudFormation template that deploys the solution for you. Unfortunately, most of the solutions from AWS are designed to stand by themselves. They don't interoperate when you have more than one deployed. We are in this situation at this point because we have already deployed the voicemail solution. The voicemail and the analytics solutions overlap each other regarding this deployment. Connect can only support one Kinesis stream, and each solution deploys its own.

To resolve this conflict, we will need to modify the template used to deploy the analytics solution. We need to adjust the template to piggyback off of the existing Kinesis stream that was deployed. To get started, download the template from `https://s3.amazonaws.com/lfcarocomdemo/glueconnect/glueconnectKinesis.yaml` and open it in your favorite editor.

The first item that we want to change is the parameter at the beginning of the file. The original template uses the parameter to set the name of the Kinesis stream. In our case, we already have one, so we need to change this parameter to be the **Amazon Resource Name** (**ARN**) of the existing stream. We will discover what this ARN is in the next section. Change the `KinesisStreamName` parameters to match what is shown in *Figure 11.2*, converting it to an ARN:

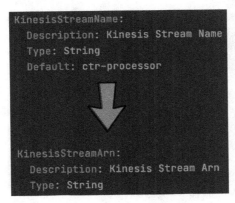

Figure 11.2 – Changing the name to an ARN

The next thing that needs to be modified in the template is to delete the Kinesis stream. Locate the resource in the template called `connectKinesisStream` and remove it from the file entirely. This resource is not required for our deployment. For reference, it looks like *Figure 11.3*:

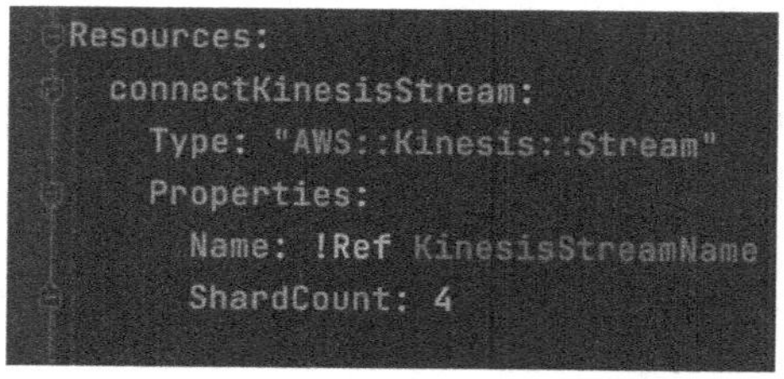

```
Resources:
  connectKinesisStream:
    Type: "AWS::Kinesis::Stream"
    Properties:
      Name: !Ref KinesisStreamName
      ShardCount: 4
```

Figure 11.3 – Deleting the stream

Since we have deleted the stream, a few sections of the template will now error out. They expect to have this resource in the file and therefore cannot access the data for it anymore. We will have to change the existing setting to the new ARN parameter that we created as the first step for all of these resources.

Look for `FirehoseStream` in the template file and locate the `KinesisStreamARN` setting. Instead of looking up the attribute for the setting, we need to change this to a reference. Change this setting to `!Ref KinesisStreamArn`. *Figure 11.4* demonstrates how the file should change:

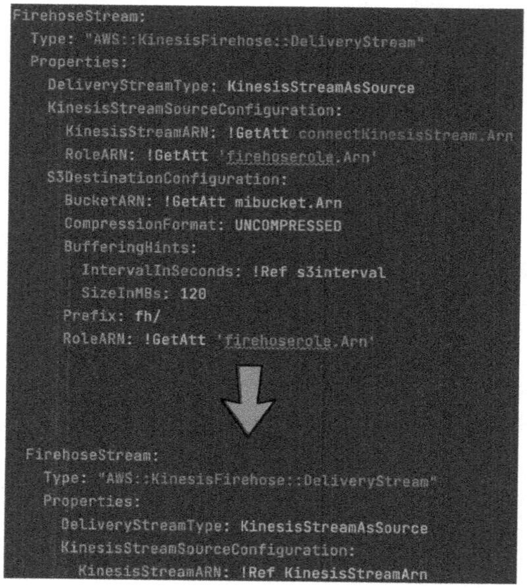

```
FirehoseStream:
  Type: "AWS::KinesisFirehose::DeliveryStream"
  Properties:
    DeliveryStreamType: KinesisStreamAsSource
    KinesisStreamSourceConfiguration:
      KinesisStreamARN: !GetAtt connectKinesisStream.Arn
      RoleARN: !GetAtt 'firehoserole.Arn'
    S3DestinationConfiguration:
      BucketARN: !GetAtt mibucket.Arn
      CompressionFormat: UNCOMPRESSED
      BufferingHints:
        IntervalInSeconds: !Ref s3interval
        SizeInMBs: 120
      Prefix: fh/
      RoleARN: !GetAtt 'firehoserole.Arn'



FirehoseStream:
  Type: "AWS::KinesisFirehose::DeliveryStream"
  Properties:
    DeliveryStreamType: KinesisStreamAsSource
    KinesisStreamSourceConfiguration:
      KinesisStreamARN: !Ref KinesisStreamArn
```

Figure 11.4 – Repairing the firehose

The second item that we need to reconfigure to remove the Kinesis resources is the IAM policy. Locate the `KinesisReaderPolicy` resource in the file. Look for the `Resource` setting and again change this to `!Ref KinesisStreamArn`. *Figure 11.5* shows how your file should change:

```
KinesisReaderPolicy:
  Type: 'AWS::IAM::ManagedPolicy'
  Properties:
    Description: Policy for writing to connect bucket
    Path: /
    PolicyDocument:
      Version: 2012-10-17
      Statement:
      - Action:
        - kinesis:Get*
        - kinesis:DescribeStream
        Resource: !GetAtt 'connectKinesisStream.Arn'
        Effect: Allow
```

```
KinesisReaderPolicy:
  Type: 'AWS::IAM::ManagedPolicy'
  Properties:
    Description: Policy for writing to connect bucket
    Path: /
    PolicyDocument:
      Version: 2012-10-17
      Statement:
      - Action:
        - kinesis:Get*
        - kinesis:DescribeStream
        Resource: !Ref KinesisStreamArn
        Effect: Allow
```

Figure 11.5 – Repairing the IAM policy

CloudFormation allows for the output of data, such as ARNs or IP addresses, that can be used later by other templates or accessed by the API. The solution template includes one of these outputs. However, this is no longer required. Locate the `Outputs` section in the template and delete it. You can reference *Figure 11.6* to check what you should delete:

```
Outputs:
  streamname:
    Description: Stream to send connect data
    Value: !Ref connectKinesisStream
```

Figure 11.6 – Deleting outputs

One of the last things we want to change is the security settings for the S3 buckets. The bucket configuration that comes with the solution doesn't prevent public access. For this solution, public access is not required so it's best to turn it off to avoid accidental exposure. Locate the S3 bucket definition in the file. It's called `mibucket`. You can see what this entire definition should look like in *Figure 11.7*:

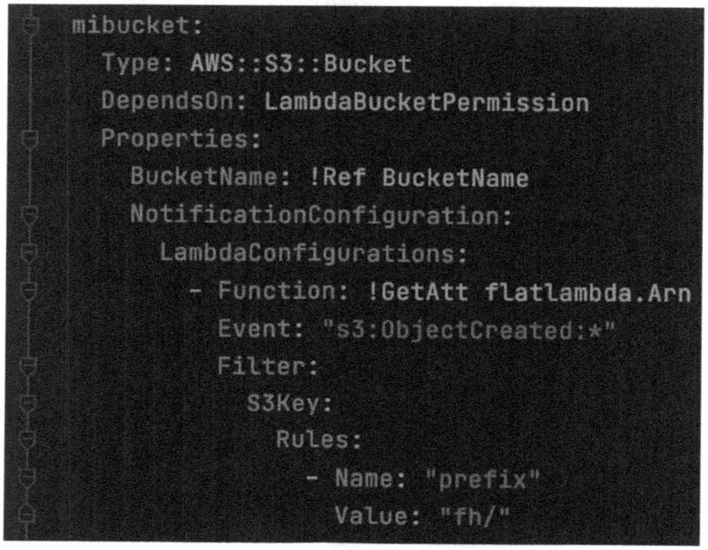

```
mibucket:
  Type: AWS::S3::Bucket
  DependsOn: LambdaBucketPermission
  Properties:
    BucketName: !Ref BucketName
    NotificationConfiguration:
      LambdaConfigurations:
        - Function: !GetAtt flatlambda.Arn
          Event: "s3:ObjectCreated:*"
          Filter:
            S3Key:
              Rules:
                - Name: "prefix"
                  Value: "fh/"
```

Figure 11.7 – Original S3 bucket

We want to add the settings that will prevent the bucket from ever having public access. To do this, append the following snippet of code under the `Properties` section of the bucket definition. To align it under `NotificationConfiguration`, spacing is essential in the YAML format used for this template:

```
<code>
PublicAccessBlockConfiguration:
    BlockPublicAcls: TRUE
    BlockPublicPolicy: TRUE
    IgnorePublicAcls: TRUE
    RestrictPublicBuckets: TRUE
</code>
```

When you are done, your template should mimic *Figure 11.8*:

```
mibucket:
  Type: AWS::S3::Bucket
  DependsOn: LambdaBucketPermission
  Properties:
    BucketName: !Ref BucketName
    NotificationConfiguration:
      LambdaConfigurations:
        - Function: !GetAtt flatlambda.Arn
          Event: "s3:ObjectCreated:*"
          Filter:
            S3Key:
              Rules:
                - Name: "prefix"
                  Value: "fh/"
    PublicAccessBlockConfiguration:
      BlockPublicAcls: TRUE
      BlockPublicPolicy: TRUE
      IgnorePublicAcls: TRUE
      RestrictPublicBuckets: TRUE
```

Figure 11.8 – Modified S3 bucket

With all of these settings properly configured, we are ready to begin the deployment process. However, before we can do that, we need to capture the ARN of the Kinesis stream deployed as part of the voicemail solution. We cover this in the next section.

Capturing the ARN from a voicemail

To retrieve the ARN, we need to access the stream through the AWS console via the Kinesis section:

1. Access the AWS console and look for **Kinesis**. **Kinesis** is located under the **Analytics** section (*Figure 11.9*):

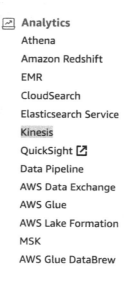

Figure 11.9 – Kinesis

2. When you access the Kinesis console, you will see the screen shown in *Figure 11.10*. You will need to click on the number under the **Data Streams** section:

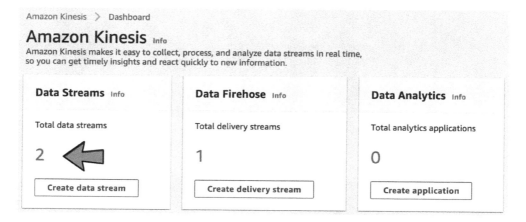

Figure 11.10 – Greeting screen

3. When you click on the number under **Data Streams**, you will be prompted with a new screen that shows all of the streams that have been created. We need the one that starts with CONNECT-VOICEMAIL, which is the name of the stack that we deployed for the voicemail solution (*Figure 11.11*).

    Click on the name in the leftmost field to access the details for the stream:

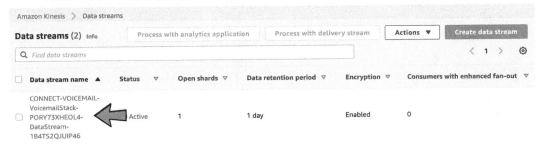

Figure 11.11 – Voicemail stream

4. A screen showing the details of this stream will appear. This is where we can get the location of the ARN for this stream. Click the icon of two squares (*Figure 11.12*) in front of the ARN to copy it. It makes sense to save this ARN in a text file or some other location for access later:

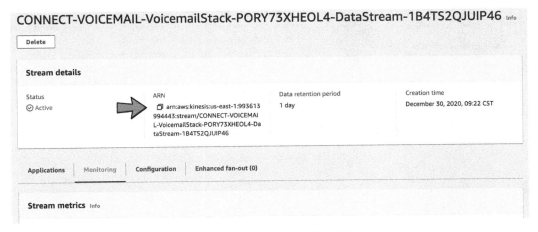

Figure 11.12 – Copying the ARN

We now have all of the information and CloudFormation changes necessary, and we can finally deploy the newly modified template.

Deploying the CloudFormation template

The deployment of the analytics solution will be similar to the deployment we did for the voicemail solution. We will want to deploy a new stack in CloudFormation that will deploy new resources. To begin the process, enter into the CloudFormation console:

1. Click on the **Create stack** button in the upper-left corner of the screen. You can reference *Figure 11.13* for a refresher:

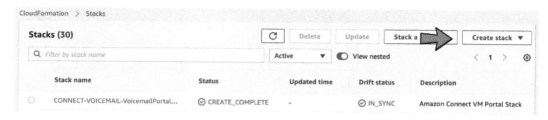

Figure 11.13 – Creating a stack

2. Since we don't have any resources already deployed that we want to import, we need to choose the **With new resources (standard)** menu item (*Figure 11.14*):

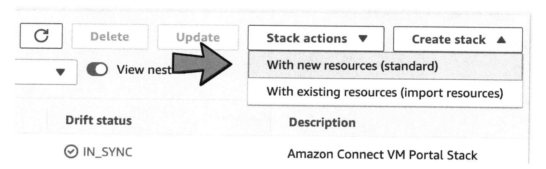

Figure 11.14 – New resources

3. When we get to the **Create stack** screen, we want to upload a template file. Choose the file that you modified to upload. Make sure not to choose the original file downloaded from AWS. It won't work with our deployment of Connect. Before you click the **Next** button, validate that your settings match *Figure 11.15*:

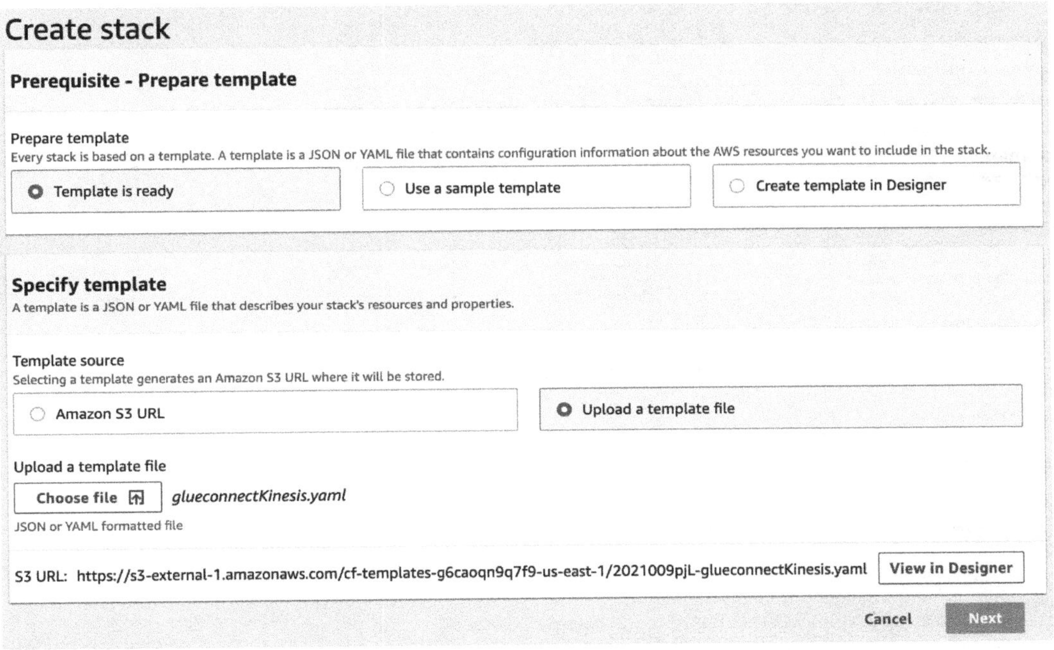

Create stack

Prerequisite - Prepare template

Prepare template
Every stack is based on a template. A template is a JSON or YAML file that contains configuration information about the AWS resources you want to include in the stack.

| ● Template is ready | ○ Use a sample template | ○ Create template in Designer |

Specify template
A template is a JSON or YAML file that describes your stack's resources and properties.

Template source
Selecting a template generates an Amazon S3 URL where it will be stored.

| ○ Amazon S3 URL | ● Upload a template file |

Upload a template file

| Choose file 🔼   *glueconnectKinesis.yaml* |

JSON or YAML formatted file

S3 URL: https://s3-external-1.amazonaws.com/cf-templates-g6caoqn9q7f9-us-east-1/2021009pjL-glueconnectKinesis.yaml | View in Designer |

Cancel   **Next**

Figure 11.15 – Creating a stack

4. The next screen displays the parameters that are needed for our modified template. I've called my stack CONNECT-ANALYTICS. You can choose any bucket name that you want, but remember that S3 bucket names need to be unique across the entire infrastructure of AWS. Not just in your account, but across all accounts. The final item that needs to be entered is the ARN of the stream that we looked up earlier (*Figure 11.16*).

The rest of the settings don't need to be changed. These settings are optional, and if you wish to change them, you can update the stack later to adjust them. When you are happy with the settings, click the **Next** button:

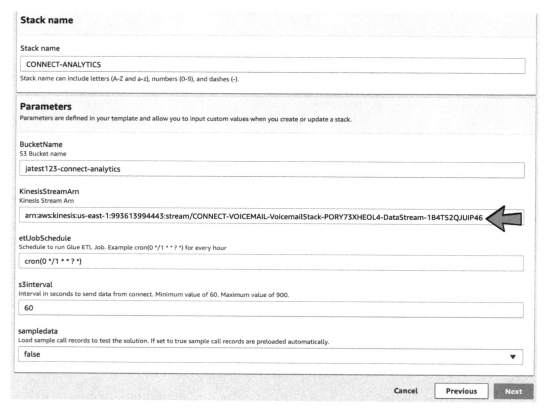

Figure 11.16 – Stack options

5.   As before, there are no changes required on the **Advanced options** page of the stack deployment. Click the **Next** button to continue:

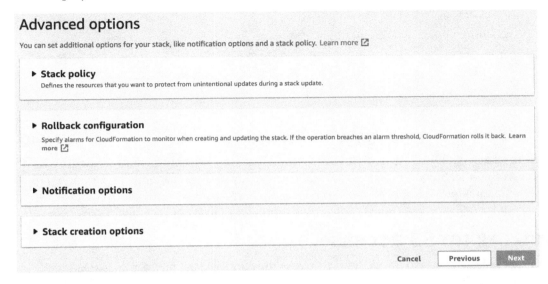

Figure 11.17 – Advanced options

6.   On the final CloudFormation screen, we need to acknowledge some special capabilities required to deploy the stack properly. Scroll to the bottom of the page and check the box to acknowledge that the stack might deploy IAM resources. After you check the box, click on **Create stack** to deploy the solution:

▶ Quick-create link
Capabilities

ⓘ **The following resource(s) require capabilities: [AWS::IAM::ManagedPolicy]**

This template contains Identity and Access Management (IAM) resources that might provide entities access to make changes to your AWS account. Check that you want to create each of these resources and that they have the minimum required permissions.   Learn more

☑ **I acknowledge that AWS CloudFormation might create IAM resources.**

Cancel   Previous   Create change set   Create stack

Figure 11.18 – Creating a stack

7.　When the stack is complete, you will see it entered in the deployed stacks list along with the voicemail stack we deployed earlier (*Figure 11.19*):

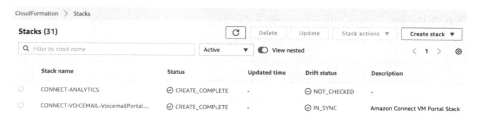

Figure 11.19 – Completed stack

With the stack deployed, we can move onto configuration. We only have to configure S3 access from QuickSight. This access control isn't deployed from the template and needs to be done manually. We will cover how to set this up in the next section.

Setting up S3 access

To configure the access to S3, we need to access the controls via QuickSight, instead of through S3. This configuration is a little bit different than most in AWS. You might think that you need to create an S3 bucket policy. However, this is not the case. I suspect that it's because of how the QuickSight service is deployed within AWS itself:

1.　To begin, find **QuickSight** in the AWS console. **QuickSight** is located in the **Analytics** section of the services list. *Figure 11.20* highlights where **QuickSight** is located:

Figure 11.20 – Accessing QuickSight

2. Once you access the QuickSight console, we need to locate the admin menu. The admin menu is located in the upper-right corner of the screen. You can use *Figure 11.21* to assist you in finding it:

Figure 11.21 – QuickSight admin menu

3. When you click on the menu, a drop-down menu will appear with several options to choose from. We want to select **Manage QuickSight** (*Figure 11.22*). This option will allow us to configure access to S3:

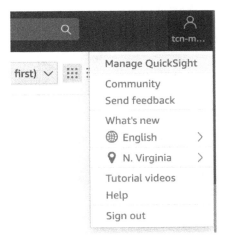

Figure 11.22 – Managing QuickSight

4. When you click on **Manage QuickSight**, a new screen will appear with a menu on the left-hand side. In this left-hand menu, we want to select **Security & permissions** (*Figure 11.23*):

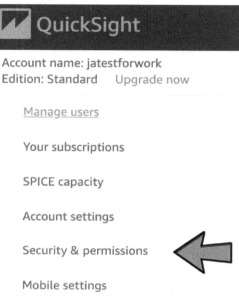

Figure 11.23 – Security & permissions

5. A new screen will appear with several options. The option that we are looking for is **QuickSight access to AWS services**. At this point, you want to click the **Add or remove** button to progress to the next step, as seen in *Figure 11.24*:

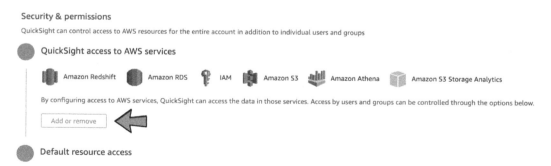

Figure 11.24 – Security screen

6. We are concerned with granting S3 access. The rest of the options should be set and won't need to be changed. S3 should already be checked, so there is nothing to do there. But we will need to drill down and tell QuickSight what buckets it should have access to. To do this, click on the **Details** link shown in *Figure 11.25*:

Figure 11.25 – S3 access

7. The menu will expand and offer you a new button to click. Click on the **Select S3 buckets** button as highlighted in *Figure 11.26*:

Figure 11.26 – Selecting buckets

8. Find the name of the bucket that you entered into the CloudFormation stack when you deployed it. In my case, my bucket was called `jatest123-connect-analytics`. Check the box on the left-hand side of the screen next to your bucket to grant access (*Figure 11.27*). You don't need to grant write access to the bucket:

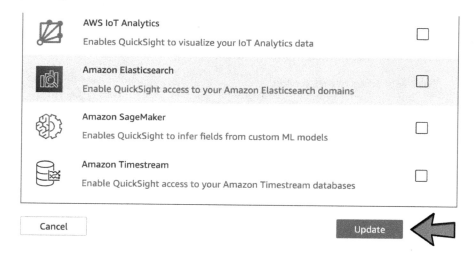

Select Amazon S3 buckets   ×

| S3 Buckets Linked To QuickSight Account | S3 Buckets You Can Access Across AWS |

Select the buckets that you want QuickSight to be able to access.

Selected buckets have read only permissions by default. However, you must give write permissions for Athena Workgroup feature.

☑ Select all

S3 Bucket	Write permission for Athena Workgroup
☑ jatest123-connect-analytics	☐

Figure 11.27 – Selecting buckets

9. When you have your bucket settings complete, scroll to the end of the screen and click the **Update** button, as shown in *Figure 11.28*, to save the access settings for QuickSight:

	AWS IoT Analytics Enables QuickSight to visualize your IoT Analytics data	☐
	Amazon Elasticsearch Enable QuickSight access to your Amazon Elasticsearch domains	☐
	Amazon SageMaker Enables QuickSight to infer fields from custom ML models	☐
	Amazon Timestream Enable QuickSight access to your Amazon Timestream databases	☐

Cancel   Update   ⇐

Figure 11.28 – Updating the settings

Congratulations, you have now configured the S3 access. QuickSight will now be able to load the data that has been processed by Glue and made into a format that is readable by Athena. The next step in our deployment process is to connect Athena to QuickSight so that the data can be visualized.

Establishing analysis

Configuring QuickSight to access the data is straightforward. In the next few steps, we will configure this connectivity:

1. From the QuickSight main screen, locate the **New analysis** button in the upper-left corner of the screen. You can look at *Figure 11.29* to identify its location:

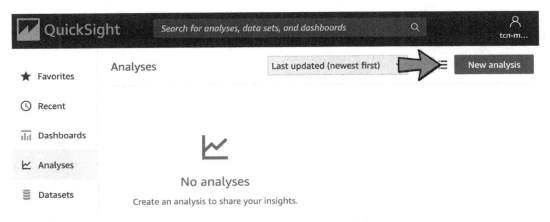

Figure 11.29 – Creating a new analysis

2. A new screen will appear, which should currently be blank unless you have existing configurations deployed in QuickSight. To connect our dataset, click on the **New dataset** button on the screen's upper left-hand side (*Figure 11.30*):

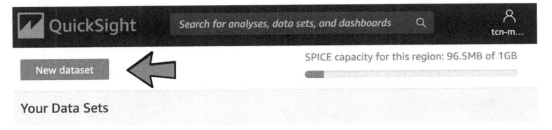

Figure 11.30 – New dataset

3. We are looking for Athena in the list of services that are available for connection. We allowed access to S3, but we want to connect QuickSight to Athena. Locate **Athena** in the list of services. It should look like *Figure 11.31*:

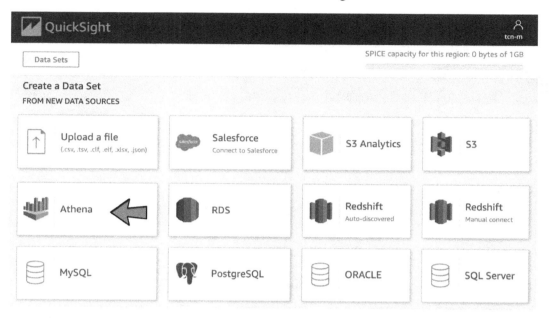

Figure 11.31 – Athena

4. Once you click Athena, a new popup will appear, as shown in *Figure 11.32*. Enter a name for the data source. I've called mine `Connect-CTR`. When you are done, click on the **Create data source** button to progress to the next step:

Figure 11.32 – Creating a data source

5. The next popup will display, asking you to choose a table from the catalog. My catalog is called `AwsDataCatalog`. The database that we are looking for will match the stack name that you gave when you deployed the solution. In my case, I used `connect-analytics`, so my database is called `connect-analytics_db`. Find the database that matches your stack name and select it. The table that we need is called **ctr**. Select the radio button next to that table. When you are done, your screen should look like *Figure 11.33*. When you are done, click the **Select** button to progress to the next step:

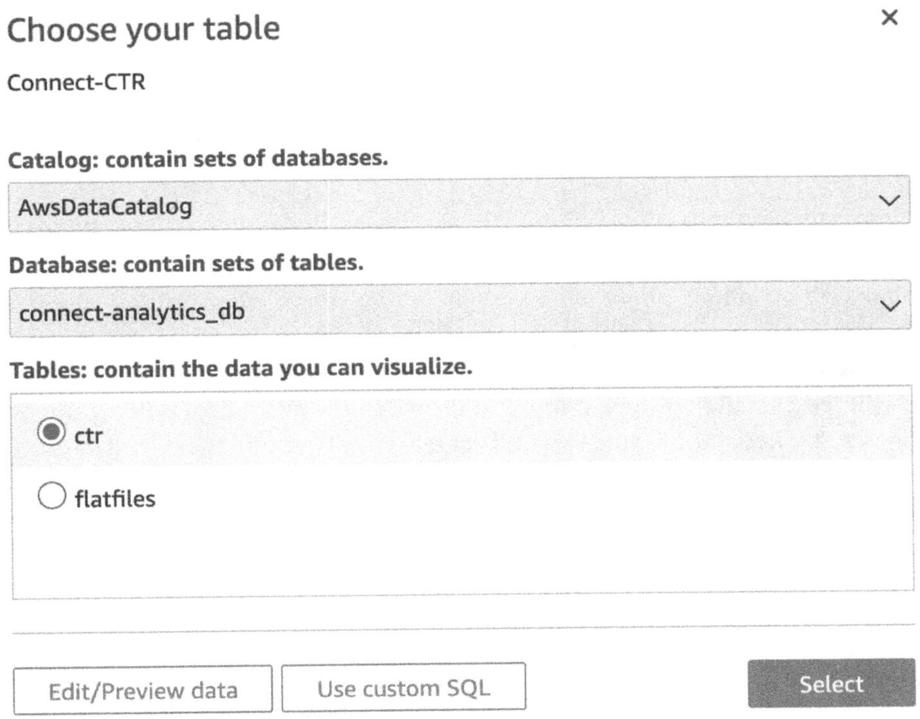

Choose your table   ✕

Connect-CTR

Catalog: contain sets of databases.

AwsDataCatalog   ⌄

Database: contain sets of tables.

connect-analytics_db   ⌄

Tables: contain the data you can visualize.

◉ ctr

◯ flatfiles

Edit/Preview data   Use custom SQL   Select

Figure 11.33 – Choosing a table

6. On the next screen, there are no changes that need to be made. To complete the setup, click the **Visualize** button to move forward (*Figure 11.34*):

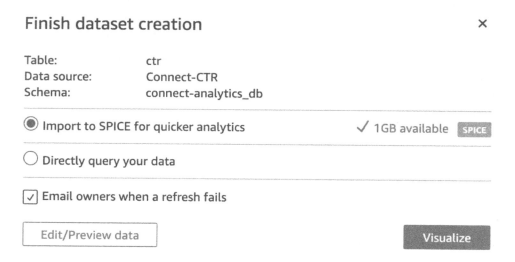

Figure 11.34 – Finishing a dataset

7. QuickSight will begin importing your data. If you have everything set up properly, you will see a small pop-up window that displays how much data is being imported, as shown in *Figure 11.35*. Since my call center isn't active and the only data available is a few test calls after the solution's deployment, I didn't have any rows imported. If your call center is live or under active testing, you will see significantly more rows imported:

Figure 11.35 – Completed

Now that the database has been imported, the final piece is actually to use the solution. We do this by creating dashboards and visualizations. This book isn't about QuickSight, so we won't go into detail on this subject. We will, however, quickly demonstrate how the process works so you can at least get started.

Dashboarding with QuickSight

We are going to create a quick visualization that shows the number of calls per agent and queue. To do this, we need to locate the necessary fields on the left-hand side **Fields list** menu (*Figure 11.36*). We are first looking for the agent.username field. This field will show how many calls have been taken per agent. To add this to the visualization, follow these steps:

1. Drag this field name to the visualization:

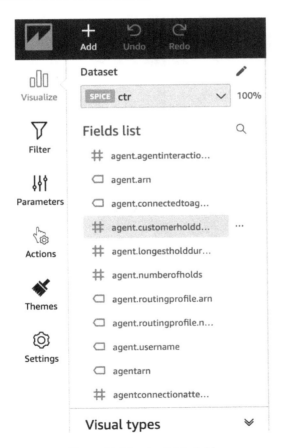

Figure 11.36 – Available fields

2. It will scan the data and automatically choose the best way to display the data. In this case, it's a bar graph, as shown in *Figure 11.37*:

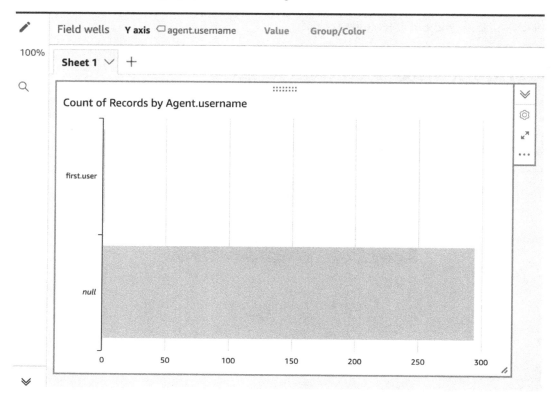

Figure 11.37 – Agent list

3. We only have one dimension at this stage. We also want to include a grouping. It would be more useful to see from which queue callers were taking calls. To do this, locate the `queue.name` field in the **Fields list** menu on the left (*Figure 11.38*). Drag this field to the visualization:

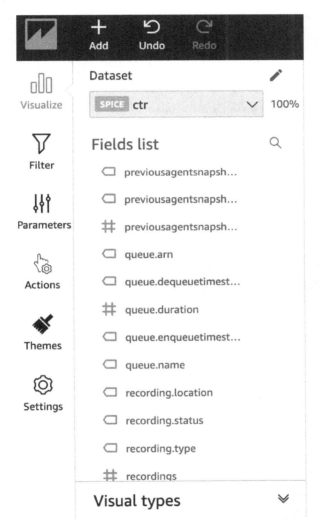

Figure 11.38 – Queue

4. QuickSight will automatically address the best way to display the data when you do this. In this case, it will group the users and the queues that they take calls from. I don't have a lot of data available, so my visualization (*Figure 11.39*) details how many calls my user `first.user` took:

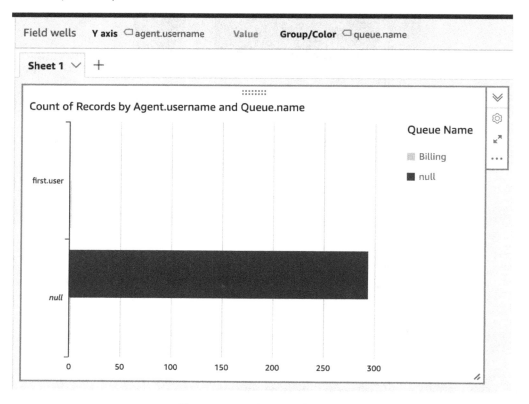

Figure 11.39 – Agent and queue

Looking at the visualization in *Figure 11.39*, you can see that my `first.user` agent took a small number of calls from the billing queue. This visualization is just a tiny sample of the capabilities of QuickSight and the data contained within the Connect CTR records.

The requirements for reporting are vast, and specific to what your stakeholders are looking for. I would suggest that you review all of the available fields in the CTR records to be aware of the potential reporting that can be used. This study will better prepare you when communicating to stakeholders around reporting.

I would also recommend studying QuickSight for yourself, to better understand of how to create dashboards and visualizations for your stakeholders. There is too much to cover in a few short pages in this book.

Summary

This chapter helped you understand how CTR records are output from the Connect instance and how, using various AWS services, these records can be processed and made consumable by QuickSight.

We started by modifying CloudFormation to meet our specific requirements before we deployed the solution. We also improved the security stance as a byproduct. From there, we granted access to S3 and, finally, created a visualization to test the overall solution.

Our call center is starting to take shape at this point. We have a lot of functionality, such as the analytics we deployed in this chapter, available to us that we wouldn't have if we were using a conventional on-premises hardware solution. In the next chapter, we want to build further upon our implementation with the advanced capabilities for sentiment analysis offered by Contact Lens.

12
Implementing Contact Lens

Contact Lens is a service that uses existing **Amazon Web Services** (**AWS**) services to provide **artificial intelligence** (**AI**) sentiment analysis and transcription of your call center's calls. Contact Lens uses the Transcribe and Comprehend services to accomplish this. The Transcribe service is used first, to convert what people are saying on the phone into text that can be more readily processed. From there, Comprehend is used to review that text and determine how the people on the phone feel.

Thankfully, Contact Lens is a solution that is integrated with Amazon Connect. So, unlike the voicemail and analytics solutions, we won't have to deploy it; we will have to just activate it. In this chapter, we will walk through the activation and user permissions needed to view the Contact Lens output. We will cover the following topics in detail:

- Enabling Contact Lens
- Assigning user permissions
- Understanding Contact Lens' capabilities
- Creating Contact Lens rules

Enabling Contact Lens

To enable Contact Lens, we need to perform two separate configuration options, the first of which is to enable Contact Lens on the instance itself. To do this, you will need to log in to the AWS management console and access the console for Amazon Connect. Follow these steps to enable Contact Lens:

1. When you reach the Connect console, you will need to access the menu on the screen's left-hand side to access the **Analytics tools** settings. You can see this option on the menu in the following screenshot:

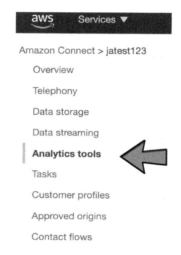

Figure 12.1 – Instance settings

2. When you select this option, the screen's right-hand side will update with the details listed in the following screenshot. To enable Contact Lens on the instance, we need to check the box highlighted here and click **Save**:

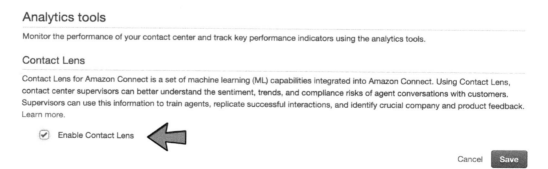

Figure 12.2 – Analytics tools

3. Once you complete this configuration, the instance is now ready to process calls and analyze them.

However, at this time, Contact Lens doesn't know which calls we want to process. By default, **recording** and **sentiment analysis** aren't enabled. If you recall, we previously talked about controlling call recording and some other features by department. This strategy allows us to determine which departments we will use sentiment analysis for. For our demonstration, let's configure the **Billing** department to perform this analysis.

To get started, we need to modify the contact flow for the billing department. Edit the billing department contact flow using the process we covered in *Chapter 6, Contact Flow Creation*. Once you have the **editing** screen up, we need to locate the **Set recording and analytics behavior** component. Your flow should look something like the one shown in the following screenshot. When you locate the component, click on the heading to edit it:

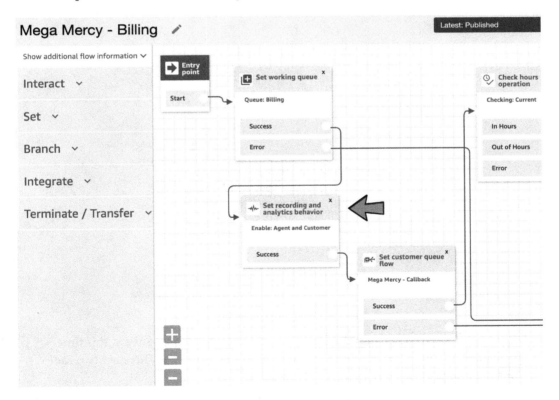

Figure 12.3 – Billing contact flow

4. When you edit your component, you will see at the bottom of the **Settings** popup that there is a checkbox to enable Contact Lens, as illustrated in the following screenshot. Check this box to activate Contact Lens:

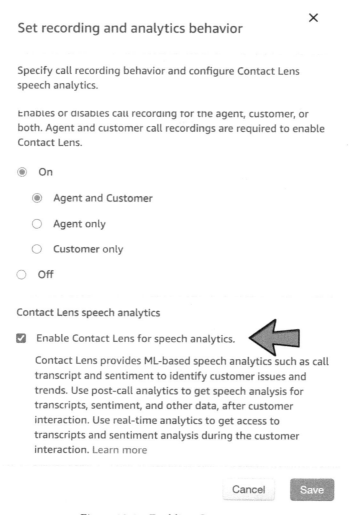

Figure 12.4 – Enabling Contact Lens

5. We aren't done conjuring up this component yet, so don't click **Save** at this time. Instead, scroll down to see additional settings available to you. There are two radio button options available for Contact Lens (*Figure 12.5*).

In December 2020, AWS announced the ability to use Contact Lens in real time versus post-call. Before this release, you were only able to analyze calls after a call had been completed. Since then, an option has been added to allow you to decide if you want real-time or standard post-call processing. Since post-call processing is more accurate, we are going to move forward with that option, as illustrated in the following screenshot:

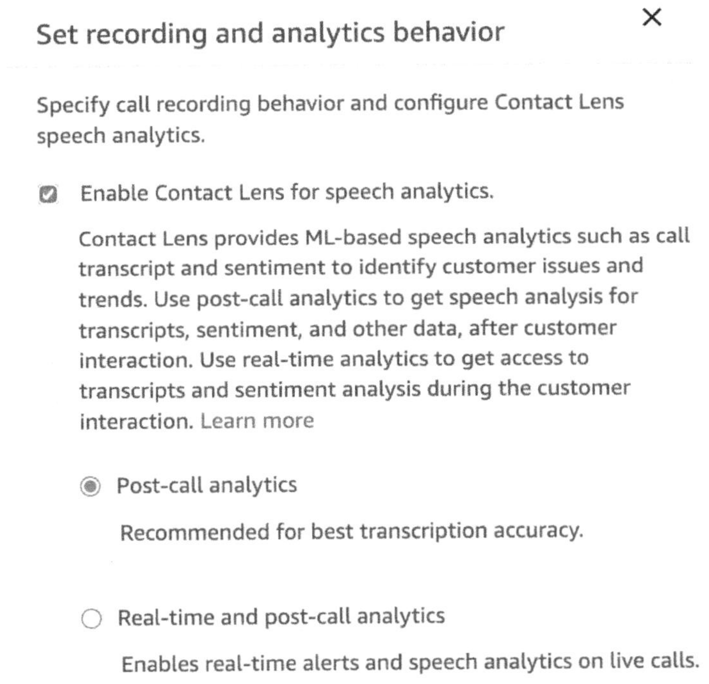

Set recording and analytics behavior   ✕

Specify call recording behavior and configure Contact Lens speech analytics.

☑ Enable Contact Lens for speech analytics.

Contact Lens provides ML-based speech analytics such as call transcript and sentiment to identify customer issues and trends. Use post-call analytics to get speech analysis for transcripts, sentiment, and other data, after customer interaction. Use real-time analytics to get access to transcripts and sentiment analysis during the customer interaction. Learn more

◉ Post-call analytics

Recommended for best transcription accuracy.

○ Real-time and post-call analytics

Enables real-time alerts and speech analytics on live calls.

Figure 12.5 – More Contact Lens settings

6. Real-time analytics allows Contact Lens to interpret your callers' sentiment as a call occurs and will display pertinent information on the real-time metrics screen for agents. If a caller is unhappy, that sentiment will be displayed on that screen. With the notification, your managers can listen in and coach the agent on how to resolve the issue with the customer.

> **Tip**
> At the time of this chapter's writing, real-time analysis has only been available for 1 month. As with most new capabilities from AWS, or any vendor, I would only use real-time analysis for non-production workloads until it has been available for at least 6 months.

There are more settings available for Contact Lens. Continue scrolling down to view the rest of the settings, which are displayed in the following screenshot:

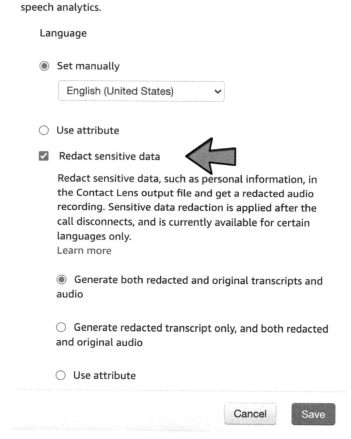

Figure 12.6 – Final settings

7. With these settings, you can set the language, which we will leave set to **English (United States)** at this time. You will also see in the preceding screenshot that there is a **Redact sensitive data** checkbox. I would recommend always turning this on. Redaction removes items such as name, address, credit card numbers, and so on. Selecting the **Generate both redacted and original transcripts and audio** option will provide your company with the greatest level of protection.

> **Important note**
> It's important to know that redaction makes a best effort to redact sensitive information, but it doesn't guarantee that all sensitive information will be removed.

When you have completed selecting the options, you can now click the **Save** button to commit the changes. We are now done modifying the contact flow. You can publish it using the **Publish** button on the screen's upper right, as illustrated in the following screenshot:

Figure 12.7 – Publish flow

After you publish the flow, I would wait a few minutes and log in to the Connect console as a test user. Make a call to your call center and request the billing department, and simulate a customer call. We will look at the output from Contact Lens later in the chapter, but it takes a few minutes for Contact Lens to process the call. Making your test call now will ensure that everything is ready to review later.

Assigning user permissions

Before we can see the Contact Lens output, we need to allow administrators and managers to access it. By default, the `Admin` and `CallCenterManager` security groups have access to Contact Lens data. If you are using these groups then no changes are necessary. If you have created your own security profiles, you need to ensure that the settings are correct for them to view Contact Lens data.

Access the security profiles via the left-hand menu, as we did before in *Chapter 5, Base Connect Implementation*. Edit the security profile that you wish to have Contact Lens capabilities. You will be presented with the following screen. Select the dropdown for **Metrics and Quality**, as illustrated here:

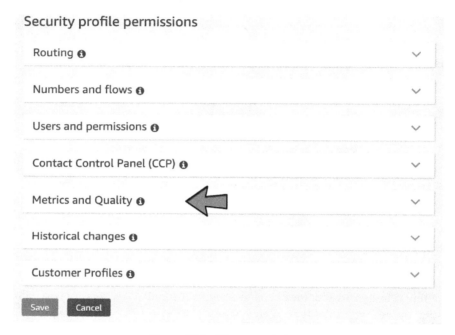

Figure 12.8 – User permissions

When this screen expands, you will be presented with all of the security settings available, as shown in *Figure 12.9*. There are three primary settings to be concerned with, as follows:

- **Contact Lens - speech analytics**
- **Recorded conversations (redacted)**
- **Recorded conversations (unredacted)**

Select the necessary options to enable access to give the relevant users Contact Lens capabilities. I would not recommend giving access to unredacted conversations. If you followed my advice about redaction previously, you won't have to worry about unredacted files; however, unchecking the **Recorded conversations (unredacted)** option on this screen adds another layer of protection.

The individual settings are shown here:

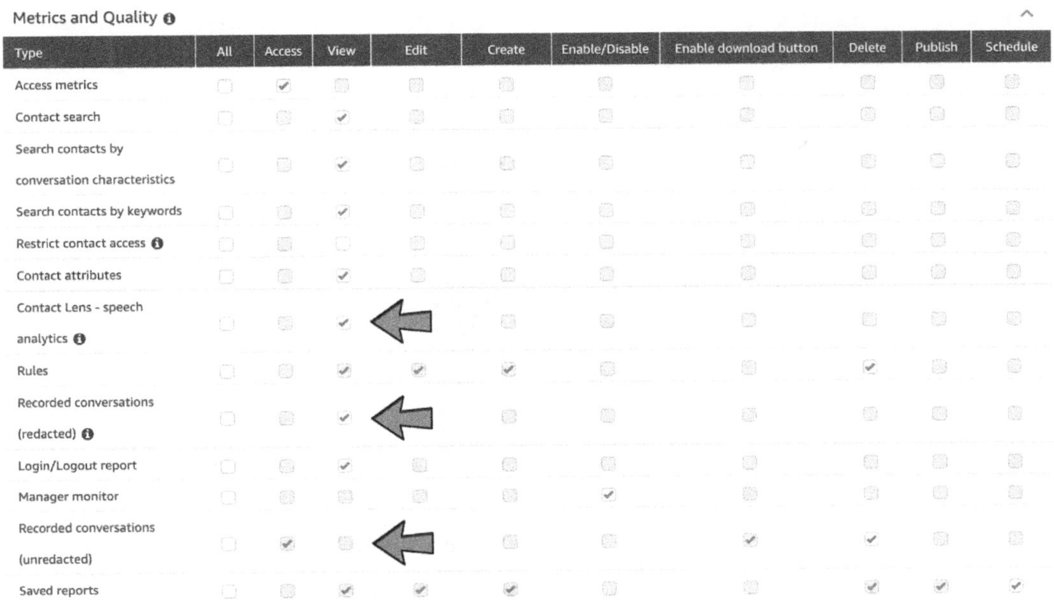

Metrics and Quality ❶

Type	All	Access	View	Edit	Create	Enable/Disable	Enable download button	Delete	Publish	Schedule
Access metrics		✓								
Contact search			✓							
Search contacts by conversation characteristics			✓							
Search contacts by keywords			✓							
Restrict contact access ❶										
Contact attributes			✓							
Contact Lens - speech analytics ❶			✓							
Rules			✓	✓	✓			✓		
Recorded conversations (redacted) ❶			✓							
Login/Logout report			✓							
Manager monitor						✓				
Recorded conversations (unredacted)		✓					✓	✓		
Saved reports			✓	✓	✓			✓	✓	✓

Figure 12.9 – Individual settings

When you are done with the changes, click **Save** to commit the settings. With all of the settings complete and your test call made and processed, it's now time to take a look at the capabilities of Contact Lens.

Understanding Contact Lens' capabilities

When Contact Lens processes data, it shows up in the **Contact search** portion of the **Connect management** interface.

The **Contact search** section is available in the left-hand menu, under **Metrics and quality**. You can see how to access **Contact search** in the following screenshot:

Figure 12.10 – Accessing Contact search

When you select this menu option, you will be presented with a screen that offers many options to limit your search. There are several criteria, but we are primarily concerned with the date fields. Since you just made your test call, make sure that the date fields are identified, as illustrated in the following screenshot:

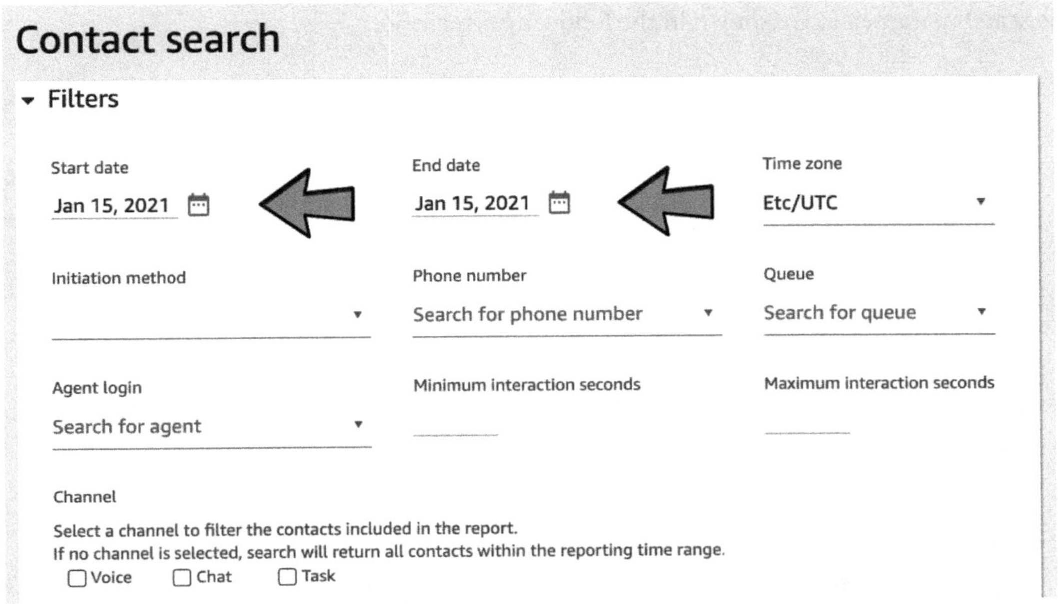

Figure 12.11 – Contact search

If you scroll down, you will see additional parameters. There is a section called **Sentiment score** (*Figure 12.12*). You can use these search criteria to narrow your findings when your call center is live—for instance, you could filter for calls where callers are upset to identify potentially problematic agent handling or product dislikes. Alternatively, you might want to find out when callers were unhappy at the beginning of the call but became happier by the end. These settings offer the granularity level required to help make your managers a force to be reckoned with, improving your business's caller satisfaction.

The search parameters are shown in the following screenshot:

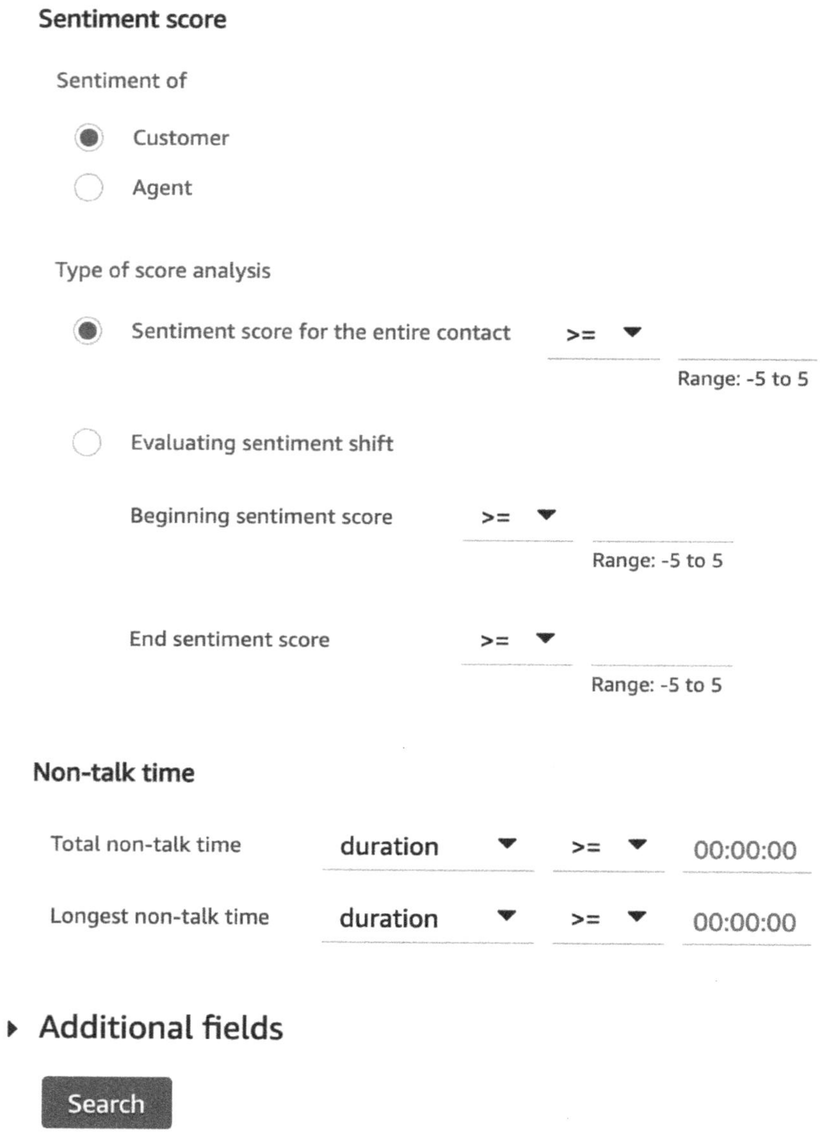

Sentiment score

Sentiment of

- ⦿ Customer
- ○ Agent

Type of score analysis

- ⦿ Sentiment score for the entire contact   >= ▼

  Range: -5 to 5

- ○ Evaluating sentiment shift

  Beginning sentiment score   >= ▼

  Range: -5 to 5

  End sentiment score   >= ▼

  Range: -5 to 5

Non-talk time

| Total non-talk time | duration ▼ | >= ▼ | 00:00:00 |
| Longest non-talk time | duration ▼ | >= ▼ | 00:00:00 |

▸ **Additional fields**

Search

Figure 12.12 – More search parameters

For now, just leave all the settings at their default setting and click the **Search** button. This action will bring up the test call that you made earlier. Your call should appear at the bottom of the screen in a list that looks like the one shown in *Figure 12.13*.

To access the Contact Lens information, click on your call using the **unique identifier (UID)** found in the first column, as illustrated here:

Figure 12.13 – Found contacts

When you select your call, you will be presented with a screen that looks like the one shown in *Figure 12.14*. You can see the call's sentiment on this screen and how much time was spent with no talk time. As you can see here, in my test call my sentiment was pretty much neutral, without many changes. Depending on what you said, your call might not have the same results:

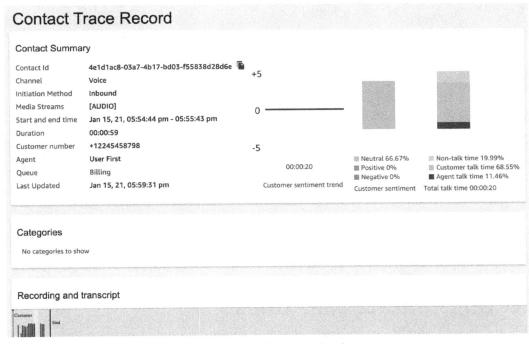

Figure 12.14 – Sentiment details

In addition to details about a call's sentiment, Contact Lens also produces a call transcription, which is a textual representation of what was said during a call. You can view the transcript, both from the caller and the agent side, at the bottom of the **contact details** screen. The transcript will appear in a similar way to the one shown in the following screenshot. Of course, what was said would be different than in my test call:

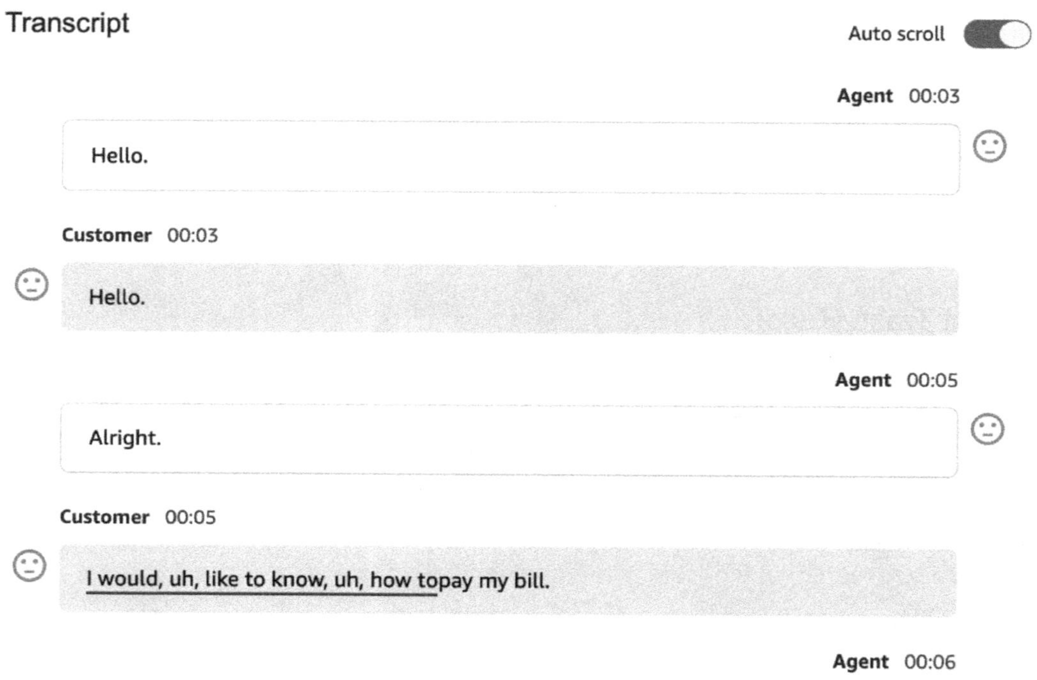

Transcript   Auto scroll ⬤

                                                            Agent 00:03

    Hello.   ☺

Customer 00:03

☹   Hello.

                                                            Agent 00:05

    Alright.   ☺

Customer 00:05

☹   I would, uh, like to know, uh, how topay my bill.

                                                            Agent 00:06

Figure 12.15 – Transcript

Now that you understand Contact Lens' capabilities, let's look at how we can expand upon those capabilities to drive even more improvement for your call center.

Creating Contact Lens rules

One of the ways in which Contact Lens can help you improve your customer experience is to utilize rules. Connect rules allow you to create criteria in the form of rulesets to identify specific things in your call center—for instance, you might want to specifically identify and track callers wanting to cancel their account. A Contact Lens rule will identify and tag specific calls based on the criteria of that rule.

A rule consists of a number of words and parameters that are found in the customer or agent communication streams. We will now create rules to identify when a caller wants to cancel their account, to demonstrate this capability. This demonstration doesn't align very well with our **Mega Mercy Hospital** scenario, but it is so common a request that I wanted to cover it anyway.

To begin creating a rule, follow these steps:

1. Find the **Rules** menu item on the **Connect management** menu, on the left-hand side. It's located under the icon that looks like a judge's gavel. I've identified it here to assist you in locating it:

Figure 12.16 – Creating rules

2. When you click on the menu item, you will be presented with a new configuration list. This list should give you all of the rules that you have created. Since we don't have any yet, the list is empty. Locate the **Create a rule** button on the right-hand side, as illustrated in the following screenshot, and click it:

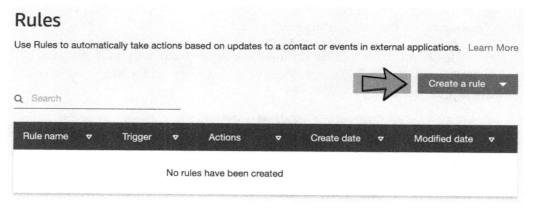

Figure 12.17 – Rules list

3. There are two types of rules that can be created. When you click the button, a drop-down menu will appear. We want to select the **Contact lens** item from the menu, as shown in the following screenshot:

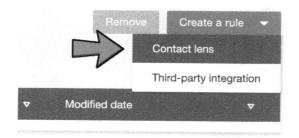

Figure 12.18 – Rule menu

4. A new screen will appear, allowing you to configure your new Contact Lens rule. To begin, name the rule using the entry point on the upper left of the form. I've highlighted it here:

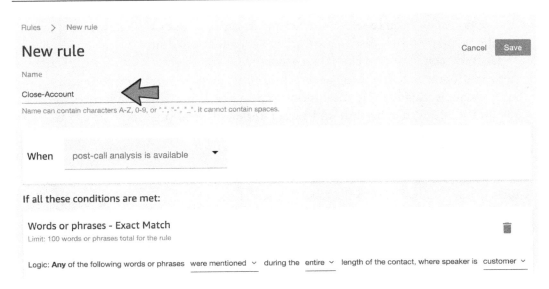

Figure 12.19 – New rule

5. When you configure a rule, there are several selectable options to control how the rule is applied. Looking at the bottom of *Figure 12.19*, you will see a section headed **If all these conditions are met:**. Everything that is listed under this heading needs to occur for the rule to trigger. You can enter more than one criteria, but between each item is an AND clause.

Everything inside the rule, meaning the words or phrases that you will be entering, is an OR clause.

Scroll down and look at the first clause box. Within this box is a logic sentence. Three options can be configured in this sentence. The first is displayed here:

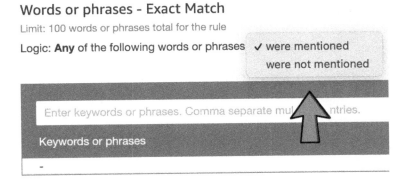

Figure 12.20 – Mention types

6. This option allows you to select whether the words or phrases were or were not mentioned. For our use case, we will select **were mentioned** since we are looking to see if someone wants to close their account, but you might want to use the **were not mentioned** selection if you are creating a rule to make sure that your agents are communicating items to the customer as expected. You might want them to mention a sale or membership, and a **were not mentioned** rule would help you identify if agents haven't been following procedure.

   The second selection allows you to select when the words are heard, either in the first or last part of the call or during the entire call. We are going to choose **entire** for our rule, as illustrated in the following screenshot:

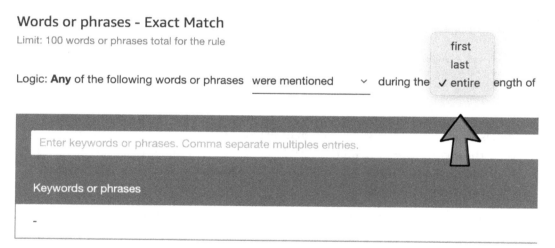

Figure 12.21 – Duration

7. The final option that we can select is to whom the rule is applied. Your options are **agent, customer**, or **either**. For the first component of our rule, we are going to select **customer**, as illustrated in the following screenshot:

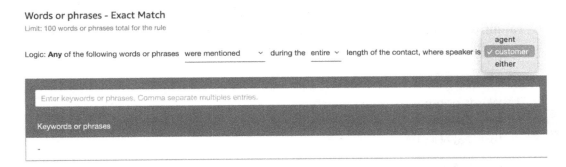

Words or phrases - Exact Match

Limit: 100 words or phrases total for the rule

Logic: **Any** of the following words or phrases were mentioned ⌄ during the entire ⌄ length of the contact, where speaker is ⌄ customer

| agent |
| customer |
| either |

Enter keywords or phrases. Comma separate multiples entries.

Keywords or phrases

Figure 12.22 – Speaker rule

8. The next step is to add the words that we want to identify for the rule. Add the words `close account` to the box and click the **Add** button at the end of the box. When you do this, the words will be added to the list below, as identified in the following screenshot:

Words or phrases - Exact Match

Limit: 100 words or phrases total for the rule

Logic: **Any** of the following words or phrases were mentioned ⌄ during the entire ⌄ length of the contact, where speaker is customer ⌄

close account   Add   ⇐

Keywords or phrases

Figure 12.23 – Words to look for

9. Next, we want to add another condition to our rule. To do this, click on the **Add condition** button shown in the following screenshot, and a new box will be added to the rule:

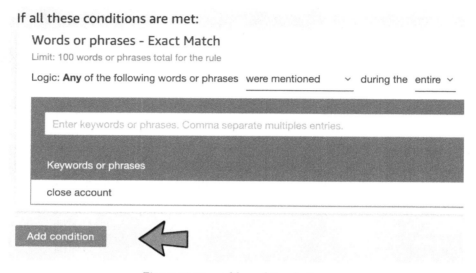

Figure 12.24 – Add condition button

10. We now want to set up our **send** condition to complete the rule. We first identified that the customer wanted to close their account. To finish the rule, we want to see whether the agent says that the account has been closed. We want to mimic the settings of the first condition except for who the speaker is. In this case, we want the speaker to be an agent. Add the words account is closed, as illustrated in the following screenshot:

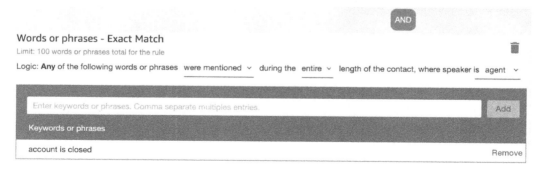

Figure 12.25 – Second set of words

11. When you are done, click the **Save** button on the upper right to save the rule. The rule will apply to all future contacts. Rules cannot go back in time; they can only be evaluated against future calls.

With rules enabled, contacts will now be tagged when the rule applies. Your managers can use this information to identify when a client asked for their account to be closed and the agent responded that the account was closed, meaning that they weren't able to convince the customer to keep the account open.

The rule function in Connect is a very powerful function that allows you to leverage Contact Lens to improve customer satisfaction. With the skills that we covered in this section, you will be able to provide several analytics that were previously unavailable.

Summary

Contact Lens' implementation is pretty simple, significantly easier, and more refined than the last two implementations that we have completed. Even though the implementation was easy, the value that Contact Lens brings to your organization is substantial. Contact Lens allows you to identify how your customers feel, which is significantly more important than any information that a conventional on-premises call center would be able to capture. Using the information we covered in this chapter, you will be able to create more rules to help specifically identify the conversations that are occurring in your call center, based on your stakeholders' needs.

We are nearing the completion of our call center implementation. The last aspect that we will cover for your call center is the implementation of text chat. We will cover this next, in *Chapter 13, Implementing Chat.*

13
Implementing Chat

As we discussed in *Chapter 1, Benefits of Amazon Connect,* the implementation of chat into your Amazon Connect instance is a major benefit to your organization. By implementing chat in Connect, you can use the same staff and skills to answer website and mobile application questions as you would on the phone. This synergy not only saves you expenses but also improves your customer experience by providing a universal feel.

The implementation of chat is highly dependent on your specific use case, be that a mobile application or a website, and what this is implemented with from a technology perspective. To understand the implementation of chat, we will take an approach similar to the one we took in *Chapter 8, Interfacing Enterprise Applications,* for the enterprise application integration. We will create a small mockup so that you can gain experience and background in the implementation of chat and then translate that into your environment. In this chapter, we will cover the following topics:

- Chat requirements
- Connect instance requirements
- Importing contact flows
- Gathering required information
- Deploying the solution
- Testing your chat experience

Chat requirements

Adding chat to your application requires the design and implementation of custom code to interface with your Connect instance. Depending on the platform and programming languages used, the individual prerequisites that are needed change and are of too great a scope to cover in this book. Instead, we will cover what is necessary to establish a chat session, as this is universally applicable. With this information, you can determine the required pieces based on your implementation: an iOS, Android, or web-based application.

Also, there are several places where chat needs to be enabled in your Connect instance as well. Chat functionality doesn't need to be enabled on all queues if it doesn't fit your overall design or requirements. We will cover both of these aspects now.

Application requirements

For your application to establish connectivity to the Connect instance, it will first need to call the **Amazon Connect Service (ACS) application programming interface** (**API**). The API has a function called `StartChatContact`. This function will initiate the contact flow for a new chat and return a token for the individual participant. In order for your application to invoke the `StartChatContact` API call, it will need to have the correct **identity and access management** (**IAM**) permissions on the correct Connect instance and contact flow. In the sample that we will be deploying, this action will be performed by a lambda function that is called via an API gateway from a website.

Once your application has the participant token, it will need to communicate with the **Amazon Connect Participant Service (ACPS)** API. The application will need to invoke the `CreateParticipantConnection` API function using your participant token. When you make the `CreateParticipantConnection` call, the ACPS will return a secure WebSocket **Uniform Resource Locator** (**URL**). Your application must connect to this URL within 100 seconds before it times out, or the process will need to be restarted. In the sample that we will be deploying, this functionality is implemented using JavaScript on the website.

Finally, after connecting to the WebSocket, your application can send and receive messages. In our sample, the sending and receiving of messages is also implemented in JavaScript on the website. For more information on the ACS API, you can review the detailed API documentation at `https://docs.aws.amazon.com/connect/latest/APIReference/API_Operations.html`. Likewise, you can also find detailed information on the ACPS API at `https://docs.aws.amazon.com/connect-participant/latest/APIReference/API_Operations.html`.

The chat implementation isn't overly complicated but you need to have the application or website as a baseline—however, based on the work we are doing in this book, this doesn't exist. Instead, we will deploy a canned sample website from an existing **Amazon Web Services** (**AWS**) solution to see how all of the pieces tie together without creating an undue burden.

Connect instance requirements

For the chat function to work within the Connect instance, we need to ensure that the routing profiles have chat enabled. If you recall, routing profiles allow you to configure which queues your agents will have access to. In addition, you can also select which channels they have access to: voice, chat, or both.

For our Connect instance for **Mega Mercy Hospital**, we will connect our chat to the billing department. Chat is usually enabled by default but let's check the routing profile, just to make sure. To check the profile, access the routing profiles through the user menu in your Connect instance. We want to locate and edit the routing profile for the billing department.

When you edit the routing profile, you will see several settings that are specific to chat. To ensure that chat is enabled, identify the checkboxes for **Voice** and **Chat** and ensure that they are checked. You can reference the following screenshot as to where these settings are located. When you are sure the settings are checked, save the profile:

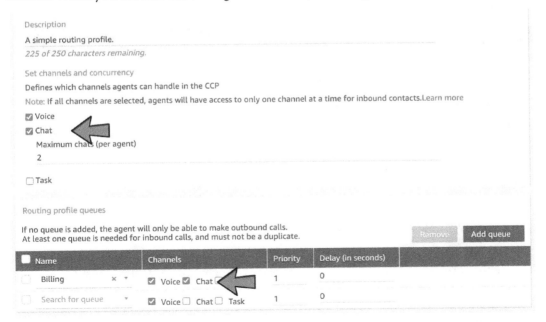

Figure 13.1 – Routing profile

In your Connect instance, you will want to ensure that chat is enabled for all profiles where you wish to have it. These are the only settings that we need to configure to allow chat on your instance. Before we can deploy our solution, we need to import some contact flows. We will do this next.

Deploying contact flows

The solution that we are going to deploy needs a couple of contact flows deployed beforehand. The solution we are using is available on GitHub. The URL we need to use to get the contact flows from is https://github.com/amazon-connect/amazon-connect-chat-ui-examples/tree/master/cloudformationTemplates/asyncCustomerChatUX. Access the repository and download the two contact flow **JavaScript Object Notation** (**JSON**) files from the contactFlows directory.

We will import these two flows using the same process as before, in *Chapter 6, Contact Flow Creation*. The following steps will demonstrate how:

1. Access **Contact flows** in the Connect instance administration. Click the **Create contact flow** button, as shown in the following screenshot:

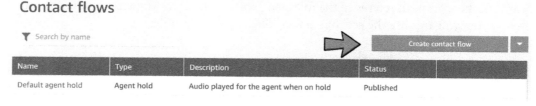

Figure 13.2 – Creating a flow

2. On the **editing** screen, click on the down arrow on the far right, next to **Save**. We want to select **Import flow (beta)** to import the first file, as illustrated in the following screenshot:

Figure 13.3 – Import flow

3. The first flow we are going to import is the disconnect flow. This flow must be imported first as the second flow depends on the disconnect flow. Select the Basic Chat Disconnect Flow JSON file and click the **Import** button, as illustrated in the following screenshot:

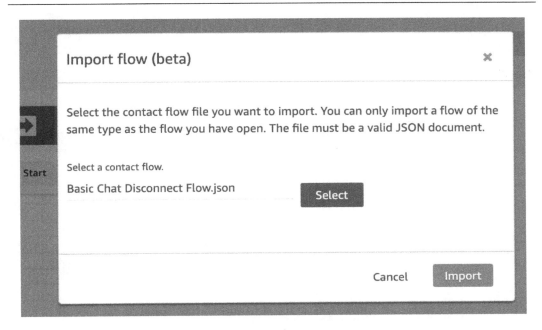

Figure 13.4 – Import Disconnect flow

4. When the flow is imported, we need to make a couple of changes. I've called my
    flow Mega Mercy - Chat Disconnect. The second change we need to make
    is to edit the **Set working queue** component, as shown in the following screenshot.
    Set the working queue to the billing queue:

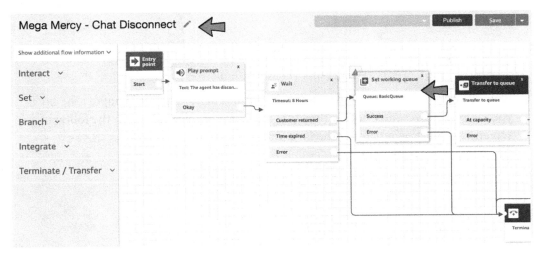

Figure 13.5 – Disconnect flow

5. When you are done, your flow should mimic the flow shown in the following screenshot:

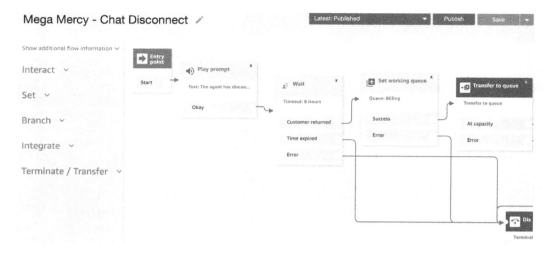

Figure 13.6 – Final disconnect flow

6. We have no other changes to make. Publish the flow to save the settings, as illustrated in the following screenshot:

Figure 13.7 – Publishing the flow

7. Now, we need to repeat the process for the second flow. When you import the flow, you should be presented with a flow that looks like the one shown in the following screenshot. Start by renaming the flow. I've changed mine to be `Mega Mercy - Chat`, as you can see here:

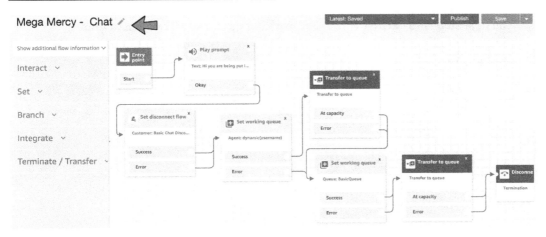

Figure 13.8 – Chat flow

8. We need to make a few changes to this flow. By default, the flow targets a specific agent instead of a queue, and we don't want that functionality. The first change we want to make is to change the **Set disconnect flow** component. When you import a flow, links to any other flow are disrupted and won't work. The **unique identifier (UID)** of those flows will not match, and we changed the name of our flow as well. Edit the **Set disconnect flow** component and change the flow to match, as shown in the following screenshot. When you are done, click **Save**:

Figure 13.9 – Set disconnect flow

9. The next step is to delete the first **Set working queue** and **Transfer to queue** components from the flow. When you are done, your flow should mimic the one shown here:

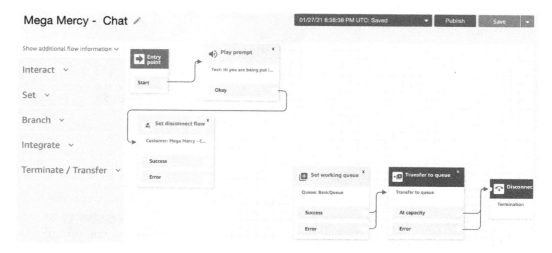

Figure 13.10 – Removed components

10. We want to connect this flow to the billing queue. Edit the second **Set working queue** component and select the **Billing** queue, as shown in the following screenshot. When you are done, save the component:

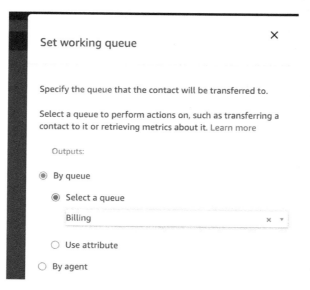

Figure 13.11 – Second queue

11. The **Disconnect** component needs to be connected to the input of **Set working queue**, as shown in the following screenshot:

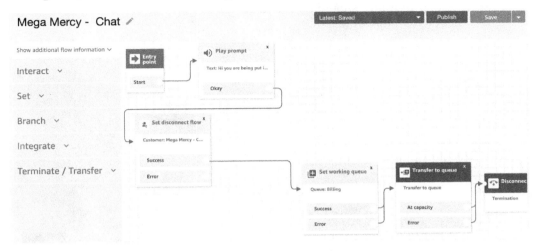

Figure 13.12 – Connect components

12. The original flow didn't have any error handling. I believe that some form of error should let the customer know that something went wrong and they weren't just cut off. To accomplish this, add a new **Play prompt** component that lets people know an error occurred. Connect the error output of the **Set working queue** component to the new **Play prompt** component. Finally, connect the **Play prompt** output to the **Disconnect** component. When everything is done, your flow should look like this:

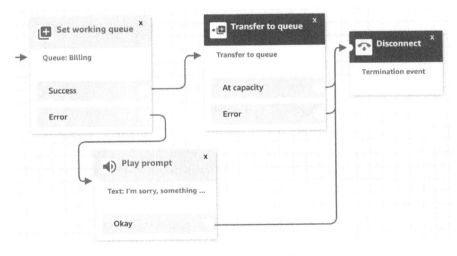

Figure 13.13 – Error handling

13. The last change we will make to this flow is to connect the error output of the **Set disconnect flow** component to the new **Play prompt** component, to finish off the error handling. Your flow should now look like this:

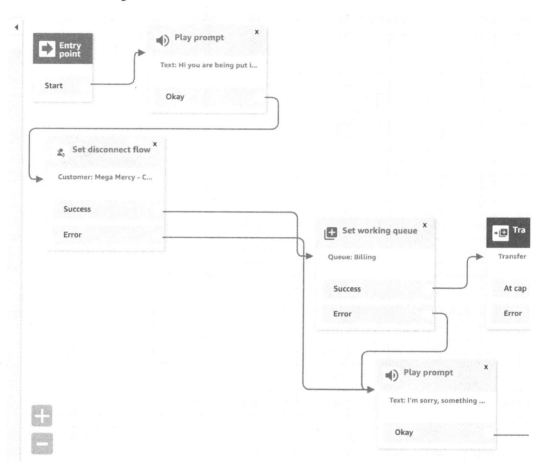

Figure 13.14 – Completed flow

14. Publish this flow to commit the changes, but don't navigate away from the **editing** screen. After publishing, we want to capture this flow's ID in our CloudFormation template later. The solution will use this to transfer the chat session to the flow using this ID. Expand the additional flow information to see the ID of the flow. The following screenshot shows you where this information is. Copy the **Amazon Resource Name (ARN)** of the flow and save it, to use later:

Figure 13.15 – Additional information

We are now done with the flows required to make this solution work. We can now navigate away from the edit screen. Next, we will gather the rest of the information we need to deploy the chat solution.

Gathering required information

For our chat deployment, we are going to deploy a canned Amazon deployment for chat. The solution will deploy a small website with a chat client via CloudFormation. As with the other solutions we deployed, we need to capture some more information to input into the CloudFormation parameters to deploy correctly.

The solution requires our Connect instance ID and the **Simple Storage Service (S3)** bucket name of where the chat transcripts are kept. Let's start by capturing the instance ID. If you recall, we have captured the instance ID for Connect before. If you don't have it handy, you can get it from the **Overview** section in the AWS management console for Connect, as we did for the voicemail solution in *Chapter 10, Implementing Voicemail*. You can see the ARN for your instance in the following screenshot. The instance ID is the UID located after the /. Save this information for use later:

Overview

Instance ARN	arn:aws:connect:us-east-1:993613994443:instance/8a41b405-9770-409b-ad21-4981c4ae1471
Directory	jatest123
Service-linked role ⓘ	AWSServiceRoleForAmazonConnect_nkNn0XOqb6PjupIuApph Learn more
Login URL	https://jatest123.awsapps.com/connect/login
Emergency access	⚠ Warning: This login method will give you full permission within the Amazon Connect instance and should not be used for day-to-day operations. Log in for emergency access. ↗

Figure 13.16 – Instance ID

For the S3 bucket for the chat transcripts, we can get the bucket name from the AWS console as well. To find the bucket name, locate the **Data storage** settings in the AWS Connect console, as illustrated in the following screenshot:

Amazon Connect > jatest123

Overview

Telephony

Data storage

Data streaming

Analytics tools

Tasks

Customer profiles

Approved origins

Contact flows

Figure 13.17 – Connect menu

The **Data storage** settings will display on the right-hand side of the screen. We are looking for the **Chat transcripts** settings. You can see these in the following screenshot. Copy the storage location of the transcripts for use later:

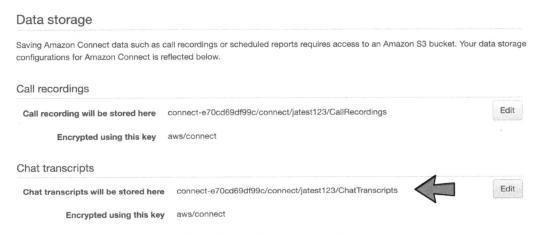

Data storage

Saving Amazon Connect data such as call recordings or scheduled reports requires access to an Amazon S3 bucket. Your data storage configurations for Amazon Connect is reflected below.

Call recordings

Call recording will be stored here   connect-e70cd69df99c/connect/jatest123/CallRecordings   Edit

Encrypted using this key   aws/connect

Chat transcripts

Chat transcripts will be stored here   connect-e70cd69df99c/connect/jatest123/ChatTranscripts   Edit

Encrypted using this key   aws/connect

Figure 13.18 – Data storage settings

At this point, we have all the information we need to continue with the solution's deployment.

Deploying the solution

With all the information for deployment in hand, we can start deploying the CloudFormation template. To begin, follow these steps:

1. Access the CloudFormation console, as we have in previous chapters, to begin the deployment process.

You will want to create a new stack, as we have done before. However, this time, instead of uploading a template, we will reference the existing one in S3 directly. Set the template source as **Amazon S3 URL** and enter `https://s3.amazonaws.com/us-east-1.amazon-connect-advanced-customer-chat-cfn/cloudformation.yaml` into the **Amazon S3 URL** location. Your settings should mimic those shown in *Figure 13.19*. When you are done, click **Next**, as shown here:

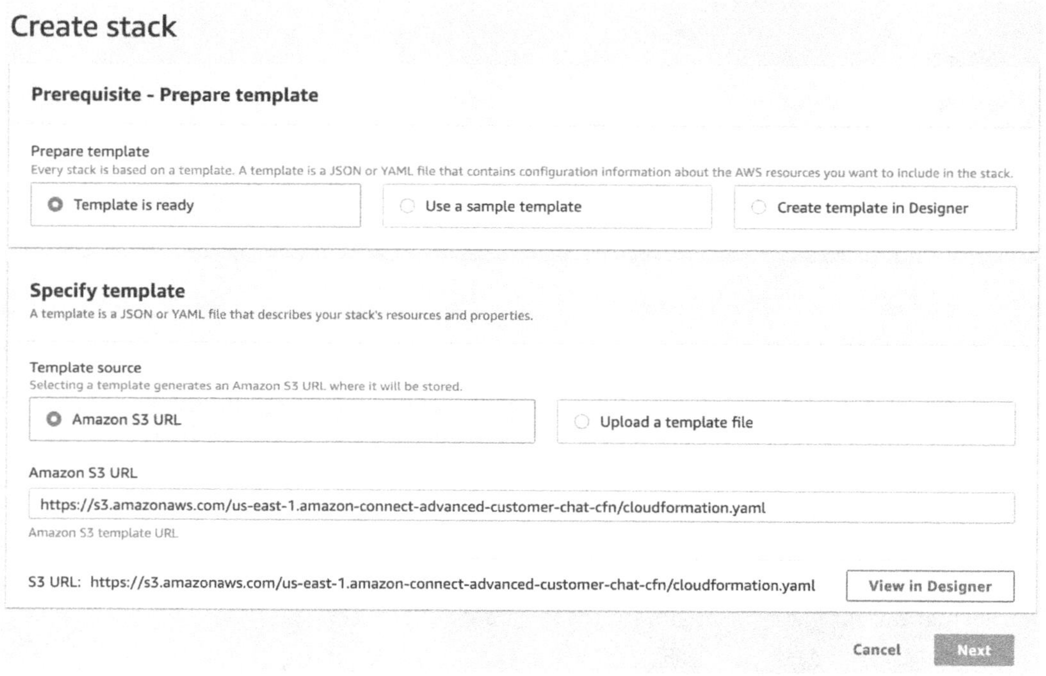

Create stack

Prerequisite - Prepare template

Prepare template
Every stack is based on a template. A template is a JSON or YAML file that contains configuration information about the AWS resources you want to include in the stack.

- ⦿ Template is ready
- ◯ Use a sample template
- ◯ Create template in Designer

Specify template

A template is a JSON or YAML file that describes your stack's resources and properties.

Template source
Selecting a template generates an Amazon S3 URL where it will be stored.

- ⦿ Amazon S3 URL
- ◯ Upload a template file

Amazon S3 URL

https://s3.amazonaws.com/us-east-1.amazon-connect-advanced-customer-chat-cfn/cloudformation.yaml

Amazon S3 template URL

S3 URL: https://s3.amazonaws.com/us-east-1.amazon-connect-advanced-customer-chat-cfn/cloudformation.yaml | View in Designer |

Cancel   Next

Figure 13.19 – Creating a stack

2. In the **Parameters** section, we need to enter in the information that we captured previously. But first, start by giving the stack a name. I've called mine CONNECT-CHAT to align to the naming convention we have already used for the other solutions.

Enter the name of the S3 bucket used for your instance. The bucket name will be the first part of the string we copied from the **Data storage** settings. Copy everything up to the first / and enter it into the field.

The website S3 bucket parameter can be made up, but remember that it must be different to all other S3 buckets in the world. If you leave this field with the original information in it, your stack will error out as the probability of someone else leaving it and already using the bucket name is high. You can refer to the following screenshot to validate your configuration:

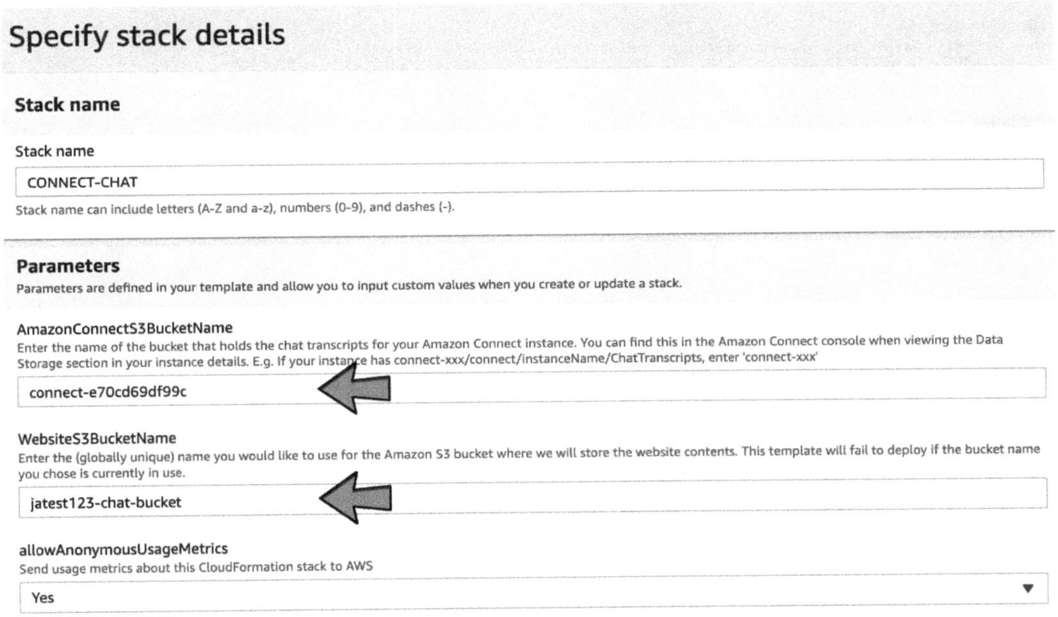

Specify stack details

Stack name

Stack name

```
CONNECT-CHAT
```

Stack name can include letters (A-Z and a-z), numbers (0-9), and dashes (-).

Parameters

Parameters are defined in your template and allow you to input custom values when you create or update a stack.

AmazonConnectS3BucketName
Enter the name of the bucket that holds the chat transcripts for your Amazon Connect instance. You can find this in the Amazon Connect console when viewing the Data Storage section in your instance details. E.g. If your instance has connect-xxx/connect/instanceName/ChatTranscripts, enter 'connect-xxx'

```
connect-e70cd69df99c
```

WebsiteS3BucketName
Enter the (globally unique) name you would like to use for the Amazon S3 bucket where we will store the website contents. This template will fail to deploy if the bucket name you chose is currently in use.

```
jatest123-chat-bucket
```

allowAnonymousUsageMetrics
Send usage metrics about this CloudFormation stack to AWS

```
Yes
```

Figure 13.20 – Stack parameters

Scroll down to see the rest of the parameters. There are three other settings that we need to configure at this point. The first is the contactflowID field. Using the ARN of the flow that we captured before, copy the UID that is located after the last / and enter it into the parameter location.

3. Next, enter the instance ID of the connect instance in the `instanceId` field. Finally, enter the transcript path for the chat transcripts. This path is everything that is located after the first / in the S3 bucket path. It is the opposite of the setting that we entered earlier. When you are done, you can check your settings against the following screenshot. When you are done, click **Next** and complete the CloudFormation deployment:

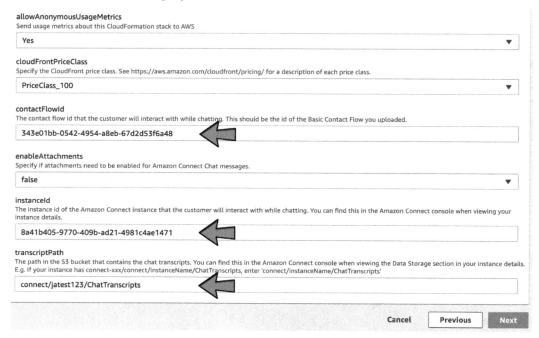

Figure 13.21 – Additional parameters

You have now completed the deployment of the solution. Wait for the CloudFormation stack to deploy. It might take a little time to deploy based on the types of components that are being configured. In the next section, we will review how to test the solution to see how it works.

Testing your chat experience

Now that the solution is deployed, it is time to test it out to see how it works. To do this, you will need to log in to the Connect instance as your test user. Your test user will need to be configured with the `Billing` routing profile. If you need to, set this routing profile on your test user first. When everything is set, log in and make the user active in the client so that you can receive a chat message.

Once you are logged in, you can access the website as a customer and initiate a chat session. To find out where the site is, access the stack via the CloudFormation console and locate the **Outputs** tab. We are looking for the `cloudFrontDistribution` output in the stack, as detailed in the following screenshot. Click this link to launch the website:

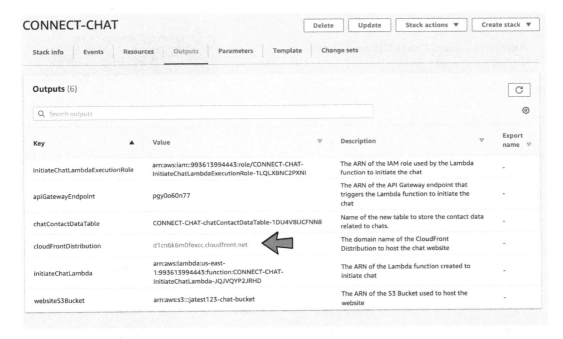

Figure 13.22 – Outputs

When you access the website, you will be prompted with a simplistic website asking for a first name and a username. Enter your name and a username and click the **Start Chat** button, as illustrated in the following screenshot. The username doesn't matter because we removed that function and connected it to a queue rather than a user:

Amazon Connect Omni-Channel Demo

Figure 13.23 – Start Chat button

The chat window will appear. It's nothing fancy, but it will mimic most chat windows you will see around the web today. When you click **Start Chat**, you will need to accept the Connect client's chat as if it were a call. When you do, a similar chat screen will appear on the agent side. Send a message from the website as a test, as illustrated in the following screenshot:

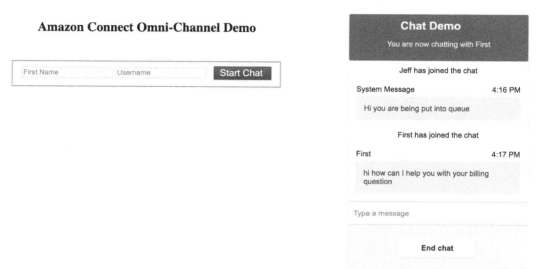

Figure 13.24 – Chat window

On the agent side, you should see something similar to *Figure 12.25*. Try sending messages back and forth to ensure that all the functionality is working. When you are done, click the **End chat** button on either end to disconnect, as illustrated here:

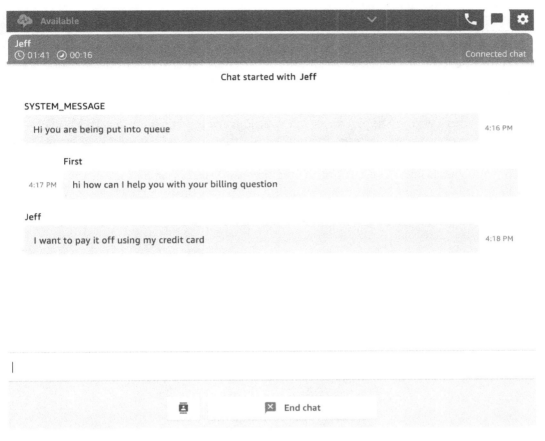

Figure 13.25 – Agent chat

Congratulations! You have deployed a working chat solution in Amazon Connect. Of course, this is a long way off from a production solution, but it should give you a good starting point to understand how all of the pieces come together. If you need more details, you can look inside the S3 bucket that the stack created and look at the **HyperText Markup Language** (HTML) files to see how the chat interface was implemented. If you would like more examples, there are a few located in this GitHub repository: `https://github.com/amazon-connect/amazon-connect-chat-ui-examples`

Summary

We have finally reached the end of our journey, not just for this chapter, where we learned how to implement the chat solution, but for the entire book. We covered the benefits of Connect and how to deploy it, and what all of the components in Connect do. There was also information on how to use complex solutions such as Lex bots, analytics, and voicemail.

Sadly, this is where we have to part ways, but your journey is just beginning. This book covered how to perform all of these functions within the AWS and Connect ecosystem, but we barely scratched the surface. There is so much more that can be done based on the needs of your stakeholders and customers. The sky—and your imagination—is the limit. Good luck!

Other Books You May Enjoy

If you enjoyed this book, you may be interested in these other books by Packt:

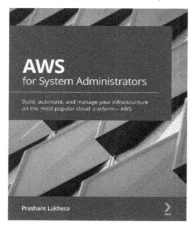

AWS for System Administrators

Prashant Lakhera

ISBN: 978-1-80020-153-8

- Adopt a security-first approach by giving users minimum access using IAM policies
- Build your first Amazon Elastic Compute Cloud (EC2) instance using the AWS CLI, Boto3, and Terraform
- Set up your datacenter in AWS Cloud using VPC
- Scale your application based on demand using Auto Scaling
- Monitor services using CloudWatch and SNS
- Work with centralized logs for analysis (CloudWatch Logs)
- Back up your data using Amazon Simple Storage Service (Amazon S3), Data Lifecycle Manager, and AWS Backup

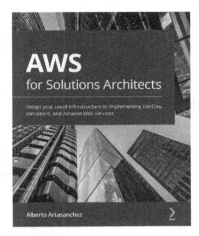

AWS for Solutions Architects

Alberto Artasanchez

ISBN: 978-1-78953-923-3

- Rationalize the selection of AWS as the right cloud provider for your organization
- Choose the most appropriate service from AWS for a particular use case or project
- Implement change and operations management
- Find out the right resource type and size to balance performance and efficiency
- Discover how to mitigate risk and enforce security, authentication, and authorization
- Identify common business scenarios and select the right reference architectures for them

Packt is searching for authors like you

If you're interested in becoming an author for Packt, please visit authors. packtpub.com and apply today. We have worked with thousands of developers and tech professionals, just like you, to help them share their insight with the global tech community. You can make a general application, apply for a specific hot topic that we are recruiting an author for, or submit your own idea.

Leave a review - let other readers know what you think

Please share your thoughts on this book with others by leaving a review on the site that you bought it from. If you purchased the book from Amazon, please leave us an honest review on this book's Amazon page. This is vital so that other potential readers can see and use your unbiased opinion to make purchasing decisions, we can understand what our customers think about our products, and our authors can see your feedback on the title that they have worked with Packt to create. It will only take a few minutes of your time, but is valuable to other potential customers, our authors, and Packt. Thank you!

Index

A

agent hold flow 36
agent whisper flow 36
Amazon Connect
  base charges 58-60
  benefits, exploring 4
  communications costs 60-62
  connecting to 154-156
  hard costs, reducing 10
  soft costs, reducing 13, 15
  user experience 4, 5
Amazon Connect Participant
    Service (ACPS) 292
Amazon Connect Service (ACS) 292
Amazon Lex
  crash course 140
Amazon Resource Name (ARN)
  about 243, 300
  capturing, from voicemail 248, 249
Amazon Web Services (AWS)
    110, 140, 293
Analytics costing
  about 65
  Athena 67
  Glue 66
  Kinesis Firehose 66

QuickSight 67, 68
API capabilities
  learning 164
artificial intelligence (AI) 125
Athena 67
automatic speech recognition (ASR) 140
AWS account prerequisites
  about 72
  federation 73
  management roles 73
  Virtual Private Cloud (VPC) 72
AWS Connect pricing page
  reference link 58

B

bot
  creating 140-154
branch components
  about 48
  check contact attributes component 50
  check hours of operation component 50
  check queue status component 49
  check staffing component 49
  distribute by percentage component 50
  loop component 51

wait component 51
business hours 19

C

callback contact flow
  implementing 200, 202
callback flow
  implementing 194
callbacks 22
caller's number
  capturing 195-199
call queues
  creating 87-89
calls
  hours of operation, setting 84-86
change routing priority 44, 45
chat
  application requisites 292, 293
  requisites 292
chat solution
  deploying 303-306
  testing 306-309
chat solution deployment
  required information, gathering 301-303
check contact attributes component 50
check hours of operation 50
check queue status 49
check staffing 49
Children's Online Privacy Protection
    Act (COPPA) 143
CloudFormation
  solution, deploying 169-173
CloudFormation template
  configuring 243-247
  deploying 167, 168, 250-254
Connect
  deploying 74-78

instance, logging into 78-80
  Lambda function, connecting
    to 173-175
Connect instance
  configuring 215-219
  requisites 293, 294
connect_lambda template
  download link 170
Contact Control Panel (CCP) 24
contact flow components
  about 37
  branch components 48
  integrate components 51
  interactions components 38
  settings components 42, 43
  terminate/transfer group 52
contact flow influencers
  about 19
  business hours 19
  callbacks 22
  integrations 24
  queues 20
  transfers 21
  voicemail 23
contact flow types
  about 34
  agent hold flow 36
  agent whisper flow 36
  customer hold flow 35
  customer queue flow 35
  customer whisper flow 35
  inbound contact flow 34
  outbound whisper flow 36
  transfer to agent flow 37
  transfer to queue flow 37
contact flows
  about 5, 54, 55
  copying 121-129

creating 102, 175-187
creating, from scratch 111-121
CRM integration 189
deploying 294, 301
deploying, in Connect 167, 168
editing 103-110
exporting 130-136
importing 130-136
information, retrieving 168, 169
integration types 189
internal application 190
ITSM integration 190
modifying 157-162
solution, testing 187-189
Contact Lens
about 9
capabilities 277-282
costing 65
enabling 270-275
rules, creating 282-289
Contact Trace Records (CTRs) 242
critical information
extracting 18
customer hold flow 35
customer queue flow 35
Customer Relationship Management
(CRM) 7, 24, 39
Customer Relationship Management
(CRM) integration 189
customer whisper flow 35

D

data flow 242
Data Processing Unit (DPU) 66
departmental flows
implementing 136-138
deployment influencers

about 24
conversation, reframing 30, 31
management 24, 26
Direct Inward Dial (DID) 58
distribute by percentage component 50
Dual Tone Multi-Frequency (DTMF) 39

E

Elastic Compute Cloud (EC2) 140
Enterprise Resource Planning (ERP) 7, 24
Extract, Transform, and Load (ETL) 66

G

get customer input 39, 40
get queue metrics 48
Glue 66

H

hard costs, Amazon Connect
circuit costs, avoiding 10, 11
demarcation extension
costs, avoiding 12
extra equipment 13
long delays, avoiding for
implementation and upgrades 12
long-term contracts, avoiding 11
hold customer 41
Hypertext Markup Language (HTML) 309

I

identity and access management
(IAM) 292
in-house applications 190
inbound contact flow 34

Information Technology Service
Management (ITSM) integration 190
Infrastructure as Code (IaC) 140, 169
integrate components
about 51
invoke Lambda 51
integrations 24
integration types
CRM integration 189
ITSM integration 190
in-house applications 190
interactions components
about 38
get customer input 39, 40
hold customer 41
play prompt 38
start media streaming 42
stop media streaming 42
store customer input 41
Interactive Voice Response
(IVR) 20, 34, 125
invoke Lambda component 51

J

JavaScript Object Notation (JSON) 294

K

Kinesis 66
Kinesis stream template
reference link 243

L

Lambda 165
Lambda costing
about 62

invocations 63
RAM 63
Lambda function
connecting, to Connect 173-175
Lambda's capabilities
learning 165, 167
Letter of Authorization (LOA) 81
Lex 8
Lex bot costing 64
loop component 51

M

management, deployment influencers
agent location 29
identity management 29, 30
monitoring 27
outbound calling 27
recording 27
region 28
management portal
using 220-224
Multi-Factor Authentication (MFA) 30

N

Natural Language Processing (NLP) 64
natural language understanding
(NLU) 140
Network Address Translation (NAT) 72
number validation 200

O

outbound whisper flow 36

P

phone number
  picking 80-84
  transferring 80-84
play prompt 38
Polly 8

Q

queues
  about 20
  quantity 20, 21
  types 20, 21
QuickSight
  about 67, 68
  analysis, establishing 259-263
  dashboard 263-266

R

recording analysis 271

S

S3 access
  setting up 254-258
Sample interruptible queue
    flow with callback
  editing 194
Security Assertion Markup
    Language (SAML) 30, 73
security profiles
  creating 90-96
sentiment analysis 9, 271
set callback number 47
set contact attributes 44
set customer queue flow 46

set disconnect flow 47
set hold flow 46
set logging behavior 45
set recording 45, 46
settings component
  about 43
  change routing priority 44, 45
  get queue metrics 48
  set callback number 47
  set contact attributes 44
  set customer queue flow 46
  set disconnect flow 47
  set hold flow 46
  set logging behavior 45
  set recording 45, 46
  set voice 48
  set whisper flow 47
  set working queue 44
set voice 48
set whisper flow 46
set working queue 44
set working queue 44
Simple Storage Service (S3) 140, 302
software as a service (SaaS) 10, 24, 72
software development kit (SDK) 140
start media streaming 42
stop media streaming 42
store customer input 41
Super-fast Parallel In-memory,
    Calculation Engine (SPICE) 67

T

terminate group
  about 52
  disconnect/hang up 52
  end flow/resume 54
  transfer to flow 53

transfer to phone number 53
transfer to queue 53
transfer group 52
transfer to agent 22
transfer to agent flow 37
transfer to external number 22
transfer to queue 21
transfer to queue flow 37
transfers 21

U

Uniform Resource Locator
    (URL) 154, 292
unique identifier (UID) 281, 297
Universal Serial Bus (USB)
    symbol 103, 157
user experience, Amazon Connect
  AI services 7, 8
  improved interaction 5, 6
  interfacing, with enterprise
      applications 6
  multi-channel experiences 8
  self-service 7
  sentiment analysis 9, 10
  surveys 9
User management
  users, adding 97-99
user permissions
  assigning 275, 276

V

Virtual Private Cloud (VPC) 72
voicemail
  about 23
  ARN, capturing from 248, 249
  settings, completing 232, 233

voicemail contact flows
    extension prompt, removing 234-238
    importing 225-231
    integrating into 234
voicemail solution
    launching 207-214
    overview 204-206
    testing 233, 234
Voice over IP (VoIP) 28

W

wait component 51

CPSIA information can be obtained
at www.ICGtesting.com
Printed in the USA
FSHW020106150421
80410FS